A Message from the
BILLY GRAHAM
EVANGELISTIC ASSOCIATION

If you are committing your life to Christ, please let us know! We would like to send you Bible study materials and a complimentary six-month subscription to *Decision* magazine to help you grow in your faith.

The Billy Graham Evangelistic Association exists to support the evangelistic ministry and calling of Billy Graham to take the message of Christ to all we can by every effective means available to us.

Our desire is to introduce as many as we can to the person of Jesus Christ, so that they might experience His love and forgiveness.

Your prayers are the most important way to support us in this ministry. We are grateful for the dedicated prayer support we receive. We are also grateful for those who support us with contributions.

Giving can be a rewarding experience for you and for us at the Billy Graham Evangelistic Association (BGEA). Your gift gives you the satisfaction of supporting an organization that is actively involved in evangelism. Also, it is encouraging to us because part of our ministry is devoted to helping people like you discover and enjoy the stewardship of giving wisely and effectively.

Billy Graham Evangelistic Association
1 Billy Graham Parkway
Charlotte, North Carolina 28201-0001
www.billygraham.org

Billy Graham Evangelistic Association of Canada
20 Hopewell Way NE
Calgary, Alberta T3J 5H5
www.billygraham.ca

Toll free: 1-877-247-2426

$\mathscr{S}$TEPS TO $\mathscr{P}$EACE WITH $\mathscr{G}$OD

1. ## RECOGNIZE GOD'S PLAN—PEACE AND LIFE

   The message you have read in this book stresses
   that God loves you and wants you to
   experience His peace and life.

   The BIBLE says . . . *"For God loved the
   world so much that He gave His only Son,
   so that everyone who believes in Him may
   not die but have eternal life."* John 3:16

2. ## REALIZE OUR PROBLEM—SEPARATION

   People choose to disobey God and go
   their own way. This results in separation
   from God.

   The BIBLE says . . . *"Everyone has
   sinned and is far away from God's saving
   presence."* Romans 3:23

3. ## RESPOND TO GOD'S REMEDY—CROSS OF CHRIST

   God sent His Son to bridge the gap. Christ
   did this by paying the penalty of our sins
   when He died on the cross and rose from
   the grave.

   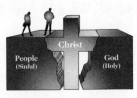

   The BIBLE says . . . *"But God has shown
   us how much He loves us—it was while we
   were still sinners that Christ died for us!"*
   Romans 5:8

4. ## RECEIVE GOD'S SON—LORD AND SAVIOR

   You cross the bridge into God's family when
   you ask Christ to come into your life.

   The BIBLE says . . . *"Some, however, did
   receive Him and believed in Him; so He
   gave them the right to become God's
   children."* John 1:12

THE INVITATION IS TO:

REPENT (turn from your sins) and by faith RECEIVE Jesus Christ into
your heart and life and follow Him in obedience as your Lord and Savior.

PRAYER OF COMMITMENT

"Lord Jesus, I know I am a sinner. I believe You died for my sins. Right now,
I turn from my sins and open the door of my heart and life. I receive You as
my personal Lord and Savior. Thank You for saving me now. Amen."

If you want further help in the decision you have made, write to:
Billy Graham Evangelistic Association
1 Billy Graham Parkway, Charlotte, NC 28201-0001

THE AUTHORIZED BIOGRAPHY

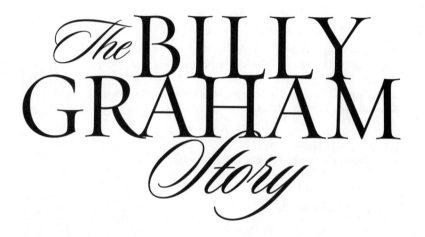

The BILLY
GRAHAM
Story

THIS SPECIAL EDITION IS PUBLISHED BY THE
BILLY GRAHAM EVANGELISTIC ASSOCIATION
BY SPECIAL ARRANGEMENT
WITH ZONDERVAN PUBLISHING HOUSE.

JOHN POLLOCK

REVISED AND UPDATED EDITION OF *TO ALL THE NATIONS*

ZONDERVAN™

GRAND RAPIDS, MICHIGAN 49530 USA

CONTENTS

Preface 7

$\mathcal{P}$ART ONE
1918–1959

1. Sunshine in the South 13
2. The Eighteenth Green 20
3. The Girl from China 28
4. Geared to the Times 36
5. Los Angeles 1949 41
6. An Hour of Decision 52
7. Harringay 1954 62
8. Ripe for Harvest 76
9. New York 1957 86
10. Under the Southern Cross 96

$\mathcal{P}$ART TWO
1960–1976

11. Reaching Out 107
12. The Reconciler 112
13. Scenes from West and East 118
14. True Friendship 124
15. Lausanne 132

PART THREE
1977–1983

16. Billy at Sixty *139*

17. Into Eastern Europe *148*

18. Tidal Wave *156*

19. Sydney 1979 . . . . *160*

20. Great Steps Forward *167*

21. Moscow 1982 and After *173*

22. New England *192*

23. Amsterdam 1983 . . . . *199*

PART FOUR
1984–present

24. The Queen's Guests *207*

25. Mission England *214*

26. Romania Awakes *223*

27. Reaching Out to Washington *232*

28. Sidelight on Amsterdam II *237*

29. China 1988 . . . . *244*

30. Mission New York State *252*

31. Moscow 1992: A Dream Come True *259*

32. Millennium Harvest *269*

33. "Light a Fire" *279*

34. "A Day of Victory" *285*

35. "Toward the Future" *294*

Notes *311*

Index *312*

PREFACE

WHEN THE HIJACKED PLANES SLAMMED INTO THE WORLD Trade Center and the Pentagon on September 11, 2001, murdering some three thousand unsuspecting people, the president of the United States, George W. Bush, immediately proclaimed a National Day of Prayer and Remembrance. For the interfaith, interdenominational service at the Washington National Cathedral, he chose Billy Graham, eighty-two years old and frail but still in active ministry, to give the address. No other clergyman, whatever his office, could so aptly bring the Word of God to America at that terrible hour.

By 2001 Billy Graham had acquired a unique respect and affection in America. And an important place in world history, as the then Vice President Al Gore had remarked five years earlier at the presentation of the Congressional Gold Medal to Billy and Ruth Graham: "In the next few years, historians and scholars will issue their conclusions as to who they regard as the five or ten most influential individuals of the twentieth century. I believe that any such list will be incomplete if it does not include the name of Billy Graham."

Between 1949 and 2003 Graham had addressed more than eighty-three million people face-to-face and at least one billion through television, radio, and satellite. More than three million people had come forward as inquirers at his crusades and missions, and evidence from all over the world suggests that a large number of them found this the beginning or deepening of their Christian lives. Yet Graham is far more than an evangelist of integrity and vision. As a Christian statesman, his profound influence on the growth and depth of Christianity across the world, and especially on the recovery of religious freedom in Eastern Europe, cannot be overestimated.

This short book aims to give the gist of Graham's story and the flavor of his character. The first two parts are abridged, with some new material, from my two authorized biographies, *Billy Graham* (1966, updated 1969) and *Billy Graham: Evangelist to the World* (1978). They were based on his private files and my own widespread research. The third part (mostly from the first edition of the present book) covers the years from 1978 to 1983. I dealt at some length with his controversial visit to Moscow in 1982, which now can be seen as a factor in the fall of Communism seven years later and thus to Billy Graham's own mission in the Olympic Stadium in Moscow in 1992. This mission is described in the new part, covering the years 1984–2003, which begins with the visit of Billy and Ruth to Sandringham as guests of Her Majesty the Queen on the eve of Mission England.

Billy Graham's life and achievements have been so full that to tell everything in a short book would make it a catalogue. In particular, the period since the previous 1984 edition has been so crowded that I have had to select vital episodes, consciously leaving out others. However, the full-length official biography is in preparation.

This book owes much to many people who gave me information directly or by correspondence or who helped in other ways. I was very glad to acknowledge many by name in the books of 1966, 1978, and 1984, some of whom are no longer living. I gladly renew my thanks.

For Part 4 of the present book, I give warmest thanks to Billy and Ruth Graham, once again, and to Franklin Graham and Anne Graham Lotz. The Billy Graham Team members gave me every assistance, and I would like to mention particularly John Corts, Chief Operating Officer until retirement, and his successor, Preston Parrish; John Akers; Blair Carlson; Viktor Hamm; Sterling Huston; Rick Marshall; and Stephanie Wills.

I am grateful to Her Majesty the Queen for her gracious permission to quote the letter written to Billy Graham in 1954 on behalf of Her Majesty Queen Elizabeth the Queen Mother, and to former President George Bush for his gracious permission to quote from his tribute to Billy Graham at Dallas in October 2002.

At Amsterdam 2000, Marie Coutu arranged and recorded my interviews and made my heavy schedule a pleasure together with her helpers, Ruth Mullen, Dawn Jobe, Kristen Jankowski, and Charlene McLeod.

At Minneapolis, Diane Holmquist and her deputy, Leslye Ashwood, were of greatest assistance, transcribing interviews, typing the chapters, and swiftly incorporating amendments, checking facts, making contacts, and forming my essential link with the BGEA office. Diane has been working with the Official Biography project for many years, and I am very grateful for her cheerful and unstinting help despite many other duties for the Association.

I am grateful to Jean Wilson and Pat Strange of the Office London for their kind help in speeding material to and from Minneapolis and in other ways. Finally, my warm thanks to Amy Boucher Pye and Angela Scheff, my editors at Zondervan, and to Amy's editorial assistant, Maryl Darko, for all they did for the book.

John Pollock

Part One

1918–1959

I

Sunshine in the South

William Crook Graham, a Confederate veteran with a bullet in his leg, died in 1910 at the age of sixty. He had a patriarchal beard and a large family, but nothing else biblical about him. He drank, he swore, and he neglected his farm and would not pay his debts.

He was born at Fort Mill in York District and after the Civil War bought the land a few miles away near Charlotte, North Carolina, which he left to two of his sons, William Franklin and Clyde. Together the sons built up a three-hundred-acre dairy farm of rich red soil, with woods and streams and gently rolling contours, and delivered milk in the city.

William Franklin Graham married Morrow Coffey of Steele Creek near Charlotte in 1916. Their eldest son, William Franklin Graham Jr., Billy Frank to his family, was born in the frame farmhouse on November 7, 1918, three days before his father's thirtieth birthday and four before the Armistice.

All four of Billy Graham's grandparents were descended from the Scots-Irish pioneers who settled in the Carolinas before the Revolution. His mother's father, Ben Coffey, had fair hair and blue eyes (like his grandson) and the tall, clean-limbed, strong-jawed physique immortalized in the North Carolina monument at Gettysburg, where he fell badly wounded. A one-legged, one-eyed veteran, he was a farmer of intelligence, spirit, and sterling honesty, with a tenacious memory and a love for Scripture and literature, which he imparted to his daughters.

In the frame farmhouse and then in the red brick home nearby, which the Grahams built when Billy was ten, with its pillared porch, paved paths, and shade of oaks and cedars, Morrow Coffey Graham kept the books, did the cooking and housework, and chopped the wood with the aid of Suzie, her black maid. A blend of determination with gentleness and affection won for Morrow the complete devotion of her two sons and two daughters: Billy Frank, Catherine, Melvin, and Jean, who was fourteen years younger than Billy.

Frank Graham was an equally strong character. At six foot two, with dark hair and a fine bass voice, he was a farmer through and through. In early manhood he had experienced a religious conversion, but his faith had lost urgency though it remained the foundation of his integrity. Straight as his back in business dealings, he was adored and a little feared by the farm hands and his children. His scanty education was offset by shrewdness and a lively curiosity. He had a dry wit and a warm and generous nature, kept in close control because agricultural bankruptcies were frequent in the Carolinas. His one indulgence was the smoking of large cigars. He scorned relaxation and hated travel. His world was the South—placid, sunny, but smarting from the Civil War and the economic depression and poverty that it had left.

The Graham farm was comparatively prosperous. Billy Frank's hero was the black foreman, Reese Brown, an army sergeant in World War I. He was a splendid person who could hold down a bull to be dehorned, had a wide range of skills, and was tireless, efficient, and trustworthy. Billy crammed down Mrs. Brown's delicious buttermilk bread, the Brown children were his playmates, and Reese taught him to milk and herd.

Billy was a bit too prankish to be of much use at first. High spirits and a love of adventure frequently cost him a taste of his father's belt or his mother's long hickory switch—such discipline was normal and expected. "Billy was rowdy, mischievous," recalls an older cousin, "but on the other hand—he was soft and gentle and loving and understanding. He was a very sweet, likeable person." His parents were strict but fair, and the house was full of laughter.

Billy Graham's early education was almost as poor as Abraham Lincoln's, a primary reason being the low level of teaching. Yet even if the teaching had been better, he would have made little use of it. By the age of eleven, he thought "horse sense" was enough education for a farmer, an attitude slightly encouraged by his father and stoutly resisted by his mother.

Billy's main interest was baseball. He had been taught the game early by the McMakins, three sons of the sharecropper on his father's farm. Mr. McMakins was a redheaded man of high temper but strict Christian principles, who had once been a southern champion bicycle racer. Billy's fondness for baseball was not matched by his skill. He barely made the Sharon High School team as a first baseman, and though he dreamed of being a professional, the dream died before he left high school. Baseball influenced him most by interfering with his studies. The one redeeming feature of Billy's early intellectual life was an exceptional love of reading history books. By the time he was fourteen, he had read about a hundred.

When Billy was young, Sunday was rather like an old Scottish Sabbath. Its highlights included the five-mile drive by car to the small Associate Reformed Presbyterian Church, which sang only metrical psalms, in Charlotte, a city then rated the most church-going in America.

Billy never thought of his parents as particularly religious. Then, when he was about fifteen, his mother joined a Bible class at the urging of her sister. Her husband remained indifferent. His energies were absorbed by the farm, especially since he had recently lost his savings in the bank failures of 1933.

Three weeks after she joined the Bible class, Frank Graham's head was smashed by a piece of wood that shot out from the mechanical saw. The surgeons believed he would die. Mrs. Graham, after calling her Christian friends to pray, went up to her bedroom to pray. When she finished, she had the assurance that God heard her prayer. Both the Grahams believed that the Lord really spoke to them in Frank's accident and full recovery. They spent more time in Bible study and prayer, and Mrs. Graham read devotional books to the children.

The adolescent Billy Frank thought it was all "hogwash." He was in a mild rebellion, though his chief wildness was to borrow his father's car and drive it as fast as it could go, turning curves on two wheels, and racing other boys on the near-empty roads of North Carolina. As Billy recalls, "Once I got the car stuck in the mud, and I had to call my father. He was more angry than I had ever seen him. He had to get mules to come and pull it out."

Physically Billy Graham developed fast, like most southern country boys. At high school he was much the ladies' man, with his height, wavy blond hair, blue eyes, tanned skin, neat clothes, and fancy ties. He was in and out of love, sometimes dating two girls successively in the same night. But Billy remembers, "[Our parents expected us] to be clean and never doubted that we would be. They trusted us and made us want to live up to their confidence."

Farm labor gave Billy the needed release of physical energy. Every day he was milking before dawn, fast and smoothly; then he helped pour the Holstein, Guernsey, and Jersey milk into the big mixer before bottling. From school he hurried back to the afternoon milking. He reveled in sweat and exertion, whether cleaning out cow stalls, forking manure, or pitching hay.

In May 1934, Frank Graham lent a pasture to some thirty local businessmen who wanted to devote a day of prayer for Charlotte, having planned an evangelistic campaign despite the indifference of the ministers. During that day of prayer on the Graham land, their leader prayed—as Frank Graham would often recall between Billy's rise to fame in 1949 and his own death in 1962—that "out of Charlotte the Lord would raise up someone to preach the Gospel to the ends of the earth."

The businessmen next erected in the city a large "tabernacle" of raw pine on a steel frame, where for eleven weeks from September

1934 a renowned, fiery southern evangelist named Mordecai Fowler Ham, and his song leader, Walter Ramsay, shattered the complacency of church-going Charlotte.

Ham, who was then pastor of First Baptist Church in Oklahoma City, charged scandals and prejudices and was a mighty protagonist for Prohibition. Despite his old southern courtesy, he tended to "skin the ministers," as his phrase was, and cared not at all that Charlotte's most powerful clergy opposed, or that newspapers attacked him. His passionate preaching left hearers with an overwhelming realization that Christ was alive.

The Grahams did not attend Ham's campaign for at least the first week—possibly because of the tabernacle's distance and their minister's guarded neutrality toward Ham. Some neighbors then took them. After that they claimed they couldn't stay away.

Billy, too old to be ordered to attend, was "definitely antagonistic," until the Ham-Ramsey campaign exploded new controversy when Ham flung at his audience a charge of fornication among the students at Central High School. Infuriated students marched on the tabernacle, the newspapers featured the sensation, and Billy was intrigued.

Albert McMakin, the second of the sharecropper's sons, now twenty-four and newly married, had been attending the campaign regularly because a few months earlier, at one of the small preparatory meetings, he had discovered that an upright life was not enough. He filled his old truck with people from the neighborhood, both whites and blacks, and telling Billy that Ham was no "sissy" but a fighting preacher, he invited him to drive it to the meetings.

Albert's party sat at the back of the largest crowd Billy had ever seen. Far away up the "sawdust trail" of wood shavings sat the choir, and when vigorous, white-haired Mordecai Ham began to preach, Billy was "spellbound," as he wrote thirty years later. "Each listener became deeply involved with the evangelist, who had an almost embarrassing way of describing your sins and shortcomings and of demanding, on pain of divine judgment, that you mend your ways. As I listened, I began to have thoughts I had never known before."

That night in the room he shared with Melvin, Billy gazed at the full moon. As he recalls, I felt "a kind of stirring in my breast that was both pleasant and scary. Next night all my father's mules and horses could not have kept me away from the meetings."

Billy's sixteenth birthday passed. Albert McMakin detected that Billy's self-righteousness was crumbling. Ham had a habit of pointing his finger. His analysis cut so close to the bone that once Billy ducked behind the hat of the woman in front, and to escape the accusing finger applied for a place in the choir, though he could not carry a tune and his vocal efforts in the bath were a merriment to all the Grahams. He was accepted and found himself next to Grady Wilson, a casual acquaintance from another school.

The maneuver was futile. By now, as Billy remembers, "[I had] a tremendous conviction that I must commit myself. I'm sure the Lord did speak to me about certain things in my life. I'm certain of that. But I cannot remember what they were. But I do remember a great sense of burden that I was a sinner before God and had a great fear of hell and judgment."

The more he struggled to assert his own goodness, the heavier his burden grew. He now had no doubt in his mind that Christ had died on the cross to bear Billy's sins, and each night the conviction grew that Christ, whose resurrection Billy had never doubted in theory, was actually alive, wanting to take away that burden. If only Billy would commit himself unreservedly, Christ would be his Savior and Friend. Billy was far less conscious of Mordecai Ham than of Christ. Yet the price of Christ's friendship would be total surrender for a lifelong discipleship—Billy would no longer be his own master. A price he was not yet prepared to pay. When Ham invited those who would accept Christ to move toward the pulpit in an act of witness and definition, Billy Graham stayed in his seat.

The inward struggle continued, at school in his desk, in the gym playing basketball, in the barn milking. He did not tell his parents (who suspected and were hoping and praying), but talked with his cousin Crook Stafford, who encouraged him to go forward although Crook had not yet done so himself. Billy moved again the next night and sat near the front. Ham's smile seemed consciously directed. Billy, quite wrongly, was certain Ham knew about him and quoted specially for him, "God commendeth his love toward us in that while we were yet sinners, Christ died for us."

Ham made the appeal. Billy heard the choir sing, "Just As I Am, Without One Plea," verse by verse, as people gathered round the pulpit. Billy stayed in his seat, his conscience wrestling with his will. The choir began, "Almost persuaded, Christ to believe." Billy could stand it no longer and went forward.

As Billy recalls, "It was not just the technique of walking forward in a Southern revival meeting. It was Christ. I was conscious of him."

A short man with dark hair and dark eyes, an English-born tailor whom Billy knew and liked, approached him and they talked and prayed. Billy had a "deep sense of peace and joy," but around him many were in tears, and he worried a bit because he felt so matter-of-fact. His father came across, threw his arms round him, and thanked God for his decision.

That night Billy Graham walked upstairs past the old family clock ticking loudly the time, day, and month, and undressed in the dark because Melvin was already asleep. The moon rode high again and Billy looked out across his father's land, then laid for hours unemotionally checking over in the context of his adolescent world what should be the attitudes of a fellow who belonged to Christ. He drifted into sleep content and at peace, with just a grain of doubt: "I wonder if this will last."

2

THE EIGHTEENTH GREEN

THE FLORIDA BIBLE INSTITUTE'S ELEGANT CREAM-COLORED, Spanish-style building in Temple Terrace, near Tampa, faced the eighteenth tee of a golf course. It had been a country club, picked up for a song by the founder, Dr. W. T. Watson, at the height of the Depression. In 1937, the Institute had thirty male and forty female students. The remainder of the rooms were used as a hotel and Bible conference center.

The Graham family drove up in a new Plymouth on a February morning in 1937 to drop Billy off at the school. In the just over two years since the Ham mission, Billy had grown as a Christian. He gave his first faltering testimony in the small jail at Monroe, North Carolina, where he had gone with a young evangelist, Jimmy Johnson, who did not regard him as a candidate for fame: "He was a typical, unpredictable, gangling tall young man," but he had a great personality and was very likeable. Billy had no firm ideas for a career, except that he no longer wished to be a farmer, and he wanted to continue his education beyond a high school level.

His parents' first choice was Bob Jones College, which was then located in Cleveland, Tennessee, because they admired several men that had gone there. Following a summer in which Billy and his great friend Grady Wilson worked as Fuller Brush salesmen and Billy's sales topped the whole list, the two boys entered Bob Jones College in the fall of 1936, shortly before Billy's eighteenth birthday.

Neither the college nor the climate suited him. Billy was soon unhappy. Two bouts of flu during the Christmas vacation and the start of his respiratory troubles increased his reluctance to return. The physician prescribed sunshine. During a family holiday with Mrs. Graham's sister in Florida, they heard about the Bible Institute. Billy finished the semester at Bob Jones with Dr. Bob's ominous words in his ears: "Billy, if you leave and throw your life away at a little country Bible school, the chances are you'll never be heard of. At best, all you could amount to would be a poor country Baptist preacher somewhere out in the sticks."

At Temple Terrace, Billy Graham burgeoned in the freedom and family spirit, the sunshine and scenery. The school was too small for baseball, though convenient for watching (through a hole in the fence) the big league training sessions. There were tennis and volleyball courts and the Hillsboro River for swimming and canoeing. On the golf course, Billy first began to caddy and then began to play. Though his father paid the modest fees, Billy worked like the other students since it was an outlet for his unceasing energy. He sought grass cutting, hedge trimming, and other jobs to develop his wiry strength. He also washed dishes, claiming he washed so fast that he could keep four girls busy.

With his nice clothes, suits regularly sent to the cleaners, bright bow ties for the evenings, Billy Graham was a favorite. A good fellow to have around, he was vital, generous, clean-limbed, and clear-eyed. Yet he was aimless, lacking serious application to lectures or study.

At an ordinary school, these virtues and defects might have left him a charming incompetent. However, the Florida Bible Institute (now Trinity College in Clearwater) put an exceptional emphasis on individual instruction. The faculty worked from the belief that the latent possibilities of each student must be fostered, and that the Holy Spirit, if allowed to operate in his own time and way, could make of a man what he would. And the dean, John Minder, with his humorous eyes and endless patience, applied this principle to Billy.

Having heard Billy give his testimony outside the dog track at Sulphur Springs, Minder invited him to stay during the Easter vacation of 1937 at the little conference center he had developed on the shores of Lake Swan near Melrose in northern Florida. On Easter Sunday evening, they drove to Palatka above the broad St. John's River to visit Minder's close friend Cecil Underwood, an interior decorator who was a Baptist preacher. They found him trying to line up a preacher at the nearby country community of Bostick. In the car Underwood suggested Minder might preach. Minder replied, "Billy's preaching tonight."

"No sir," said a horrified Billy. "I've never preached before."

"Well, you are preaching tonight," said Minder. "When you run out, I'll take over."

Billy had secretly prepared and practiced four sermons on themes taken from a famous Baptist preacher, each to last forty-five minutes.

They drove up to the church, stepped through the beagles and hounds that had accompanied their masters, and joined a congregation of twenty-five or thirty cowboys and ranchers. The song leader, a man of odd jobs from junk collecting to fishing, led off in a raucous marching hymn, pausing occasionally to spit tobacco juice into the boiler. Underwood introduced Billy, whose knees knocked and palms and brow were sticky. Billy began loud and fast, and worked through all four sermons in eight minutes. But Underwood noted that "his delivery was impressive, even that first sermon, because of his sincerity."

Back at Temple Terrace, Minder asked Billy to preach to the young people at his church, Tampa Gospel Tabernacle. That night Billy could hardly sleep. He studied, prayed, and sweated, and he crept outside the next morning to practice preaching to the squirrels and rabbits. Sunday evening left Billy sure he would never make it as a preacher. His audience, however, so appreciated this dramatic, forceful youth that before the summer semester was over, Minder invited him to take charge of the young people's department.

By early 1938, at age nineteen when Billy had been at Temple Terrace for a year, he was still an overgrown undisciplined boy without purpose. Three major upheavals turned him into a man of overriding purpose and intense conviction.

Two Christians whom he had admired were accused of serious moral defections. Billy was shaken. He determined that nothing should ever be allowed in his life, known or unknown, that could harm the name of Christ. Furthermore, he realized that this could not happen unless he took his vocation as a Christian seriously.

An even stronger influence began to shape him. Temple Terrace had become a vacation attraction to prominent evangelicals from the north and the south. Billy had the inestimable benefit of rubbing the shoulders (or at least wiping the boots) of the great. He listened attentively as they discoursed on the decline of religion in America—church budgets low, church buildings emptying, church preaching blunted and confused. These old stalwarts who had seen the fires die down had one theme: We need a prophet. We need a man to call America back to God.

A "tremendous burden" began to weigh on Billy Graham. On walks at night across the golf course and along the open streets laid out for housing estates never built, he faced his future. He believed he would not be a preacher: He was too poorly educated. Yet he began to sense an unmistakable call. Praying aloud as he walked the empty countryside, he answered that call in Moses' words at the burning bush: "They will not believe me, nor harken unto my voice. . . . I am not eloquent."

During these days the president's secretary, Brunette Brock, would often say, "Billy, God has called you to preach." During the walks at night, he struggled with excuses. His indifferent background might indeed keep him a mediocre preacher "somewhere out in the sticks." Yet any sacrifice appeared trivial beside Christ's sufferings or the world's needs. As for eloquence, the Lord had told Moses, "Go, and I will be with thy mouth, and teach thee what thou shalt say." Billy hesitated because for him the call was absolute. If he accepted, he must henceforth have no other ambition, no other occupation but the proclaiming of God's message, everywhere, to everybody, always.

One night in March 1938, Billy Graham returned from his walk and reached the eighteenth green immediately before the school's front door. He recalls, "The trees were loaded with Spanish moss, and in the moonlight it was like a fairyland." He sat down on the edge of the green, looking up at the moon and stars, aware of a warm breeze from the south. The tension snapped. "I remember getting on my knees and saying, 'O God, if you want me to preach, I will do it.'"

In the days following, "I used to walk those empty streets in Temple Terrace praying. I would pray sometimes three or four hours at a stretch. And then," he recalled a quarter of a century after, "in the most unusual way I used to have the strangest glimpses of these great crowds that I now preach to." He certainly did not see himself as the preacher, and scarcely believed great crowds would ever come together again to hear the Gospel, but the daydreams or visions flashed across his consciousness. "I think I saw myself as participating in some way in what Billy Sunday and D. L. Moody had witnessed—big stadiums, big meetings."

Some weeks later, he faced a third upheaval: The girl whom he hoped to marry was no longer sure. Emily Regina Cavanaugh, one year older than Billy, had a sparkling personality and was intelligent, musical, vivacious, and dedicated. Billy had loved her from the moment he first saw her. During the summer vacation of 1937, he had proposed by letter. In February 1938, she had accepted. They did not expect to marry for three or four years, but their friends and families rejoiced. Early in May, Emily told Billy that she was again uncertain and asked him to pray.

In a basement room every day for fifteen minutes, Billy prayed that they should marry—if, and only if, it were God's will. Emotional suspense bred spiritual development, for he had seldom related prayer to specific matters before this time. This was different than the wide sweeping vistas of the world's need. And never before had he seen such answers.

Emily found herself deeper in love with Charles Massey, a senior classman whom Billy admired. Before class night in May 1938, each of the boys ordered from Larson, the florist, a twenty-five-cent corsage for his girl. Billy exclaimed, "I'll buy a fifty-cent one. Emily must have the best."

Emily did not wear it. During the party she asked to speak to Billy outside. They sat on one of the swings on the riverside, and she told him gently that she was going to marry Charles. They parted friends.

Billy sought John Minder, who consoled him by the Scripture verse, "The God of all comfort ... comforteth us in all our tribulation, that we may be able to comfort them which are in any trouble." Billy bravely rejoined the social evening.

"One of two things can happen in a time like that," comments Billy. "You can resist and become bitter, or you can let God break you. And I determined to let God have his way."

"Every letter he wrote home," recalled his mother years later, "he was heartbroken; you could read that between the lines. But instead of it depressing him, he turned to the Lord and the Lord sustained him. Every letter was full of that."

Billy threw himself into his newly accepted commission to preach. "I now had a purpose, an objective, a call. That was when the growing up began, and the discipline to study."

At first he was forced to create most of his opportunities. "I would take two or three students with me, or somebody that would sing, and go down on a street corner." On Sundays he would hold seven or eight street-corner services. Once he began preaching in front of a saloon full of prostitutes and drunken people on Franklin Street, which in those days was Tampa's worst. "I stood right in the door, preaching to the people sitting at the bar. The barkeeper came out and ordered me away, and I wouldn't go. He just shoved me down, and I half fell and half tripped into the wet street. I got my clothes messed up. I remembered the words of Jesus, and felt that I was suffering for Christ's sake. It was quite tactless the way I went about it, zeal with no knowledge; but those were experiences that helped develop me."

The first time he gave the "invitation" or altar call was at Venice on the Gulf shore in the only church, a converted meat market. The parents of a Bible Institute girl had telephoned for a preacher. The morning service seemed sluggish, so Billy and his soloist spent the afternoon praying on the dirt floor of the garage of their hosts, who were out encouraging the local youths to attend. The church that evening was crowded.

Billy thought his sermon indifferent, but when he gave the invitation, thirty-two young men and women came forward. The superintendent of the Sunday school remarked afterward, "There's a young man who is going to be known around the world!"

Billy secured a regular invitation to the Tampa City Mission. He was made a chaplain to the trailer parks. He visited the prisoners at the Stockade. "That's where I started my discussion groups. I had them ask me questions. A lot of them I couldn't answer, but I did it deliberately not only to help them, but to try to sharpen my mind."

Billy was always seeking to educate himself. Most ministers acquire learning and then, from the superiority of pastorate or priesthood, begin to impart. Billy learned to preach while his fund of knowledge was limited. "I had one passion, and that was to win souls. I didn't have a passion to be a great preacher; I had a passion to win souls. I'd never been trained as a public speaker. I had to learn in the best way I knew." His stock of sermons was small, but he knew exactly what he would say. He did not write them out except in outlines, but he practiced them even to cypress swamps and alligators. He was not perfecting a technique. "It was all unconscious. I wasn't practicing gestures; I was practicing my material, learning my material. I felt I was not prepared to preach a sermon until I had practiced it many, many times."

He preached too loud. He preached too fast. He dramatized and was dubbed "the preaching windmill," but the tramps, alcoholics, prisoners, and the northern winter visitors in the trailer parks knew what Billy meant. His goal, whether preaching or speaking with individuals, was not to promote an idea but to bring them to know the living Christ. Dedication to a cause or an idea might have hardened or narrowed Billy Graham; dedication to a Person sweetened him. The biggest fault was lack of balance. He practiced and prayed so hard during the day that by the time he came to the pulpit in the evening, he was worn out. His mind refused to relax at night. Light sleeping became the insomnia that has troubled him ever since.

In the summer of 1939, John Minder departed to California for six weeks, leaving Billy in charge of the Tampa Gospel Tabernacle, where he learned the hard labor of ministry to the poor. During his last year at the institute, while war came to Europe far away, he was in growing demand at obscure churches and chapels in different parts of Florida. With his parents' approval, he became a Southern Baptist. He was ordained in 1939 by the St. John's Association at Peniel, Cecil Underwood's white-painted clapboard church under the cedar trees between Silver Lake and Lake Rosie.

At graduation in May of 1940, the class valedictorian, Vera Resue, her mind on the war and the spiritual darkness engulfing the world, and without thought of an individual, uttered words that years afterward were seen to be prophetic. At each critical epoch of the church, she said, God has "a chosen human instrument to shine forth his light in the darkness. Men like Luther, John and Charles Wesley, Moody, and others who were ordinary men, but men who heard the voice of God. . . . It has been said that Luther revolutionized the world. It was not he, but Christ working through him. The time is ripe for another Luther, Wesley, Moody. There is room for another name in this list."

3

THE GIRL FROM CHINA

A BROWN-HAIRED, HAZEL-EYED GIRL OF TWENTY, A SECOND-year student at Wheaton College near Chicago, was in the entrance to East Blanchard Hall in the fall of 1940 when she noticed a blond fellow running down the steps. "He was tall and lanky and just dashed past," and she thought, *There's a young man who knows where he's going!*

The father of one of her friends had told Ruth Bell to keep an eye out for a young minister and remarkable preacher called Billy Graham coming to campus, but she had not met him yet. Some days later she was part of a group of students meeting for prayer before going out to teach Sunday school or for similar work. They divided into small parties in the lobby of Williston Hall and went into different rooms. "We would take turns praying, and all of a sudden I heard a voice from the next room. I had never heard anyone pray like it before. I knew that someone was talking to God. I sensed that here was a man that knew God in a very unusual way."

Billy Graham had entered Wheaton as a freshman. Keen for a university education, he had seized an opening offered in Florida by relatives of the new president of Wheaton, V. Raymond Edman, though it would mean living in the unfamiliar world of the northern states. To work his way through college, Billy had joined a senior, Johnny Streater, in running a truck, and it was Streater who effected the introduction between Billy and Ruth in the lobby of Williston Hall outside the college cafeteria. Billy fell in love at first sight.

Ruth and Billy went together to the glee club's *Messiah* on a snowy Sunday afternoon and afterward to supper at Professor Lane's. Billy recalled that he "could not believe anyone could be so beautiful and so sweet." They stood for a long time talking beside a tree near the college entrance. Later, Billy wrote to his mother that this was the girl he would marry. Ruth had not yet fallen in love with Bill, as she always calls him. However, that very first Sunday night, she knelt beside her bed in prayer. She said to the Lord, "If I could spend the rest of my life serving you with Bill, I would consider it the greatest privilege imaginable."

Ruth McCue Bell was born of Virginia parents in North China where her father, a Presbyterian surgeon, had helped develop a substantial missionary hospital, despite civil wars and Japanese occupation.[1] Dr. Bell described his daughter in childhood as "an interesting mixture of deep spirituality and mischievous fun." The second of three sisters with a younger brother, she had spent most of her life in the Orient. At Wheaton, her housemother wrote of her in 1943: "Very attractive, beautiful to look at, and excellent taste in dress. The most beautiful Christian character of any young person I have ever known. And she has the intellectual qualities to make a success in any work she would choose to undertake. She ranks very high in the qualities of poise, forcefulness, and courtesy."

Ruth had many admirers. That first Sunday night, back at Professor Gerstung's home where he roomed, Billy slumped in a chair and, as Gerstung recalls, "bemoaned the fact that he had no chance with Ruth because he had so little to commend him."

Ruth soon thought otherwise. "There was a seriousness about him; a depth. He was much older in every way than the other students on the campus, not just in age. He was a mature man; he was a man who knew God; he was a man who had a purpose, a dedication in life; he knew where he was going. He wanted to please God more than any man I'd ever met." She recognized that he was a very intelligent man, though in no sense an "egghead." Her one reservation was that, though there was plenty of fun in his personality, "he was so very serious about life in general. He didn't have enough time to go to ball games. Every date we had was to a preaching service of some kind. Yet for all his terrific dedication and drive, there was a winsomeness about him, and a consideration for other people, which I found very endearing."

Love grew, but Ruth's ambition was to be a pioneer missionary in Tibet, and for this she was prepared to renounce romance. Billy, though closely interested in foreign missions, had no indication that God called him to be a missionary. He believed that Ruth was essentially a homemaker, not a pioneer, and that when she married, it would be to him. He bided his time. The Bells returned on furlough in the spring of 1941. In the summer Ruth and Billy became engaged.

Back at Wheaton, Ruth again feared that to marry him would deny a clear missionary call, unless he too were bound for Tibet. He prayed but had no leading there. Finally Billy asked her, "Do you believe that God brought us together?" Ruth did, unquestionably. Billy pointed out that the Bible teaches that the husband is head of the wife: "God will lead me and you will do the following." Ruth agreed, in faith.

More than anyone, Ruth broadened Billy's mind. She had no need to polish his manners or graces, as D. L. Moody's were polished by his wife, but she was cultured, traveled, with a love of art and literature. She saved his seriousness from degenerating into stuffy solemnity, and preserved from extinction the light touch, the slice of small boy. Moreover, Ruth and her family, loyal Presbyterians, eased Billy Graham from his unspoken conviction that a vigorous scriptural faith could not dwell within the great denominations, and underlined Wheaton's lesson that a strong evangelical should focus his vision on the entire horizon of Christianity.

Billy, who expected to go on to theological seminary, chose a nontheological subject as his major at Wheaton: anthropology, a new, exciting course under an able professor, Alexander Grigolia.

Billy got good grades and might have made the honor roll had not his life again taken an unusual turn in the fall of 1941.

Dr. Edman wished to be relieved of his part-time pastorate of the United Gospel Tabernacle of Wheaton and Glen Ellyn, a small independent church served previously by student pastors. On his recommendation, the deacons offered it to Billy Graham, who was spending his vacation preaching in youth crusades in Florida.

The Tabernacle hired a small hall. Virtually no more than a preaching center, it was the church of many students and faculty. In the words of an associate professor, Billy's delivery was "rapid, earnest, forceful, simple, a very direct approach. He had a message he wanted to get across, and it came right through without hesitation and stumbling." There might be extravagances, mispronunciations, a touch of Mordecai Ham and the sawdust trail, but the hall was always packed. Ruth's memory, endorsed by that of Wheaton contemporaries, is that "you weren't impressed with his earnestness, you weren't impressed by his gestures. You were impressed that there was Someone speaking to you beside Bill. There was another voice than his."

The Tabernacle, and later his presidency of the Christian Student Council, interfered with studies, but Billy thirsted for learning. He became one of the circle of the hospitable, wealthy Professor Mortimer Lane, a much traveled former public servant, who combined knowledge of the Bible with a gift for imparting an understanding of politics and economics. Billy became fascinated by the American political and economic scene.

After the events at Pearl Harbor, Billy offered himself as an Army chaplain. He was told to finish college, and his professors persuaded him not to volunteer for combat duty. As the Army required him after graduation to do a year at seminary or in a pastorate, he accepted one without consulting Ruth, to her considerable indignation. Western Springs was a typical semirural, high middle-class suburb of Chicago: straight streets, houses with unfenced lawns, and ten or more places of worship including a well-supported Methodist center—and one mortgage-ridden Baptist church in a basement, which appointed him to be pastor immediately on graduation.

Billy and Ruth were married on Friday, August 13, 1943, at Montreat, the Presbyterian conference center in the mountains of North Carolina where the Bells had settled when the war prevented return to China. After a week's honeymoon in a room at a cottage in Blowing Rock, high in the Blue Ridge Mountains, the Grahams returned to Illinois and made their home in a four-room apartment in Hinsdale, a neighboring community, since they could not find a place in Western Springs. They were one block from the main line of the Burlington Railroad, and for the first week every train sounded as if it were going straight through the living room.

Billy endured Ruth's early adventures in cooking without complaining, and Ruth the muddle on Billy's desk and his habit of treating the top of the bathroom door as a towel rack. They differed in temperament and in many ideas. "If you agree on everything, there's not going to be much growth for either one," Ruth commented long after. "I don't think happy marriages are ever accidental. They are the result of good, hard work." The Grahams's love for one another fast grew deep and abiding.

The church people enjoyed Billy's sermons, were amused by the loud socks and ties, and gratified by Ruth's poise and smartness despite a restricted wardrobe. Billy organized house-to-house calls, sought out storekeepers, especially those that other ministers preferred not to know, and with Bob Van Kampen launched the Western Suburban Professional Men's Club, meeting over dinner seven times a winter, to which Billy personally persuaded business executives of highest rank and tightest schedules. Soon he had more than three hundred men dining to listen to an evangelistic speaker.

Billy was deepening his understanding of the importance of a pastor in the work of evangelism, but a little church in a suburb seemed trivial in the midst of a world war. He waited impatiently for his chaplaincy commission.

Then, early in October 1943, a telephone call came from Tor-rey Johnson, pastor of a flourishing church and professor of New Testament Greek, but best known around Chicago for his broad-casts. Billy, almost not believing his ears, heard the suggestion that his Village Church take over Johnson's *Songs in the Night*—forty-five minutes of preaching and singing carried live by one of Chicago's most powerful commercial stations at 10:15 P.M. each Sunday.

The cost would be over $100 weekly, and the station required an initial contract for thirteen weeks. The pledged income of the Village Church was $86.50 a week; yet the people raised among themselves enough for five broadcasts.

Billy was now flying high. In Chicago lived a Canadian-born, thirty-seven-year-old bass baritone named George Beverly Shea, who was a famous Christian soloist and broadcaster, especially on the American Broadcasting Company's *Club Time*, a program of hymns. One of his own compositions, "I'd Rather Have Jesus," was already popular. Billy went to the radio station where Shea was pro-gram manager and announcer and received a polite brush-off from the receptionist. After turning to go out, Billy thought, *No, I've come to see him. I'm going to see him.* And he walked straight in.

Beverly Shea was gracious and guarded, but Billy was persis-tent. *Songs in the Night* with Beverly Shea came on the air from Western Springs in January 1944.

Young people from all over the Chicago area would hurry out after their own evening church services to see and hear Beverly Shea in person. Letters came, money came, covering not only the broadcast but enabling Billy solemnly to burn the mortgage of the church in a pie plate. Billy's southern accent, now deliberately tamed, was an immediate hit with the Yankees. And he preached in the way that was to become specially his: Against a backdrop of the latest news and world events, he would proclaim the urgent rel-evance of Christ in such manner that the listener longed to know him. Billy urged immediate decision.

Then, in the spring of 1944, Torrey Johnson offered an even greater opportunity. Johnson was concerned about the hundreds of servicemen who swept into Chicago every weekend, tough, cynical, sex-starved, indifferent to God and man. On the last Saturday night of April 1944, he found an answer. He was present in First Baptist Church at Minneapolis, where a thirty-year-old businessman named George M. Wilson had organized a Youth for Christ Rally, in the belief that the Gospel could reach servicemen and unchurched civilians too, if clean excitement was linked with an uncompromising Christian message. Johnson immediately formed Chicagoland's Youth for Christ and booked Orchestra Hall, with three thousand seats, next door to the USO Center, for twenty-one Saturday nights. Most of Chicago rated him foolish.

For the preacher at his opening rally, he chose Billy Graham. Johnson could have had any famous preacher but wished to work with the young ministers who shared his vision and had an instinctive understanding of their generation. Johnson had not the slightest doubt that for an evangelistic sermon to youth, Billy Graham had no equal.

Johnson saw him "thrilled at the prospect but dreadfully afraid he might fail." On Saturday evening, May 20, 1944, they gathered in the stage room of Orchestra Hall. Billy paced up and down, biting his nails, palms sticky, throat dry; he claimed it to be the worst fit of stage fright of his life. They prayed together and walked onstage. With one consent, they kept their eyes to the main floor, daring to hope that this at least would be full. They glanced higher and saw the lower balcony full too; and, to their wonder, the upper. Only the high "peanut gallery" was thin. Someone reckoned a total of 2,800, mostly service personnel, were present.

After a swift program of songs, instrumental music, community singing, Bible reading, and prayer, Billy began to preach. Words came tumbling. "As my nerves relaxed, I felt I was merely a mouthpiece and soon became unaware of the audience." At the invitation to commit their lives, Billy marveled to see forty-two people come forward, a high number for the times.

In October, Billy was commissioned a second lieutenant in the United States Army, with orders to await entry to a chaplains' training course at Harvard Divinity School. Then he got mumps.

The mumps took the most virulent and painful form. His temperature raged and one night Ruth thought he was dying. Billy was in bed for six weeks, emerging thin as a lath, and thankful to go to Florida, helped by a listener's gift.

Torrey Johnson was in Florida too. In Miami out in a fishing boat under the Florida sun, which Billy so loved, Torrey outlined a plan to coordinate Saturday night rallies across the country, to capture and inspire American youth. Since the Army would relegate a convalescent to a desk, Billy should now resign his commission and his church, and with such funds as Johnson could raise, become the first full-time organizer and evangelist of Youth for Christ.

Billy, like Johnson, saw it as a spearhead of return to a forthright Christianity—in America, Canada, the world.

4

GEARED TO THE TIMES

DURING 1945 BILLY GRAHAM TRAVELED THROUGHOUT THE United States and Canada, hurrying back whenever he could to Montreat where the Grahams lived with the Bells and later in their own home next door. Their first child, Virginia (known as Gigi, Chinese for "sister") was born in September. Billy and Ruth missed each other terribly. It was harder on the wife left behind, but a missionary childhood had prepared her for frequent goodbyes.

Billy and the Youth for Christ pioneers believed in a combination of efficient organization and daring faith. Their Saturday night rallies went in for bright solos, choirs, and bands. They wore loud hand-painted ties and bright suits, so all the world might know Christianity to be no dreary faith. Clothes and excitement were essentially contemporary American, but rally organizers learned to cut back on the noise and the glamour and the lights if Billy Graham was preaching. A long musical program meant a short sermon. As Billy put it, "If I preach short we're not going to do the job of winning souls."

The motto was "Geared to the Times, Anchored to the Rock." At a time when denominational leaders were convinced that the great Christian doctrines no longer might be preached with emphasis, Youth for Christ demonstrated that young men and women would respond to the unashamed proclamation of a Christ who worked miracles, shed his blood on the cross, rose bodily from the dead, and could transform the lives of any who accepted him. The

Bible became alive again, not a document to be mutilated or a set of propositions to be defended, but a living Word.

Once the war ended, Torrey Johnson wished to introduce Youth for Christ to Britain and Europe. He selected Billy for his four-man team, but since they daringly decided to cross the Atlantic by air, they could not obtain passages until March 1946.

They rushed through England, Scotland, and Ireland in three weeks. The American's blend of seriousness and boyishness left hosts at a loss. They were astonished, for instance, when at the Manchester rally, Billy and the soloist went to the phone booth during the intermission, and preached and sung to a rally at Birkenhead over a previously booked landline.

Billy was not generally regarded as showing the greatest potential in the team. He endeared himself as "a man of much courtesy and Christian gentlemanliness." When the others were considered somewhat indifferent and know-it-all Americans, Billy was soaking up the British scene. "Learning was an insatiable desire with me. I burned to learn, and I felt my limitations of schooling and background so terribly that I determined to try to do all I could through conversations, picking everything I could from everybody."

Billy Graham fell in love with Britain. He had begun with a tendency to dismiss the clergy as neither geared to the times nor anchored to the Rock, but he now knew that a genuine revival must come through the mainstream denominations. The southerner who had scarcely met an Episcopalian began even to grasp the peculiar significance of the Church of England.

During the summer of 1946, he raised money in America, and in October was back in Britain with his own team—Cliff and Billie Barrows.

A year before, Billy had gone to Ben Lippen Bible Conference in the North Carolina mountains to address a youth night. The conference song leader had left. Billy was offered an athletic Californian, who was twenty-two years old and on his honeymoon. He accepted Cliff Barrows dubiously under the impression that this was a newly graduated college kid. Doubts were instantly dispersed when Cliff's skill and sunny disposition, aided by a fine voice, a trombone, and the piano playing of his wife, Billie, extracted every ounce of song from a delighted audience.

Barrows, son of a farmer in the San Joaquin Valley, had studied sacred music at college. Ordained a Baptist minister in California, Barrows spent nearly a year as an assistant pastor in Minnesota, with special responsibility for song leading and youth.

Billy had money enough for six months in Britain, provided they were frugal. Their target was not correspondingly modest: "We are asking God for a thousand souls a month, and a thousand young people to respond to the challenge of the mission field." The meetings began in an obscure small Welsh town called Gorseinon, where Billy and George Wilson of Minneapolis, who had come over to help set up the tour, were guests of a mining family. The two of them stayed in one bed and were so cold because of the national fuel rationing that they went to bed right after the meeting with clothes on. Breakfast every morning was a tomato stuffed with bread. For a whole week they never saw meat.

Billy and the Barrows spoke in twenty-seven cities and towns of the British Isles at 360 meetings, between October 1946 and March 1947. A David and Jonathan bond was forged. They were alike in dedication, in ability to work without stint, but Cliff was not highly strung, and no one ever saw him bite his nails. Young Cliff had a secret hope that he too would become an evangelist in his own right, yet he consistently pushed Billy forward. The two steadily evolved methods slightly less brash and noisy, although to the British and Irish, the very idea of a song leader with a trombone was sensational. And Billy went on learning, spiritually and intellectually, from whoever he could.

At Birmingham, where in 1946 over 90 percent of its million citizens were said never to attend a church regularly, adverse reports of Youth for Christ's "showmanship" in America caused cancellation of the city hall. Ministers snubbed the organizers, and the first night of a ten-day campaign drew only two or three hundred people.

Stanley Baker, one of the ministers who had refused to help, a middle-aged Baptist, heard the phone ring and found himself, as he wrote a week or two later, "linked with a wounded spirit and a pained heart. He wasn't bitter, he didn't chide me; he hadn't one word of a lecture; he merely wondered.... Within an hour I sat in Billy's hotel room.... His was the nearest spirit to my Lord's I have ever met." Baker at once began calling ministers, and Billy visited some twenty people. One by one they began to help. Billy moved into the Grand Hotel instead of staying at a home in the suburbs, and for several nights, two or three ministers remained into the late hours praying with him for a blessing on Birmingham.

Numbers rose nightly. They secured the city hall after all for a packed Saturday and Sunday, and scores came forward, young and old. The Lord Mayor hastily reissued a cancelled invitation for tea. The Bishop of Birmingham, the extreme liberal, Ernest Barnes, asked the twenty-eight-year-old Billy to address a diocesan gathering on Evangelism in the Twentieth Century.

The British nation as a whole remained unaware of Billy's existence. The national press ignored him. Many evangelicals remained cautious, but an Anglican clergyman, Tom Livermore, arranged a Graham-Barrows youth campaign centered in his southeast London parish in February 1947. The worst winter for a hundred years combined with the national fuel crisis produced an icy fogbound church and darkened streets along which young and old stumbled through the snow. Billy, bounding up the pulpit looking to Londoners like a film star, said Livermore, "had a tremendous appeal to the ignorant and unlettered and the rougher element of the boys and girls." The same was true in the fog-enclosed, bomb-shattered port of Southampton, where Joe Blinco, a Methodist pastor and evangelist, felt this man "was fresh from God; his message had a freshness about it—cleanness in the sense that a mountain might be cleaned out by the wind and the rain."

Blinco, by origin and ministry a man of the people, also recognized Billy's social concern. It might be still naive or dogmatic, but "Billy, from the very first time I remember him, spoke always against the background of the tragic situation in society." And Blinco thought Billy had so strong a world vision that he discounted it as American big talk, until he came to know Billy better.

When the tour ended with a conference of two hundred and fifty leaders in youth work, summoned by Billy to Birmingham in March, several Britons had begun to believe that Billy Graham should return for a campaign not limited to youth. They had caught a gleam that could pierce war weariness, and the defeatism, the little-mindedness that had settled on much of British religion.[2]

5

LOS ANGELES 1949

B Y THE SUMMER OF 1949, THE THIRTY-YEAR-OLD BILLY GRAHAM had become much more than an evangelist to youth. Though not yet known nationally, he had a growing reputation in North America as an evangelist for "citywide campaigns," as they were called, the phrase carrying more potential than accuracy.

He was in demand at Bible conferences. After one conference a fellow-speaker wrote to Billy: "I do thank God for the transparency of your life and the sweetness of your spirit. No wonder he uses you so mightily, and I pray that you may ever be kept so humble and so sweet in the will of the Lord." Billy's personal character was the foundation of his message, and he was already very concerned to remove the tarnish that had settled on American mass-evangelism since the great days of D. L. Moody.

Billy was also now the reluctant, if energetic, president of Northwestern schools, a large interdenominational Bible school, seminary, and liberal arts college it Minneapolis, the pleasant city of lakes and woods and nearly half a million inhabitants in the heart of the Scandinavian region of America. Against his better judgment, he had accepted the deathbed pleas of its founder, the veteran evangelical, W. B. Riley. The presidency of Northwestern was a diversion from evangelism. But it stretched his mind, gave Billy invaluable training in finance, promotion, and administration, helped teach him delegation and the molding of a team, and how to tap the right sources of advice. It brought several colleagues who would work with him on a wider field, while Minneapolis became the natural center for the administration of his expanding ministry. And Northwestern's tensions and difficulties put into his spirit the steel without which no man comes to greatness.

Billy now faced a date with destiny: a three-week campaign in his first major city, Los Angeles, with Cliff Barrows, Bev Shea, and Grady Wilson as his team in late September 1949. "I want to see God sweep in," he told a somewhat hesitant committee, "because if Los Angeles could have a great revival, the ramifications and repercussions would sweep across the entire world." Yet when the committee accepted his conditions, he was almost sorry. Billy was in the thick of a spiritual battle within his own soul.

His close friend and former colleague in Youth for Christ, Charles Templeton, had become unsure of the integrity of Scripture. "Billy, your faith is too simple," he insisted. Billy took Templeton seriously, but the more Billy debated and read, the more confused he grew.

Could he, in the middle of the twentieth century, continue to accept the authority of the Bible? Could he, with the apostle Paul, "declare unto you the gospel ... how that Christ died for our sins according to the scriptures; And that he was buried, and that he rose again the third day according to the scriptures?" This was not loss of faith but loss of balance, yet the terrific pain at the base of his skull, which plagued him in the spring of 1949 and puzzled the doctors, was probably, as Billy suggested, caused by nervous tension and exhaustion.

In June the team held a ten-day campaign at the railroad city of Altoona, Pennsylvania. Local preparation had been scanty and the ministers were at each other's throats, but Billy believed the cause of failure lay in himself, his nagging uncertainties.

After Altoona, Billy felt that he must decide once and for all either to spend his life studying whether or not God had spoken, or to spend it as God's ambassador, bringing a message that he might not fully comprehend in all details until after death. Must an intellectually honest man know everything about the Bible's origins before he could use it?

Billy believed that his special gift lay in the "invitation" to receive Christ. He was primarily a "doorkeeper in the house of God," helping people to enter. Once entered, they would be aided by others to appreciate the treasures of the house and learn more fully to serve. At a Bible conference in Michigan in July 1949, Billy was talking with his old Florida friend Roy Gustafson and became very serious. Roy said, "He looked at me with those piercing eyes and he said, 'Roy, when I come to my invitation I sense God come on me, and I feel a power at that invitation that's peculiar.'" And now might he be preaching a doubtful Gospel derived from a not wholly trustworthy Bible?

At the same conference, Roy and another friend were with Billy when the aurora borealis lit up the sky. They began talking of the Second Advent. Suddenly Billy said, "Oh, if somehow the Lord could use me a little bit." They decided to have their prayer time under the stars and northern lights. In a few moments they heard a strange, muffled voice. Billy lay face down in the wet grass praying: "Lord, trust me to do something for you before you come!"

In the last days of August, Billy and Templeton went to California as faculty members of a student conference at Forest Home, five thousand feet high in the pine-laden air of the San Bernardino Mountains behind Los Angeles. One evening, in serious discussion, a mutual friend reported a remark by Templeton: "Poor Billy. If he goes on the way he's going, he'll never do anything for God. He'll be circumscribed to a small little narrow interpretation of the Bible, and his ministry will be curtailed. As for me, I'm taking a different road."

Templeton is sure that he never made such a remark; but whatever his actual words, these were the ones to reach Billy.

Billy was deeply disturbed and hurt. After supper, instead of attending evening service, he retired to his log cabin and read again the Bible passages concerning its authority. He recalled someone saying that the prophets used such phrases as "the Word of the Lord came" or "thus saith the Lord" more than two thousand times. He meditated on the attitude of Christ: "He loved the Scriptures, quoted from them constantly, and never once intimated that they might be wrong."

Billy went out in the forest and wandered up the mountain, praying as he walked, "Lord, what shall I do? What shall be the direction of my life?" He knew he had reached a crisis. He saw that intellect alone could not resolve the question of authority. He must go beyond intellect. He thought of the faith used constantly in daily life: Was it only in things of the Spirit that faith was wrong?

"So I went back and I got my Bible, and I went out in the moonlight. And I got to a stump and put the Bible on the stump, and I knelt down, and I said, 'Oh, God; I cannot prove certain things, I cannot answer some of the questions Chuck is raising and some of the other people are raising, but I accept this Book by faith as the Word of God.'"

Six weeks later, Billy wrote from Los Angeles to his college staff at Minneapolis: "You would have been thrilled if you could have seen the great tent packed yesterday afternoon with 6,100 people and several hundred turned away, and seen the scores of people walking down the aisles from every direction accepting Christ as personal Savior when the invitation was given."

The committee had worked hard, everything was soaked in prayer, and Billy had never seen such numbers in a citywide campaign. In the third week as the scheduled closing date drew near, several committee men were ready to stop, well satisfied even if most of the millions who lived in the fast-moving, thrusting city and county of Los Angeles, from Hollywood to Chinatown, had not been aware of the "canvas cathedral" or Billy Graham. Others, however, urged continuance, citing the rising interest and attendance. Right up until Sunday afternoon Billy hesitated, for he had never previously extended a campaign. As he and Cliff prayed, they decided to announce a short extension and meanwhile, like Gideon in the book of Judges, to "put out a fleece"—watch for a sign.

The sign came by way of a phone call in the early hours from Stuart Hamblen, a massive Texas cowboy, broadcaster, and song-writer, in his late thirties, who was already a legend on the West Coast.

Stuart Hamblen was a dance-band leader, great hunter, race horse owner, gambler, and heavy drinker. And, as he later said, "a hypocrite." He was the son of a Methodist preacher in Texas, he had "left it all behind," yet he ran a children's Cowboy Church of the Air.

His tiny wife, Suzy, had prayed for him for sixteen years. She had seized an opportunity to introduce him to Billy Graham shortly before the campaign began, and Stuart had taken to a fellow southerner and interviewed him on his radio chat show. He even attended with Suzy the first week, sitting in the front row feeling patronizing, and then entertained the Grahams to supper.

In the second week, Billy's long finger seemed pointed right at him: "There is somebody in this tent who is leading a double life." Hamblen genuinely believed such remarks were deliberately aimed. After one more night, he fled to the Sierras on a hunting trip, not returning until midnight on the supposed final Sunday, October 16.

Unwillingly, Hamblen was beside Suzy in the front row on Monday night. "When Billy Graham got up and preached a terrific sermon, I said, 'Oh, that is a lot of malarkey, he is lying.' When they took up the collection, I said, 'That is a racket!' When they sang some wonderful hymns, I said, 'That singing is lousy.'" The long finger pointed again. "There is a person here tonight who is a phoney." Stuart Hamblen rose from the seat in a fury, shook his fist at Billy, and stormed out in the middle of the sermon.

He went from bar to bar but the drinks turned sour on him. "At last I gave up and started home, and on the way Christ spoke to me." Hamblen fought back. He was still fighting when he stormed into the bedroom where Suzy was asleep, got her out of that bed, and yelled, "Let's pray." They prayed, but Hamblen said, "I still couldn't make connections."

About 2 A.M. Stuart said that since Billy was the man who had upset him, they would wake him. Billy answered the phone, could hear that Stuart had been both drinking and crying, and told him to "come right on down" to the apartment hotel where the Grahams and the Grady Wilsons shared an efficiency suite.

Stuart, with Suzy trailing behind, pounded on the apartment door. It was opened by Billy in pants and sweater. Stuart roared, "I want you to pray for me."

Billy replied, "No, I'm not going to do it." Stuart nearly knocked him down.

"Come in, Stuart," Billy said, "and I'll tell you why."

Billy knew that Stuart Hamblen was like the Rich Young Ruler and refused to help him to a selfish, easy faith. At one point in their talk, Billy even said, "Go on back home. If you're not going to go all the way and let Jesus Christ be the actual Lord of every area of your life, don't ask me to pray with you, and don't waste anybody else's time."

At last about 5 A.M. Stuart promised to give up all that was "mean and wicked" in his heart, and they prayed together. Stuart said, "As I knelt by that chair, I felt I was kneeling at the feet of my Jesus. 'Lord,' I prayed, 'you're hearing a new voice this morning.'"

That very day Stuart Hamblen told his radio audience that he had given his life to Christ. "I've quit smoking and I've quit drinking. Tonight at the end of Billy's invitation, I'm going to hit the sawdust trail." The sensation was enormous. Hundreds of newcomers flocked to the big tent.

On the next Sunday, and again the following week, Hamblen went on the platform to say, "I didn't know what it was like to be a real Christian. Do you know the thrill of it all? I like to talk about it. Boy, I talk about it everywhere." This included the bars he had most frequented. He learned that, quite seriously, the betting in

Gower Gulch and along Hollywood Boulevard that Hamblen "wouldn't keep it up," dropped from 100–1 to 20–1; after his second testimony, to 10–1.

The campaign was extended.

At the end of that week Billy, Cliff, and Bev Shea put out another "fleece," praying for a clear sign whether to extend once again.

The night on which they had to make up their minds, Billy arrived at the tent to find the place swarming with reporters and photographers—a new, overwhelming, and distracting experience. Flashbulbs exploded everywhere. Billy in the middle of the sermon had to ask a man to climb down from a stepladder he had placed right in front of the platform. All sorts of questions were flung at him afterward, and the next day the Los Angeles *Examiner* and *Herald Express* carried banner headlines. The dispatch was featured in the other papers across the country, and picked up by Associated Press. Someone told Billy, "You've been kissed by William Randolph Hearst."

Twenty years later Billy found out what lay behind that "kiss."

Among the large staff in the bedridden Hearst's Californian home worked a middle-aged maid. Hedla had come in 1947 from Chicago, where she used to hurry home from Moody Church to listen to *Songs in the Night*. At Los Angeles, she went to the canvas cathedral during that third week of the crusade, and the next morning, when Hedla was helping the nurse make Hearst's bed, he questioned her closely. He had given some newspaper support to Youth for Christ and this may have left a vague memory of the name Billy Graham, which the Hamblen sensation revived. Hearst listened to the maid's warm account of the services. That afternoon he gave his famous order to "puff Graham."

One of those who heard Stuart Hamblen's testimony on the radio was a twice-convicted wiretapper, Jim Vaus, the prodigal son of a prominent Los Angeles minister. He was driving home after clinching a dangerous deal, but his wife, Alice, knew nothing of his criminal activities.

Vaus was amused, then impressed by Hamblen's words. The next day, on an idle Sunday afternoon drive with Alice, on the spur of the moment Vaus took her to the big tent to "see what this fellow Graham is like."

They managed to squeeze on the edge of a bench. Vaus despised the crowd and rated Cliff Barrows and his trombone enthusiastic but amateurish. "Then Billy Graham stepped to the center of the platform, and I couldn't find anything wrong with him.... Something about the ease with which he moved, the flash in his eyes, the conviction in his voice, gripped me. His message wasn't new; I had heard it lots of times. What amazed me was there weren't any jokes. It was all Bible. And I knew he was telling the truth."

Billy moved rapidly back and forth on the platform, facing one block of seats, then another. He walked an estimated mile during fifty minutes. Every word of his machine-gun-like delivery was audible throughout the entire tent because he wore, on his tie, a microphone attached to a long cable, controlled by Cliff Barrows. Jim Vaus, as he listened, wrestled with his conscience. The companies he had swindled, the equipment stolen, the money he would make, persuaded him not to believe.

When Billy began the invitation, Vaus clenched his fists. An elderly personal worker with more zeal than tact, gripped his arm and would have been knocked into the sawdust had he not begun praying with bowed head. Vaus heard Billy, who had no idea of his existence, say, "There's a man in this audience who has heard this story many times before, and who knows this is the decision he should make. Yet again he's saying no to God. He is hardening his heart, stiffening his neck, and he's going out of this place without Christ. And yet this may be the last opportunity God will give him to decide for Christ."

Vaus fought in his mind.

Billy said again, far away up at the platform, his voice coming clear through the amplifiers: "The only time a man can decide for Christ is when the Holy Spirit of God has brought conviction to his heart. If God is bringing conviction to your heart you dare not say no. This is your moment of decision."

Jim Vaus muttered, "I'll go."

In the smaller tent, he was oblivious of his counselor, of the others around, of Alice kneeling beside him making her own commitment. Vaus himself was "busy talking to God." He prayed, "Lord, I believe; this time from the bottom of my heart.... It's going to be almost impossible to straighten out this bewildered, tangled life of mine. But if you'll straighten it out, I'll turn it over to you, all of it."

As the Vauses left the tent, a news photographer ran up. Vaus's first reaction was to flee publicity, but then thought it was the best way to make known his break from crime.

"Wiretapper Vaus Hits Sawdust Trail." The news flashed throughout America, by radio, hitherto impervious to religious revivals, and newsprint. Soon both *Time* and *Newsweek* featured "the new evangelist," and when Louis Zamperini, Olympic runner and war hero, was converted, the headlines screamed again.

The campaign was now the topic of all Los Angeles, and the crowds pressed to the big tent in such numbers that, despite enlargement, it could not contain them. On the seventh Sunday, it was full at midday for a 2:30 P.M. service, and the street blocked by those unable to get in.

In the final week, alcoholics and prostitutes and broken bits of humanity, too shy to enter the tent, would ask for personal workers. Before each service, church people stood shoulder-to-shoulder in every inch of the prayer tent, the leader's desk piled so high with written requests that many could not be mentioned.

The atmosphere in the big tent had nothing of the supposed emotion of a revivalist meeting. It was like an immense divine service. The people came because Billy preached with authority. He brought world affairs right into the canvas cathedral. He preached in the shadow of international crisis, and he preached straight from the Bible.

He had stopped trying to prove that the Bible was true and just proclaimed its message. "I found that I could take a simple outline and put a number of pertinent Scripture quotations under each point, and God would use this mightily to cause men to make full commitment to Christ.... I found they were desperately hungry to hear what God had to say through his Holy Word."

The numbers who came forward reached totals of two or three hundred a night—a figure which in those days seemed fantastic. For every person prayed with, ten or twenty had to be addressed in a group because of the lack of workers. For the first time, Billy began to hear about divorced couples being reunited in the counseling tent.

None of the three who hit the headlines had easy growth as Christians. Louis Zamperini, a famous Olympic runner who came forward, suffered doubts and despondency during the rebuilding of his life. Vaus had the hardship of restitution. Hamblen was fired from his $1,000-a-week program because he refused to advertise beer. Every opening closed, until his friend, actor John Wayne, hearing he had not taken a drink in thirty days, said, "Tell me truthfully, Stuart, have you wanted one?"

"No, John. It is no secret what God can do."

When Wayne suggested, "You ought to write a song about 'It Is No Secret What God Can Do,'" Stuart Hamblen found his new vocation. Jim Vaus and Louis Zamperini both found theirs among delinquent boys, Vaus in New York and Zamperini in California. These three were representative of some 4,000 men, women, and children who came forward, and additional hundreds whose decisions for Christ were not recorded.

The campaign extended from three weeks to eight. Billy wrote that in a campaign like this, all he could think about was preaching. "Morning, noon, and night I am thinking about sermons, preparing sermons, and more preaching. I forget the world, my own personal affairs, and everything."

He had quite run out of sermons. When Ruth came west again, she found him begging outlines from preacher friends, and reading every recommended book he could borrow or buy. "I remember his desperate straits in Los Angeles, probably the best thing that ever happened to him—this suddenly having to get down and study, especially the Bible. He was thrown back on simple, straight *biblical* preaching." He was now exhausted and could not sleep properly, but he had discovered that the weaker he become physically, the stronger he become spiritually.

He set Sunday, November 20, as closing day. The big tent, enlarged to 9,000 seats, overflowed. No one could estimate the audience, almost certainly the largest of its kind since Billy Sunday's New York campaign of 1917. And no one could have believed that fourteen years later the turnstiles of the Los Angeles Coliseum would click up 134,254, with 20,000 more outside the gates, to hear Billy Graham on the last night of the Los Angeles Crusade of 1963.

On Monday Ruth and Billy took the train to Minneapolis. The conductor treated them as celebrities. At Kansas City reporters boarded the train, and at Minneapolis several prominent clergy joined with Northwestern faculty and the local press to provide a hero's welcome. The Grahams at last realized that Billy had been catapulted into fame. They were bewildered, frightened lest they fail their Lord in these new opportunities, uncertain whether this were a climax or a beginning, yet tremendously encouraged.

"I feel so undeserving of all the Spirit has done," wrote Billy, "because the work has been God's and not man's. I want no credit or glory. I want the Lord Jesus to have it all."

6

An Hour of Decision

CLIFF BARROWS WROTE TO A FRIEND ON JANUARY 13, 1950, from Boston, Massachusetts: "It is our firm conviction that New England is in the midst of a great awakening, and revival fires seem to be spreading not only throughout the city but in many other sections across this area."

Three years earlier Billy Graham had agreed to bring his team for New Year's meetings in Boston. Predominantly Roman Catholic with large minorities of Unitarians and Christian Scientists, reserved, proud, and confident of its intellectual supremacy, no city in America might more surely snuff the fire lit at Los Angeles. Instead, the meetings spilled out from Mechanics Hall and historic Park Street Church to Boston Garden, the city's largest indoor arena, where on Monday, January 16, 16,000 squeezed in, leaving so many outside that Billy had to deliver an unscheduled address from the steps. Newspapermen said Franklin D. Roosevelt himself had never drawn such numbers in Boston. That night, with Ruth beside him, Billy said, "[I] felt as great a power in preaching as any other time in my ministry up till then. And when the appeal was given, more than a thousand people responded to receive Christ."

It was all unbelievable, yet wonderful because it was spontaneous. No counselor training, no careful buildup, no advertising except for New Year's Eve occurred. The team promised to return in the spring. After the service the Grahams took a train to Canada for a speaking engagement in Toronto. Speeding west across Massachusetts, Billy felt compelled to get off at Worcester and again at Springfield, to call Boston to say he would stay in New England. Again and again the feeling came to him that now was the hour. Invitations had poured in from universities, schools, cities. Any town of New England would book its largest hall to hear Billy Graham. The press would carry his words across the nation. If the team stayed in New England for six months, he felt, God might light a fire in America that never would be put out.

Billy was used to acting on impulse. But he was desperately tired, and he was frightened of the press. "Whatever I said was being quoted. I didn't have the experience to say the right things. And I was afraid that I was going to say something that would bring disrepute on the name of Christ." At Niagara Falls where they stayed a day and a night, Billy again said, "[I] felt tremendously impelled to call back to Boston and say we would continue." He let it pass, and afterward believed that he unwittingly "disobeyed the voice of God."

Yet to return would have meant abandoning a long-prepared campaign in Columbia, South Carolina. And the three weeks in Columbia, first in an auditorium, then in a hurriedly built "wooden cathedral," and finally in the Carolina Stadium, showed that Los Angeles and Boston were only a beginning. As he waited to preach at that closing rally in the stadium on March 21, 1950, with the governor and several distinguished men in the audience, Billy felt the quiet expectancy, and "a deep longing and hunger on the part of thousands for a personal encounter with God."

Columbia brought into the team the veteran Willis Haymaker, who had set up campaigns for many evangelists between the wars. He taught the Graham team the basic facts of organization. He had a gift for making local leaders prepare together, and above all, he emphasized prayer as the secret of revival, getting thousands to pray. He introduced also the word *crusade* to describe Billy Graham's evangelism, pointing out that a crusade was not confined to the actual meetings, it included preparation and follow-up. "A crusade goes on and on." Billy was soon speaking of the "crusade to bring America to her knees in repentance of sin and faith toward God."

After Columbia in the south, the team whirled through twenty New England towns from Rhode Island to Maine. A corps of national pressmen had attached itself. At nearly every place, Billy had to deliver a second talk to the overflow crowd in the street, often in the rain, and at Houlton, Maine, on the Canadian border, the only auditorium large enough was the airport hangar. At one point Billy was close to abandoning the tour because of exhaustion. Alone in a hotel room, he kneeled on the floor in prayer, and before he finished he could feel strength returning to his body.

The climax came with four nights in the Boston Garden arena and a great open air rally on Boston Common on Sunday, April 23. The day before the rally, Billy wanted to pray where he would preach, and he strolled up Monument Hill, where the platform was still being constructed, with several friends. One of these friends was John Bolten, a German-born industrialist who had rededicated his life to Christ during the January meetings.

As they prayed, John Bolten had such inward conviction that afterward he took Billy for a walk alone. "Billy," he said, "I believe God's telling me you are going to preach in the great stadiums of every capital city of the world the Gospel of our crucified Lord. I believe the world is ripe and ready to listen."

One morning the following summer, while attending a conference at Ocean City, New Jersey, Billy and Cliff drove over the bridge across the bay to play golf.

That same morning a Philadelphia clergyman, Dr. Theodore Elsner, happened to wake up late at the family summer cottage in Ocean City, which he and his son-in-law Fred Dienert, a Philadelphia advertising agent, had rented. Elsner was president of the National Religious Broadcasters. As Elsner shaved, he prayed for Billy Graham, who he knew was nearby. As he prayed, a definite sense came to him that Billy Graham was the man to fill the gap left by the recent death of Walter A. Maier, the famous weekly radio preacher who had had the ear of America. Maier had preached a clear evangelical Gospel in the context of the social, political, and moral state of the nation.

At noon, Elsner drove off to find a lunch counter. He felt a strong impression that he should cross the bridge, although he could easily get a sandwich in Ocean City. On the mainland at Somers Point, he saw a roadside diner and walked in. There sat Billy, Cliff, and a third golfer, Phil Palermo. Elsner ordered a sandwich but barely touched it for exhorting Billy, until Billy in enthusiasm began to pace up and down the diner. "How am I going to get on radio?" he asked. "Who's going to help me?"

Elsner told him of his son-in-law, Fred Dienert, whose senior partner, Walter F. Bennett of Chicago, had handled many religious programs.

On reflection, Billy rejected the idea. A national weekly program could be almost a full-time occupation. When next month, at a conference in northern Michigan, two well-dressed strangers introduced themselves as Walter Bennett and Fred Dienert of the Walter Bennett Advertising Company, Billy charmingly sent them away. They reappeared at Montreat, and told him that a peak Sunday afternoon time would shortly be available coast-to-coast on the American Broadcasting Company's network, for an initial thirteen week contract at a total of $92,000, a sum which to Billy appeared astronomical.

Shortly afterward Billy began a six weeks' crusade at Portland, Oregon, where a huge, wooden temporary auditorium had been specially erected. Bennett and Dienert pursued him by phone and telegram to explain that the program cost about $7,000 a week. If he raised $25,000, he could go on the air, for after three weeks the gifts of listeners would certainly maintain it. No one on his staff had ever seen Billy lose his temper, but he now became irritated with these most persistent partners and refused to see them when they came to Portland. Ten days later, they were back again. He used the rear elevator and even the fire escape to avoid them in the hotel lobby. They waited a week, received an appointment at last, only to find that Billy had escaped to Mount Hood for his rest day, a Monday.

On Tuesday morning at Mount Hood, Billy and Grady were having breakfast when a call came from Texas from Howard Butt, a friend of their own age, heir to the grocery chain. Butt said that if it were true that Billy might go on radio, he and their mutual friend, Bill Mead, head of a bakery business, wanted to give $1,000 each to start a fund.

When Billy returned with Grady to the Multnomah Hotel at Portland on Tuesday afternoon, he avoided Bennett and Dienert and retired for his usual rest. Grady walked in with a message that the partners had booked a flight home that evening.

Billy told Grady to send for them.

Bennett and Dienert found Billy pacing back and forth, dressed in his pajamas and the golf cap he always wore to keep his hair straight when he rested. He told them he was undecided, but reported the offer of $2,000 and supposed he might contact other wealthy men if only his time permitted.

"Billy," said Fred Dienert, "I don't think the money is going to come from a lot of big people." Bennett and Dienert suggested telling the Portland audience about the opportunity.

Billy said, "Boys, let's pray."

He knelt by a chair. Walter and Fred lowered themselves to the bedside, and "Billy really poured out his heart to God." They had never heard a prayer of such childlike directness.

"Lord, you know I'm doing all that I can," was Fred Dienert's memory of the words of Billy's prayer. "You know I don't have any money, but I believe we ought to do this. You know, Lord, I'll put another mortgage on; I'll take the little I have and put another mortgage on.

"Lord, I don't know where the money is, and if I did know where it is, I'm too busy to go out and get it.

"I feel the burden for it, but it's up to you, and if you want this, I want you to give me a sign. And I'm going to put out a fleece. And the fleece is for the $25,000 by *midnight.*"

Walter and Fred stole away. In the taxi to the airport they agreed, in awe, "You could feel the presence of God there. You could feel a state of expectancy. God was listening to Billy. Something is going to happen." At the airport, therefore, they turned around and drove to the crusade, seating themselves unrecognized at the back. A huge crowd had come, which they appraised with satisfaction at about 20,000. When the plates were passed, the amount ought to be raised.

The moment came for the offering toward crusade expenses, and Billy did not say a word about radio.

The offering taken, Billy spoke of the radio opportunity. He said he felt he should take this available time for God rather than let it go to a tobacco company or suchlike; that he had no money nor the time to raise it. "But if any of you folks would like to have a part, I'll be in the office back here at the close of the service tonight." When he mentioned $25,000, a lot of money in 1950, Billy heard a ripple or two of laughter.

Bob Pierce, founder of World Vision and fresh from the Korean battlefront, gave the address that night, reporting at length. Billy followed with the basic points of the Gospel, gave the invitation, and then said, "Shall we pray. Every head bowed, every eye closed... You come, as everybody in this place prays for you. You come ... you hundreds of you come...."

People had far to move from the ends of the building and the overflow seats outside. The time passed slowly. Billy stood at the podium, saying a word or two at intervals. Pierce then rose to address the hundreds who had come forward. Walter looked at Fred. Neither thought many of the audience would wait to see Billy at such a late hour. Fred murmured, "But God is faithful. Whatever he starts, he finishes."

At last the audience was released. A long line soon formed near the back office, where Grady held an old shoe box. Scribbled pledges and dollar notes were thrust in. A lumberman from Idaho left a $2,500 pledge. A couple of youths asking, "Dr. Graham, is chicken feed acceptable?" threw in a handful of change and a dollar, and Billy said, "God bless you. Thank you." An old lady in a worn black dress produced a $5 bill. A businessman said he had been one of Dr. Maier's most ardent supporters, that Billy should certainly pick up Maier's torch. The man pledged $1,000, with the promise of more.

Grady gave the box to the crusade chairman, Frank Phillips, and the team went to their favorite eating place, where Bennett and Dienert joined them. Frank Phillips entered excitedly saying that the tally, including the promised $2,000 from Texas, was just $23,500.

They all looked at Billy. "It's a miracle. You're as good as on the air!" Billy, almost in tears at the generosity and trust of the people, firmly said no. The fleece was for $25,000 before midnight, so $25,000 it must be. The devil might have sent the lesser sum to tempt him. When the two partners offered the balance, Billy refused them.

A subdued team returned to the hotel shortly before midnight. Billy went to his room, Grady to the mail desk, where he was given three envelopes delivered by hand.

In each was a pledge from someone unable to wait in the line: one for $1,000, two for $250. Together they made up the $25,000.

Grady Wilson kept the shoe box in his shirt drawer overnight. The next morning he was told by the bank that if, however briefly, he entered cash and checks under his name, he would be liable for income tax, nor could it go tax-free under "Billy Graham Radio Fund" unless this were a properly constituted body. He put the money temporarily into the account of the Portland crusade, and Billy called George Wilson, business manager of Northwestern Schools in Minneapolis.

Wilson flew west, bringing articles of incorporation that he had had drawn up the previous year against some such eventuality, and Billy, Ruth, Cliff, and the two unrelated Wilsons signed them to form the Billy Graham Evangelistic Association. The others firmly overrode Billy's strong opposition to the trumpeting of his name. The name would identify, and the name was trusted.

As for a title of the radio program, Ruth vetoed "The Billy Graham Hour." She saw that whereas the name of Billy Graham would rightly endorse the Association, it would be "the height of poor taste" on a program primarily designed for millions without definite faith in Christ, to whom it might imply the building of a personal following for a preacher. It was she who suggested "Hour of Decision."

Meanwhile, unknown to the Grahams, Bennett had arrived at the American Broadcasting Company's Chicago office to sign the contract on Friday afternoon, only to be told that the New York headquarters had changed their minds and would not sell time to Billy Graham. The decision was final.

Bennett and Dienert flew to New York that night. Although ABC's executive offices were always empty on a Saturday morning, a vice president entered unexpectedly. He had missed the board meeting but had learned of it by memorandum. "After a lengthy discussion he agreed that we were entitled to a review. He even contacted one of the top executives on the golf course to set up a meeting for Monday morning. The network deliberated for two days and on Wednesday announced the program's acceptance."

In Minneapolis, George Wilson set up a one-room office on Harmon Place, a few yards across Loring Park from Northwestern, and hired a secretary, which seemed enough, for they might not get many gifts or spiritual inquiries.

Billy's friends urged him to speak quietly and slowly on radio, in contrast to his preaching. He rejected the advice. In a careful study of newscasters, commentators, and radio preachers, he detected that those who spoke fast won the largest audience. He modeled himself on Walter Winchell and Drew Pearson, both subsequently his personal friends. He would cover as much ground as he could, touching social and international issues, packing in illustrations and Bible quotations, each message to be "straight evangelism calculated to stir the Christian and win the person outside the church to Christ.... Fast, hard-hitting."

The *Hour of Decision* (a half hour of time, the word *hour* in the title follows the normal custom of American radio) went out over 150 stations on ABC network on Sunday, November 5, 1950, from Georgia where Willis Haymaker had set up the Atlanta crusade in a specially constructed tabernacle on the baseball field of the Atlanta Crackers at Ponce de Leon Park. Cliff Barrows introduced and led the crusade choir and audience. Grady Wilson gave a Scripture reading. Bev Shea sang.

Then Billy Graham stepped to the microphone. Three days before, the Chinese had massively intervened in the Korean War and were about to inflict a heavy defeat on United Nations forces. In a wide-ranging address, Billy emphasized the urgency of the hour and pleaded for a nationwide movement of prayer: "Faith, more than fighting, can change the course of events today. United, believing, self-humbling, God-exalting prayer now can change the course of history."

Only at the close did he sound a direct evangelistic call: "A crucified and a risen Christ will forgive sins, lift burdens, solve problems, and give assurance of salvation to many. This experience can be yours, whoever you are, and whatever your circumstances may be, if by faith you will open your heart to Jesus Christ. Right now you can say an eternal yes to Christ, and you can become a partaker of eternal life."

The program caught on rapidly. Soon it had earned the highest audience rating ever accorded a religious program. In eighteen months, it was rated higher than most news commentators in daytime Sunday listening.

It made Billy's voice familiar across America and many countries overseas. But an attempt to use the new medium of television was short lived, and it was a few years before Billy broke into television in a different way, greatly widening his ministry.

The *Hour of Decision* had a considerable influence on his development as a preacher. Whereas each crusade or rally brought a different audience and sermon material could be used over and over again, the *Hour of Decision* demanded every week a fresh address of highest caliber, which disciplined him all the more to study the Bible and theology, and to observe and assess contemporary events. And the necessary founding of the Billy Graham Evangelistic Association enabled him to cut away from the traditional "love offering." Billy and the team became salaried members of BGEA. Henceforth, wherever they served, they gave their services free.

7

*H*ARRINGAY 1954

A T THE AGE OF THIRTY-FIVE, BILLY GRAHAM COULD LOOK BACK
on a meteoric rise. He had become the best-known preacher
in America, and by using outdoor stadiums, his crusades with their
blend of warmth and reverence had reached out to thousands reluctant to attend churches or indoor halls. He now faced the problem
of follow up, so Billy brought in Dawson Trotman, founder of the
Navigators. Under Trotman's guidance, the team began to develop
the process that integrated an increasing proportion of those who
came forward into the local churches.

Quick to seize opportunities and to recruit experts, Billy made
feature films of crusades. With *Mr. Texas,* based on the story of a
convert at the Fort Worth, Texas, crusade, he had pioneered the use
of drama blended with factual reporting as a means of film evangelism. He had become a widely read writer—through a weekly syn-
dicated column, *My Answer,* and by his first best-seller, *Peace with
God,* a book that remains a classic, in use all over the world. Over
the years, Billy would hear again and again from men and women
brought to Christ through reading it.

The Washington, D.C. crusade in February 1952 had made
Billy Graham well known to political leaders. He became a per-
sonal friend of two future presidents and of President Eisenhower.
He had also paid a pastoral visit to the frontline troops during the
Korean War.

There had been opposition and many pitfalls, but even allowing for the hand of providence, it is a wonder more mistakes or

misjudgments had not occurred. The team was preserved by their sincerity and integrity, by humility and their devotional roots, and by their grasp of the basic truths of the faith. Billy himself had antidotes to losing his head or letting it swell as he shot from obscurity to fame. One was his sense of humor, which bubbled in private and in spontaneous public comments that often disarmed a hostile audience and were generally far funnier than the rehearsed stories he told. "At home he was loads of fun and a horrible tease," recalls his second daughter, Anne (born 1948). "He hiked all over the mountain with us, told us crazy, pointless jokes, and let the dogs come in the house, grinning as he did, with us kids giggling and Mother glaring."

Beyond any other human support was his mountain home at Montreat and the inestimable contribution of Ruth. They had bought a six-room graystone house in a small shrub garden on Assembly Drive, across the road from the Nelson Bells. Billy's father-in-law was now practicing as a surgeon at Montreat. The road led to the wooded mountains below the Blue Ridge, where Billy could hike. In 1950 the Grahams had bought, for an absurdly low price ($12 per acre) about 200 acres of wild mountain land, which had been two neglected farms. As Billy describes it, "There were two little cabins on the place, 18 springs, and 120 apple trees. A dirt road led up and into the property. It was about 3,600 feet altitude—about 800 feet above Montreat. I used it as a place for study, meditation, and prayer. Our entire family loved to take hikes with our Great Pyrenees dog, Belshazzar. In order to keep fit, I started at our little home in Montreat and trotted the full mile to the top of our property."

The Grahams's third daughter, "Bunny," Ruth Bell Graham, had been born in December 1950, and their elder son, William Franklin, in July 1952. Ruth loved to join Billy at least part of each crusade, but the Grahams remembered the tears of Billy Sunday's widow who told them she had been on the road so much that none of the family grew up in sympathy with their ministry. Ruth would say, "A mother, like the Lord, needs to be a very present help in times of trouble. A mother has to be with the children. Personally, I love it." Occasionally, she was wistful because Billy was away so much, and found it a little hard at first when her husband began to be treated as public property, but their unanimity of aim, her thrill at the unbelievable spiritual opportunities now opening, and her basic qualities enabled her to adjust quickly. As a former member of the team put it, "Ruth has a warmth and vitality about her and a depth that one does not often see. She's utterly unconscious as far as one can tell of her own personal attractiveness.... She is a perfect hostess, and you can't help but feel at home."

If a happy home life and the influence of Ruth were important, so too were Billy's sense of humor and also his thirst for knowledge. Billy would pick any brain, read any book, and explore any situation. Even more important was a continuing sense of inadequacy: "The Lord has always arranged my life," he once said, "that I have had to keep dependent on him. Over and over again I went to my knees and asked the Spirit of Wisdom for guidance and direction. There were times when I was tempted to flee from problems and pressures and my inability to cope with them; but somehow, even in moments of confusion and indecision, it seemed I could trace the steady hand of God's sovereignty leading me on."

And now, approaching England by sea for the best prepared of all crusades to date, Billy was about to need in full measure his dependence on divine wisdom and his trust in the sovereignty of God.

On Monday, February 22, 1954, one day short of Southampton, the first steward of the *United States* tapped on the Grahams's door and handed him a radio news sheet. Billy was stunned to read, datelined London: "A Labour Member of Parliament announced today that he would challenge in the Commons the admission of Billy Graham to England on the grounds that the American evangelist was interfering in British politics under the guise of religion."

The Grahams were mystified until the London crusade director, Jerry Beaven, came through on the radio telephone.

It appeared that Hannen Swaffer, a columnist on the left-wing *Daily Herald,* had discovered a prayer calendar prepared in Minneapolis. In a descriptive piece under a picture of London appeared the sentence: "What Hitler's bombs could not do, socialism with its accompanying evils shortly accomplished." Cleverly touching up the small letter *s* to a capital, Hannen Swaffer under the headline, "Apologize—or stay away!" had written a blistering article pillorying Billy Graham as a political adventurer in disguise, who had "more gravely libelled us than anyone has dared to do since the war," by attacking the former Socialist (Labour) government. Taking their cue from Swaffer's "disclosure," the London press was in uproar, hot for Billy Graham's scalp.

The piece had been unknowingly taken from an uncorrected proof of a brochure for American donors. On English advice, the word "socialism" had been corrected to "secularism" before the brochure's publication; the two words were synonymous to Americans and no political reference had been intended. Billy did not even recall the details of the brochure and had never seen the calendar.

Beavan sent an explanation to the press; Billy and George Wilson in Minneapolis wired apologies to the Member of Parliament, but Swaffer, a Spiritualist, followed up with an attack on "the wild fanaticism of Billy Graham's evangelism."

Momentarily, Billy was engulfed by certainty that all was over and by the injustice of the accusations. Then, swiftly and instinctively, he turned to the Bible. Opposition was inevitable; Christ must triumph. When they reached Le Havre, it was no effort to send by the *Daily Herald's* reporter a friendly greeting to Hannen Swaffer.

Coming up Southampton water, the ship was boarded by pressmen and photographers. They ignored a film star to crowd round the Grahams, who realized later that the "socialism" furor had been a blessing in disguise by making Billy front-page news.

The reporters were hostile. One even asked Ruth, "Is it true your husband carries around his own special jug of water for baptism?" After a TV interview on the dockside, the Grahams entered customs. When the customs officer said, "Welcome to England and good luck, sir. We need you," Billy was eternally grateful for the encouragement, swiftly followed by a dockworker's "God bless you, sir. I'm praying for you."

At Waterloo the Grahams stepped into a sea of happy singing people. Londoners had converged on the terminus until platform ticket machines gave out, post office vans and taxis were held up, and a harassed official exclaimed, "If these are Christians, it's time we let out the lions!" It was the greatest crowd at Waterloo since the arrival of Mary Pickford and Douglas Fairbanks in 1924. The Grahams left the station to the sound of two thousand voices singing Wesley's hymn, "And can it be that I should gain / An interest in the Saviour's blood?"

On the day before the crusade was to begin, *The People* newspaper hurled abuse at "Silly Billy." The copy read, "Being bulldozed into loving God by ecstatic young men who talk about him with easy familiarity is something which makes the biggest British sinner shudder." The atmosphere at the press conference was of cynicism mixed with disdain. Hugh Gough, suffragan Bishop of Barking and the only Anglican leader supporting him, said, "Well, Billy. If you are to be a fool for Christ's sake, I'll be a fool with you."

The opening day, Monday, March 1, broke cold and cheerless. Billy spent most of it preparing and praying in his hotel room. The weather got worse. Billy, his nerves tense, developed a splitting headache. Two U.S. senators, whose intention to attend the crusade had been announced, cried off, murmuring something about political implications. Billy believed that the U.S. ambassador, who had washed his hands of him at the socialism dispute, had urged them to stay away. Billy had a "terrible sinking feeling." As he recalls, "I dropped immediately to my knees in prayer and committed the entire matter to the Lord."

Before the Grahams drove out to Harringay Arena in North London, a garbled phone message convinced them that it was barely a quarter full. On their arrival, the forecourt was empty. They could, however, see crowds streaming toward the greyhound stadium beyond. Billy said to Ruth, "Let's go face it and believe that God has a purpose in it."

Willis Haymaker came toward the car. "The arena is jammed! It is full and running over, and thousands are on the other side!" Billy, a little dazed, walked through the door to his special room, to a great sound of hymns from the arena. There stood two smiling senators, saying "Billy, we just couldn't let you down!" They had hurried from the Prime Minister and would shortly leave for a formal dinner, but were determined to speak on Billy's behalf.

Squads of pressmen and roaming photographers did not make for an atmosphere of worship. (The London dailies had sent an extraordinary array, including theater and literary critics, foreign and industrial correspondents.) From the moment the choir burst into a verse of "Blessed Assurance, Jesus Is Mine," followed by the stately cadences of the opening hymn, "Praise to the Lord, the Almighty," the service had a genuineness and reverence, which puzzled the press, still attempting to relate Billy to "snake-handling fundamentalists" and hysterical demagogues.

Billy preached on John 3:16: "God so loved the world, that he gave his only begotten Son, that whosoever believeth in him should not perish, but have everlasting life." With his microphone looking like an oversize tie pin, he darted back and forth. For English ears on that first evening, he talked too fast and seemed inclined to shout, so his voice became expressionless and less effective, but its impact remained unspoiled. "I believe there is a worldwide hunger for God. I believe this great crowd is evidence of that hunger for God in London, and," he went on, daringly as it seemed to his audience, "before three months have passed, I believe we are going to see a mighty revival in London and throughout Great Britain."

At the last moment before preaching, Billy had hesitated whether to give an invitation on this first, press-distracted night. Bishop Gough said, "Give it." To the surprise and gratitude of the London executive, 178 people, "mostly young but scarcely to be described as of one distinct type," moved quietly forward, some of them crying.

Numbers were slightly down the second night because of a blend of snow flurries and rain. After that, there was never an empty place throughout three months, despite rearrangement to accommodate more than 12,000. On the first Saturday afternoon, Harringay was filling so fast for the evening service that Billy took an unannounced meeting in the arena for the first 5,000, who then left. Signs posted in the tube (or subway) stations stating that Harringay had reached capacity did not stop Londoners from heading there. They would not disperse. At 9:15 the arena was emptied again and Billy preached a third sermon. The counseling room had already expanded three times, for London's first week was bringing forward inquirers in numbers that America had produced only at the last.

The influence of the crusade from the beginning was extraordinary. A change of atmosphere could be felt not only in London but across the country. Suddenly, it became easy to talk about religion. Billy Graham was the topic in homes, as well as in factories, clubs, and public places, giving tongue-tied Christians the opportunity of their lives.

From the first night too came the singing in the tube. "From the seemingly endless queues waiting at the station for tickets one hears wave after wave of song rolling back toward the street," ran a letter in the *Daily Telegraph*. "The tube trains are packed with these singing multitudes, and there is a smile on every face. This quite spontaneous demonstration of Christian joy is most impressive, and one cannot fail to observe the effect it has on the passengers who board the trains at subsequent stations."

They sang the great hymns of the church. They sang "Blessed Assurance" with its chorus, which Cliff had made the signature tune of the crusade. One song caught on right across London: "To God Be the Glory, Great Things He Hath Done." Words and tune are nineteenth-century American, yet until London they had not been known to the team, who now adopted the hymn as their own for its apt expression of their message, experience, and goal.

By the third week of March, the opposition had melted. The press had turned from vociferous suspicion to a respect that soon became admiration and support.

From London and all southern England, the crowds flocked to Harringay, from curiosity, conviction, or by invitation of churches or friends. Many came because of the change in others. When a typist saw a colleague suddenly stop being disgruntled, when a store manager was handed back stolen goods by a contrite customer, they wanted to know why.

A large percentage of those who came forward were between the ages of fifteen and twenty-five, the younger ones often being members of church youth groups whose leaders had prayed and worked for their decisions. In older age groups, many had lost their early background of religion. Decision cards showed more than half of no regular church connection. In every Harringay audience, many had never been to a religious service other than a wedding or a funeral; or they were like the pickpocket who said to the stranger beside him as they started for the front, "Now I must give you back your wallet I took a few minutes ago!"

Malcolm Muggeridge, not then a Christian, commented on BBC television: "One or two at first, and then the movement gathering momentum, as the choir sings quietly. I looked at their faces, so varied, so serious, and for me this was far and away the most moving part of the proceedings." As the weeks wore on, Billy Graham put less and less force into the invitation. "I felt," he said, "like a spectator standing on the side watching God at work, and I wanted to get out of it as much as I could and let him take over."

On Monday, March 29, the Greater London crusade extended itself nationwide.

The American Broadcasting Company's engineer traveling with the team to supervise *Hour of Decision* broadcasts had the idea of using long-distance phone lines. The BBC used them, and long ago a speech by Lloyd George had been relayed from a hall in London to a hall in the provinces. After some hesitation, the post office offered terms.

The first relay was laid to a movie theater just across the Thames River. The next night 2,000 people in Glasgow heard Billy Graham in London. Soon the post office had more applications than they could manage. The services were often clearer to a relay audience than in the arena with its echoing amplifiers, and the message came in stark simplicity unaided by atmosphere or the personality of the preacher. In hired theaters, concert halls, city auditoriums, and churches, Britons heard Billy Graham.

In London, the crusade went from strength to strength. On Saturday afternoon, April 3, Trafalgar Square was packed as it had not been since VE day. On Good Friday, April 16, sunny and warm, an open-air rally in Hyde Park, at which the police estimated there were more than 40,000 people, covered half a square mile. Billy spoke with great power on "God forbid that I should glory, save in the cross of our Lord Jesus Christ."

Holy Week had been designated a rest period without meetings, but the team sensed that it would be an error to break the momentum. Even Sundays were filled. On April 25, Billy preached at Cambridge in the packed University Church, with the service relayed in two neighboring churches. On another Sunday, he preached in Birmingham at the annual service of the British Industries Fair. Almost every day he met leading men in church and state, individually or in groups.

The strain was immense. Each week Billy looked thinner, and the circles under his eyes blacker. A distinguished physician prescribed vitamin pills. They had such a good effect and looked so small that Billy, prescribed one a day, took four!

If London exhausted him physically (and a man much over thirty-five could scarcely have stood the strain), the Greater London crusade gave Billy Graham new stature.

America had followed his troubles and read of his triumphs with such avid interest that he now became a household name to his countrymen. And Harringay influenced his ministry permanently. He learned to speak more slowly and quietly; in dress, he abandoned the loud ties, which had suggested superficial showmanship. Similarly, Cliff Barrows stopped using his trombone to stir the singing. The entire team was steadied and matured by working with British Christians, and was encouraged by reaching not only a capital but a nation.

The crusade already had drawn a million and a half and had been extended again and again until it was announced that the closing service, on the evening of Saturday, May 22, would be held in London's largest outdoor stadium, Wembley, where the soccer league's Cup Final is played. The bookings became so heavy that the smaller White City Stadium, a few miles south, was taken for an additional service the same afternoon. When that was not enough, an overflow crowd had to listen in a neighboring soccer field.

The last day of the Greater London crusade, May 22, 1954, brought weather as unfavorable as the first. Nothing else was the same for Billy as he awoke, weary. The previous evening Harringay had filled so early that two-and-a-half hours before the service, the BBC broadcast police warnings that people should stay home if they didn't have a ticket. And the morning news was of special trains and coaches converging on London, and of people camping out, despite the cold and wet weather, to make sure they had a seat at White City or Wembley, where the Lord Mayor would be present and the Archbishop of Canterbury, Geoffrey Fisher, once so cautious and negative about Billy, would give the benediction.

After Billy's sermon at White City, some 2,000 inquirers walked out of the stands and crossed the running track toward the platform to stand in the drizzle. The police said the roads around

Wembley were chaotic with traffic. Too late to hire a helicopter, the team moved across by a bus under police escort to reach Wembley in time for tea with the Archbishop, Lord Mayor, and other distinguished guests. As Billy, who said he didn't know where he was going to find the strength for the sermon, looked out of the window, he was amazed to see every seat in the enormous oval already filled and the gates opened with the overflow allowed to swarm onto the precious turf. That cold, wet evening witnessed the greatest religious congregation, 120,000 by turnstile count, ever seen until then in the British Isles.

On the platform during the first half hour, which was being broadcast, Billy glanced at the Archbishop and other great men near him and was suddenly tempted to switch from his simple message to "something impressive in an intellectual framework." He rejected the temptation and preached again in simplicity, without trace of his weariness, ending: "You can go back to the shop, the office, the factory, with a greater joy and peace than you have ever known. But before that can happen you must commit yourselves to Jesus Christ. You must make your personal decision for him. And you can do that now. Choose this day whom ye will serve!"

The *News of the World* described the scene that followed: "There was no emotional hysteria, no tension ... only a very deep reverence.... Within minutes thousands of men, women and teenagers were moving to the track. They were of all ages, of all classes of society. Husbands and wives were hand in hand with their children, young men walked forward alone." The Archbishop stepped to the microphones and prayed.

Afterward, as the team's bus inched slowly through the crowds waving goodbye and singing, "To God Be the Glory," Billy stood up and said, "I want all of us to bow our heads right now and give thanks to God for all he has done and is doing. This is his doing, and let none fail to give him credit."

When Billy had prayed, Bev Shea, with the whole team joining, began to sing softly, "Praise God from Whom All Blessings Flow."

On the day after Wembley, Billy Graham went to Oxford University to address a packed congregation. On Monday, lying in bed in his London hotel, which he was to leave that night for a vacation in Scotland, he was summoned at short notice to 10 Downing Street by Sir Winston Churchill.

Billy had invited the Prime Minister to Wembley. Papers concerning Harringay were placed before Churchill, and he consulted his party's chief whip before deciding not to attend. One of his principal private secretaries, Sir John Colville, who had met Billy at a luncheon, asked the Prime Minister if he would see him, but Churchill refused. However the reports of Wembley so impressed him that Sir Winston agreed to give Billy five minutes, intending merely to be civil. As the hour approached, Sir Winston paced back and forth, saying he was nervous about the encounter: "What do you talk to an American evangelist about?"

At the stroke of noon, Billy Graham was shown into the Cabinet room. Sir Winston stood at the center of the long table, an unlighted cigar in his hand. Billy was surprised to see how short a man he was. Sir Winston motioned Billy to be seated and said he had been reading about him and was most happy to have him come, claiming they needed "this emphasis." Then he asked, "Do you have any hope? What hope do you have for the world?"

Billy was naturally overwhelmed at meeting privately the greatest man of the age, but did not forget why he had been allowed the privilege. He took out his little New Testament and answered, "Mr. Prime Minister, I am filled with hope."

Sir Winston pointed at the early editions of three London evening papers lying on the empty table, and commented that they were filled with rapes, murders, and hate. When he was a boy, it was different. If there was a murder, it was talked about for fifty years. Everything was so changed now, so noisy and violent. And the Communist menace grew all the time. "I am an old man," he said, and repeated the phrase at different points in the conversation nine times. Several times he added, "without hope for the world."

Billy said again that he was filled with hope. "Life is very exciting even if there's a war, because I know what is going to happen in the future." Then he spoke about Jesus Christ, and began right at the beginning, turning from place to place in the New Testament and explaining, just as he would to a common inquirer in his hotel room, the meaning of Christ's birth, death, resurrection, and ascension, and how a man is born again. He moved quickly, inwardly agitated lest he should not put across the essentials in the short time granted him.

Billy got the impression that Churchill was very receptive. He made little comment but listened closely—a different attitude from that which Churchill is reported to have shown to ecclesiastical dignitaries. He sat well forward in his chair, drinking in every word.

The five minutes that he had scheduled for Billy had become forty, and the clock showed twelve-thirty, when at last Sir Winston stood up. "I do not see much hope for the future," he said, "unless it is the hope you are talking about, young man. We must have a return to God."

Harringay had encouraged that return throughout the nation. At the final ministers' meeting in Central Hall, Westminster, the Bishop of Barking said: "A new flame of hope has been lit in our hearts, new courage and new faith. A fire has been lit which will continue, please God, if we are willing to obey the guidance of God's Holy Spirit in the days and years to come."

The widespread feeling in the country was nowhere more beautifully expressed than in a private letter written on behalf of Queen Elizabeth the Queen Mother, by her Treasurer, in reply to Billy Graham's invitation to attend the closing service at Wembley:[3]

"I write at the desire of Queen Elizabeth the Queen Mother in reply to your recent letter, to which Her Majesty has given, since she received it in Scotland, a very full and sympathetic consideration.

"Her Majesty bids me tell you of the deep interest with which she has followed the course of your visit to England.

"The immediate response to your addresses, and the increasing number of those who are anxious to hear them, testify both to your own sincerity and to the eagerness with which a great host of the people of this country welcome the opportunity to fortify their religious belief and to reaffirm the principles which you proclaim.

"It is not possible for Queen Elizabeth the Queen Mother to be present on the 22nd, but she wishes me to tell you how impressed she has been by the spiritual rekindling you have brought to numberless Englishmen and women whose faith has been made to glow anew by your addresses.

"Her Majesty would like to pay her tribute both to the manner of your presentation and to its result, and to wish you Godspeed in your task."

8

RIPE FOR HARVEST

SIXTY THOUSAND PEOPLE STOOD IN THE RAIN AND MUD WHEN
Billy Graham preached on Monday, June 7, 1954, at Cliff College in Derbyshire; outside hotels on his journey, people gathered in the streets, hoping to see him; in Glasgow, for discussions with Scottish church leaders, the police had to hold back the crowds.

Billy became alarmed and confused. The expectancy was immense. He had invitations to all the major cities of Britain. He wondered whether he should abandon his imminent preaching tour in continental Europe, and crusades scheduled in America, and after a rest return to Britain in the late summer for as long as needed.

Weighing on him even more than canceling crusades was a fear lest "there was too much interest in me as a person. . . . There might be a Billy Graham sect forming, and I might do something to hurt the church in Britain." He laid his fears before the Archbishop of Canterbury. Dr. Fisher advised Billy to wait a year.

With other counselors divided and plans already forward for 1955, he decided to accept Fisher's advice. Years afterwards, with hindsight, Billy regretted that fatigue had affected his judgment: He should have stayed.

Meanwhile, Billy flew to Scandinavia, Holland, and West Germany. So great was the interest generated by London that long-planned, one-day meetings were changed to huge stadium rallies. But the night after the rally at Düsseldorf, Billy woke with a stabbing pain in the small of his back. A specialist diagnosed it as a kidney stone. Against medical advice, Billy flew on to Berlin where he was to preach in the Olympic Stadium: The Berlin Wall had not yet been built and thousands would cross from the Eastern zone. The Communist newspapers were attacking him, and Billy could not imagine then that twenty-nine years later he would preach in East Berlin and cities of eastern Germany and be invited back again when the wall had fallen and Germany was reunited.

On the morning before the rally, the pain returned. Billy refused a stronger painkiller because it would make him sleepy. He mused to John Bolten, at his bedside: "Why is God doing this to me? . . . I know what it is. I have just had a wonderful crusade in England. God has blessed me beyond imagination, and now I'm going to preach in Hitler's stadium before 100,000 people. And I would have probably talked to them in my own strength. God is humbling me. He is not going to divide his honor with anybody. He is telling me to lay everything at his feet and ask him to fill the empty Billy with his own strength."

They drove in a long motorcade down Hitler's route. Bolten, who had known Hitler personally and had broken with him in 1928, reflected how "a young Timothy with a very different message now went the same road to the same place." Instead of Nazi songs, the hymns of the Reformation echoed round the stadium. Where the swastika had stood was the text: "I am the Way, the Truth, and the Life." When Billy preached, no one could tell that he was sick.

Billy preached also in Paris, then sailed home on July 1 to a hero's welcome in New York harbor. He refused a most lucrative contract for a film on his life and returned to Montreat, where the small house on Assembly Drive received endless phone calls, an avalanche of mail, and became a focus for inquisitive tourists. A good rest seemed impossible—until fresh pains led to removal of the kidney stone, and orders to cancel engagements for six weeks.

That winter of 1954–55, while Billy Graham, Cliff Barrows, and Bev Shea held crusades in America, the British Isles were looking forward to the six weeks' All-Scotland Crusade based on Kelvin Hall, Glasgow. For the first time, Billy would come with the official endorsement of the churches to lead a united effort to reach an entire land—the land of his ancestors.

The preparations had a vital influence on the team's development. In previous crusades, clergymen had been invited by letter to send likely counselors to the classes, and perhaps seven or ten would come from each church. At Glasgow, the clergy were nervous about what might be taught. Jerry Beavan and Charlie Riggs therefore explained the training program to groups of a hundred ministers each from the city and surrounding counties. Many of these sent in fifty or more names: Nearly 4,000 persons took the classes. The highest number before this point had been Harringay with 2,500; in America it had been much smaller. From here on, the team always explained follow-up to the clergy first.

A solid cross-section of church people began to learn how to be counselors. To many Scots, this use of the Bible was new. Furthermore, many were converted in the counseling classes, which thus became one of the most important aspects of the crusade.

Billy Graham arrived at Glasgow on the morning of March 9, 1955, waved to by singing groups as the train from the south rushed through wayside stations, and welcomed at St. Enoch Station by an enthusiastic crowd. "Glasgow Belongs to Billy," ran the headline in a paper that evening.

Billy had no fear of empty seats the first night of Kelvin Hall. The crusade being intended for all Scotland, the majority of the space had to be reserved for organized parties. Tickets for the entire six weeks were taken before the start, and an annex with closed-circuit TV, holding 3,000, was hurriedly arranged. For unreserved seats, people were lining up outside Kelvin Hall throughout the cold afternoon.

Many ministers had questioned whether Billy should invite public decisions. To come forward, rather than to wait behind, or file into another room, was most un-Scottish. In reply to the doubts of the chairman, Tom Allan, Billy said, "Let's see what happens." Allan could detect in him—and before every subsequent meeting—"an inner and very finely controlled tension.... A man under immense strain but somehow living on top of the strain." Once Billy had prayed with his friends and the meeting began, he seemed to Allan transformed: "All the strain is gone, and from then on the man has forgotten himself."

The first night, attended by a galaxy of notables, was most unemotional and somewhat chaotic, with coughs, photographers, and constant movement on creaking boards in different parts of the hall. The choir was superb. Bev Shea, recovering from laryngitis, only sang one verse. During the early part of the service, Billy had a moment of lost confidence, perhaps because everybody anticipated a great victory, whereas at Harringay they had half-expected failure. But when he rose there was a great hush. "I have never felt an audience so close to me before," Billy wrote to Ruth. "It seemed that the hearts were open and the Lord pouring it in. I tried to talk quietly and deliberately. I could feel the power of the Holy Spirit moving in the audience.

"Then came the moment of decision. Would they come? Would they respond?

"I asked them to bow their heads, and then quietly gave the invitation. At first not a person moved. My heart began to sink a little. My faith wavered only for a second, and then it all came flooding back to me that millions of people were praying and that God was going to answer their prayers. Then great faith came surging into my heart, and I knew they would come even before I saw the first one move. I bowed my head and began to pray. Then I glanced up and people were streaming from everywhere. I saw some of the ministers with their clerical collars, on the platform, begin to weep."

The All-Scotland crusade did not have to make its way as at Harringay, but was borne along in a floodtide of goodwill and spiritual hunger.

Every audience was a true cross-section of social levels. Whereas Harringay had reached directly only a small proportion of artisans and manual workers, in Glasgow almost all parishes cooperated including those mainly of dockers and steelworkers.

And the crusade reached the unchurched by a new scheme: Operation Andrew. Introduced to the team during Harringay, Operation Andrew (named from the incident in the gospels when Andrew brought Simon Peter to Jesus) encouraged churches to charter coaches on which members could travel only if they brought along nonchurchgoers. Churches were invited to book reservations at Kelvin Hall according to the spirit of Operation Andrew. "The idea," says Riggs, "was to go out after the uncommitted, the unchurched, and bring them in a group."

In Glasgow the scheme was experimental and unpolished, but it became a vital factor in the ever-widening influence of the Graham crusades throughout the world.

On Good Friday the service at Kelvin Hall was carried live by television and radio throughout Great Britain. Billy had approached the occasion somewhat fearfully, for he must preach simultaneously to three audiences, each requiring a different approach: viewers, listeners, and those present in the hall. Determined that nothing should be theologically ill-digested, he took an opportunity to pick the brains of James Stewart, Scotland's foremost theologian, and he was also determined "to make the Gospel so simple that the smallest child might understand." In his preparation, as he meditated on the Cross, he felt his "unworthiness and sinfulness."

Good Friday in the Britain of 1955 was still predominantly a religious day. There was only one TV channel, and that night, with his sermon about the Cross, Billy reached more people than any other preacher in Britain before him, including a television audience second only to the Coronation. In public houses, rough men sat with their eyes glued to the screen in complete silence; at soccer games the next day, it was the main topic at halftime. The service was watched in Buckingham Palace and in every kind of dwelling. Not only was it, in the professional opinion of *TV Mirror,* "unmistakably superb television," but the content was crystal clear, proclaiming Christ's death in man's place so plainly that the issues, even if rejected, could not be misunderstood.

Throughout the next week, Scotland from the Outer Hebrides to the East Coast was linked to Kelvin Hall by a national relay mission. The haphazard landline relays from Harringay were the inspiration for the brilliantly conceived plan of a veteran Scots evangelist of the Church of Scotland, D. P. Thomson, who organized thirty-seven relay centers, each with trained counselors and its own evangelist to take over after Billy's invitation had been heard from Glasgow. The relay mission ended with a rally at Tynecastle Stadium outside Edinburgh. During the final two weeks, the services in Kelvin Hall were relayed to many centers in England, Wales, and Ireland.

The All-Scotland crusade ended in glory with two stadium rallies at Glasgow. It had seen a great reaping where others had sown, and created immense expectancy. The next General Assembly of the Church of Scotland gave Billy Graham a thunderous welcome. The son of staunch Scottish Presbyterians said that this was "one of the most historic moments of [his] entire ministry."

After a brief vacation, the team traveled south. Wembley Stadium had been reserved for a week, a daring innovation. Billy had never yet returned to a city for a second crusade, and no stadium of comparable size had been reserved for seven nights.

Every factor weighed against it. The new Prime Minister, Eden, called a general election that absorbed energies and interest. Billy drew greater crowds—50,000 or 60,000 every night—than any politician, but the London newspapers, recovering from a strike, gave little coverage. The weather was atrocious: It poured every night except for two, and those were bleak. Many people who had taken free reservations stayed away leaving empty seats, and though attendance far exceeded Harringay, even the final congregation of 80,000 seemed a contrast to the unforgettable close of 1954.

The rain, however, did not stop inquirers swarming across at the close of each service, about 3,000 a night—numbers that also dwarfed Harringay. These gave a fine opportunity to converts of 1954, some 400 of whom were among the counselors. Many of the organizers, however, were disappointed. Billy himself found Wembley, quite apart from the rain, one of his hardest crusades, for it was his first with an audience so far away as to be almost impersonal.

All adverse factors would have been outweighed had the foremost church leaders identified themselves with this new attempt to reach the unchurched. Archbishop Fisher and many diocesans had written warmly about Harringay, but none of them supported Billy at Wembley.

In contrast to the hesitation of high ecclesiastics, the British royal family stretched out hands in friendship. Billy and Ruth spent forty-five minutes with the Queen Mother and Princess Margaret at Clarence House and were touched to discover a detailed knowledge of the meetings in London and Scotland and of their family life. Much of the conversation revolved round spiritual matters. The Duchess of Kent (Princess Marina) paid a private visit to the Wembley service. On Sunday, Billy preached before the Queen and the Duke of Edinburgh, the Queen Mother and Princess Margaret, and a small congregation of royal household and estate workers at the Chapel Royal, Windsor Great Park. "I preached in utter simplicity. . . . I had prayed so much that I knew that however simple and full of mistakes my sermon was, God would overrule it and use it." Afterward the Grahams had lunch with the Queen, the first of several lunches or other private meetings over the years.

The Queen's invitation was a fitting tribute to the fourteen months in 1954–55 in which Billy Graham and his team had influenced British religion to a marked degree. Churches were revived, many putting evangelism into their programs for the first time. The crusades in London and Glasgow had presented clergy and ministers with a pastoral opportunity unparalleled in the first half of the twentieth century. They gave British Christianity a strong impetus throughout the later 1950s. Too many churches, however, held back, debating the pros and cons instead of recognizing the hour. Had they maintained the momentum, the 1960s might have been as different for Britain nationally, despite the flooding in of secularism, as they were for the thousands who through the crusades of 1954–55 found faith or vocation.

These were the lasting fruit, especially the young. There was a sharp increase in the number of men offering for ordination, and of men and women training for lay or missionary service. By 1959, the Bible Institute in Glasgow had more students than it could house. In 1966, during Billy Graham's next London crusade at Earls Court, the future Bishop of Norwich, Maurice Wood, brought together one night seventy men and women training for full-time service as a result of Harringay or Wembley. By the last decades of the century, many converts of these crusades were in positions of leadership or high responsibility, including Eileen Carey, the wife of the then Archbishop of Canterbury. And they served not only in Britain but wherever Britons served the churches: Billy Graham frequently met or heard of such men and women when he held overseas crusades.

The fame of the British crusades led to Billy's first major opportunity away from the West in January 1956. Invitations had poured in from every part of the world, and he had accepted one from India. It had been endorsed by almost every church and mission except Roman Catholic, the first time in India's history that such multiplicity of Christian endeavor had united behind one man, and preparations had been made on a scale never before known.

The meetings were of a size unprecedented for a Christian preacher, and public interest was almost as great among Hindus as within the Christian minority. At each place Billy preached basically the same address on the text, John 3:16, and spoke in short sentences for easy interpretation. "When I gave the invitation," he wrote to Ruth from Madras, "all you could hear was just the tramp,

tramp, tramp of bare and sandaled feet as they were coming forward quietly and reverently.... I have never seen such sincerity and devoutness on the faces of people. This was God. Yes, the same God that was with us at Wembley and Harringay and Kelvin Hall has been with us here in India."

India captivated Billy. He warmed to the indefinable sense of exhilaration in the cold weather season. He loved the sights and sounds, the jostling of ancient and modern, the gracefulness of the people, the abundant life of the cities and the placid timelessness of the villages. Its poverty tore at him, and he had to be rescued from throwing his change to beggars.

In the last days of January, he reached Kerala, the heart of South India's ancient indigenous Christianity. He spoke at Kottayam Cathedral to a congregation that included the Jacobite Catholicos of the East in red robes, bearded Mar Thoma bishops in purple or white, and the famous Bishop Jacob, leader in the formation of the Church of South India.

The next morning, Billy was awakened early by the blaring of amplifiers in the specially enlarged college athletic field below the bishop's house. He peeped out and saw a great prayer meeting in progress under arc lights. He preached that night to a concourse that could not be counted, but was believed locally to be far in excess of 75,000. The quiet reverence and intentness, even the silence of food vendors and bookstall keepers during the service, brought home to Billy the strength of Christianity in South India. He saw that the key to the evangelization of India lay among Indians themselves, a conviction by no means universally held by Western missionaries in 1956. He resolved to do his utmost to aid Asians to preach Christ to Asians.

Billy was already doing so. At Madras, as he preached, his Tamil interpreter, Victor Monogoram, became so involved in evangelizing, as distinct from merely translating, that his own ministry received new power. At Delhi, the interpreter was an outstanding intellectual, Dr. Akbar Abdul-Haqq. Haqq had nearly refused to interpret because he had never done such work. As he recalls, "I was not interested in this sort of outreach at all, even though I was curious to find out how God was using Billy Graham." During the first of the Delhi meetings, Billy sensed that his interpreter was "God's chosen vessel for this type of evangelism in the Orient." He startled Haqq next day by saying, "I'm not the man to be used for spiritual awakening here. It has to be an Asian. I think you are the man."

By the end of that year, Akbar Haqq had joined the Billy Graham Team and begun his great ministry of Good News Festivals in India, preaching also at American universities and as an associate in many of Billy's crusades.

Billy capped his Indian tour by one-day rallies in six countries of the Far East, each leading to full crusades later. In India, his visit had heartened and stirred the churches and awoke widespread desire for revival and evangelism.

To Billy himself, the tour of 1956 brought renewed conviction "that human nature is the same the world over, and that when the Gospel of Christ is preached in simplicity and power, there is a response in the human soul."

9

NEW YORK 1957

BILLY GRAHAM RETURNED FROM INDIA TO A NEW HOME. THE house on Assembly Drive had long been too small and too public. Tourists not only peered through the hedge—thirty-one were counted on one Sunday in August—they forced themselves into the yard, even into the house, and gave the children money to pose for photographs. In 1955, friends at Montreat and elsewhere surprised the Grahams by raising a fund for the building of a house on their remote mountain land. Ruth's romantic sense of history came into full play. She scoured the mountains buying old timber from disused cabins and brick from an ancient schoolhouse to build a place that fitted exactly into its background and soon looked a hundred years old, even to the split-rail fences. Inside she evoked an informal country house atmosphere that spanned the centuries. "I want it to be a home that everyone can feel at home in, whether mountain folk or the wealthy."

Here, Billy could "recharge his batteries," reveling in the woodland sights and sounds and the superb view in the North Carolina mountain air. The study—designed by a friend in Greensboro, prefabricated by his firm, and shipped to Montreat—was so placed that no one needed to quiet the children and their friends when their dad was working. And all the time he could squeeze from the relentless pressure of preparation and correspondence, phone calls, and interviews, Billy spent with the children, except for golfing, which kept him fit. Ruth described their home as a "Noah's Ark of happy confusion"—children, dogs, a cat called

Moldy, and at one stage, three Hampshire sheep. "They can keep down the grass," said Billy, "and we've got to have sheep and goats and things like that so the kids will learn the facts of life."

"Bill," replied Ruth, "why don't I just tell them and save us all that trouble?"

Then one day Billy was feeding this small flock with apples when an ungrateful ram butted him down the steep rocky hillside. He sustained a painful hairline fracture in his left tibia, torn ligaments of the left knee, cuts, bruises, and much hilarious kidding from all over the world.

In the early months of 1957, Billy spent most of his time in Montreat, studying, praying, preparing sermons, and seeking to deepen his spiritual life. As Billy recollects, "I also knew I needed rest and exercise to be prepared physically for the demanding road ahead of us. Those were days of peace, relaxing in the spring sun, and spending time with Ruth and the children." And time after time he walked to the top of the mountain behind their new home and, as Billy recalls, I stood there "for hours at a time, calling upon God and exercising what little faith I had in believing that New York City could be touched by the Gospel of Jesus Christ."

A crusade in the city of Wall Street, of Broadway, Madison Avenue, and Harlem and all that those names connoted—diverse population, fierce competitive spirit, hustle and sophistication, and absorption in material things—might be a disaster. Protestants were in a minority to Roman Catholics and Jews, churchgoing in Manhattan was low, and a contemporary expert likened evangelism in New York to "digging in flint."

Billy Graham accepted an invitation from the Protestant Council of the City of New York, representing 1,700 churches of 31 denominations, and from a number of independent bodies. All the leading churches would cooperate, at least in name, for a six-week crusade beginning on May 15, 1957, in the old Madison Square Garden. The committee took an option for a further five months.

During the two years of preparation, Billy's acceptance of the invitation brought some of the most violent opposition he had experienced. The *Christian Century,* at that time very much against him, derided the coming crusade: "The Graham procedure ... does its mechanical best to 'succeed' whether or not the Holy Spirit is in attendance. At this strange new junction of Madison Avenue and Bible Belt, the Holy Spirit is not overworked; he is overlooked." Extreme fundamentalists, including some older men whom Billy had revered, attacked him for being sponsored by "modernists," although the crusade was not organized by the Protestant Council (which included many liberals) but by an executive committee of fifteen men who shared Billy's basic outlook and goals. And no one controlled the preaching except Billy, who intended "to pull no punches in presenting Christ and him crucified."

While enduring these attacks, Billy met a succession of problems that were far too big for him and threatened to destroy the crusade—including the death of Dawson Trotman in a boating accident (which meant switching the leadership of counseling and follow-up training) and the crusade director's resignation for personal reasons. Charlie Riggs took over. "I did not think Charlie could do it," Billy recalls, "except I had this peace—that Charlie so depended on God and the Holy Spirit that I knew the Lord could do it through Charlie."

The scale of the preparation looked immense. In order to provide adequate numbers for each night, 4,000 people practiced for the choir, 5,000 took counseling classes, and 3,000 volunteered as ushers. And the New York churches were increasingly wholehearted, largely through the work of a comparatively new team associate, Billy's young brother-in-law from Canada, Leighton Ford, who won the clergy's confidence to a marked degree. And during the team's devotional retreat, as the crusade drew near, Leighton Ford gave a "searching, challenging, convicting message," through which, wrote Billy, "We were all broken by the Holy Spirit." By the end of the retreat they felt cleansed and anointed for the task ahead.

When Billy reached New York, he felt physically fitter and spiritually better prepared than before any previous crusade, yet "more inadequate and helpless." There had been ample predictions that he would fail. "From human viewpoint and by human evaluation, it may be a flop," Billy commented. "However, I am convinced in answer to the prayers of millions that in the sight of God and by heaven's evaluation it will be no failure. God will have his way, and in some unknown and remarkable way Christ will receive the glory and honor."

"We have not come to put on a show or an entertainment," Billy began in his first address on the opening night. "We believe that there are many people here tonight that have hungry hearts—all your life you've been searching for peace and joy, happiness, forgiveness.

"I want to tell you, before you leave Madison Square Garden this night of May 15, you can find everything that you have been searching for, in Christ. He can bring that inward deepest peace to your soul. He can forgive every sin you've ever committed. And he can give you the assurance that you're ready to meet your God, if you will surrender your will and your heart to him.

"I want you to listen tonight not only with your ears, but the Bible teaches that your heart also has ears. Listen with your soul tonight. Forget that there's anyone else here. Forget me as the speaker, listen only to the message that God would have you to retain from what is to be said tonight.

"Shall we pray: *Our Father and our God, in Christ's name we commit the next few moments to thee, and we pray that the speaker shall hide behind the Cross until the people shall see none, save Jesus.*

"*And we pray that many tonight will reevaluate their relationship to God, others will consider, for the first time perhaps, their need of God, and that many shall respond and surrender themselves to him as they did 2,000 years ago on the shores of Galilee: for we ask it in his name. Amen.*"

Billy Graham's prayer on that opening night was answered. From the start, the crusade made an unprecedented impact on the city of New York and broke all records. The total attendance of more than two million was the highest of any event in the history of Madison Square Garden. More than 60,000 people came forward, swamping the follow-up system until it was reorganized. They were a cross-section of society: "the socially prominent and the outcast, the rich and the poor, the illiterate who could not sign their own decision cards and the university professor; racial lines were freely crossed and Negroes and Puerto Ricans were among the large groups." A team associate, Dr. Robert O. Ferm, who questioned a large number one year later, wrote that "the utter fascination of listening to the reports of converts would convince the skeptic that a work of grace had been done. The person who actually made the decision retains a warm and vibrant faith that has been able to survive and persist through many discouragements and above many obstacles."

The press gave extensive coverage. *The New York Times* printed the entire text of Billy's sermon on several occasions. *The Herald Tribune* allowed him space on the front page to write whenever he wished. There were critical articles too. The great theologian Reinhold Niebuhr in *Life* magazine stated that Billy's evangelism "neglected to explore the social dimensions of the Gospel." Niebuhr admitted that Billy "had sound personal views on racial segregation and other social issues of our time," but alleged that "he almost ignores them in his actual preaching."

Niebuhr based this opinion on the newspaper accounts of the crusade and on occasional attendance. The *Associated Press* religious writer, George W. Cornell, sitting at the press desk night after night, disagreed with this view. He wrote a private letter to Billy: "I have read various criticisms of you from those who say you do not stress the full social implications of Christ's demands (the horizontal aspects, as you put it), but I have concluded that the critics simply have not paused to listen to you, but have been so dazzled by your external successes that they don't see its roots." Nevertheless, Niebuhr's criticism was taken to heart, and Billy increasingly touched on a whole range of social issues.

President Mackay of Princeton Theological Seminary wrote: "Men have been made aware of the sins of the heart and of society. It is unfair to demand that Billy Graham should have offered a blueprint for the solution of complicated social issues in our highly industrialized mass society." But this was just what his critics did demand, for they rejected his belief that the root evil of human society is the unregenerate human heart.

Ethel Waters, celebrated black singer and actress, made a spontaneous retort on television to the question whether the crusade would fail: "God don't sponsor no flops!"

Her remark was heard by Lane Adams, the former fighter pilot and nightclub singer who had postponed ordination to direct the crusade's outreach to entertainers. He offered her a seat in the reserved section. During her long stage and screen career, Ethel Waters had never lost the consciousness of God that had come when she was converted at the age of twelve, and as she walked into Madison Square Garden that first night, she said, "[I] felt that my Lord was calling me back home."

After the first week, Waters joined the choir of fifteen hundred voices in order to secure a reserved seat every night and sang at each service for eight weeks. "So many things I had pondered about for a lifetime, the Lord cleared up during these weeks." Cliff Barrows learned of her presence when the choir signed a petition for the extension of the crusade, and asked her if she would sing a solo. She sang the song that she made famous on Broadway: "His Eye Is on the Sparrow." As Waters recalls, "This time, however, it was to be very different. The glitter and heartache of the stage had disappeared. . . . There was just myself, standing before 18,000 people, saying, 'I love Jesus too,' the only way I could say it—by singing 'His Eye Is on the Sparrow.'"

On five nights in the final eight weeks, Ethel Waters sang that song. When the crusade ended, she had readjusted much in her life, for as she put it, "I found that I could no longer act every role I was offered and continue to glorify my Lord." She played in the feature film based on the New York crusade, *The Heart Is a Rebel,* and visited crusades year by year at her own expense to sing in her inimitable style until her death in 1977.

The coming of Ethel Waters, who in her own way became virtually a member of the team, was one of the crusade's long-term effects on the Billy Graham story. But by far the most significant was the breakthrough into television.

It was not premeditated. A few days after the crusade began, Fred Dienert said to Billy: "Wouldn't it be wonderful if we could take this crowd to the nation, if the people at home could see what's going on, and the people coming to Christ." Billy, recalling the great influence on Britain of the Kelvin Hall telecast on Good Friday 1955, agreed. Bennett and Dienert sounded the networks about televising the crusade coast-to-coast but encountered skepticism, even ridicule. Then the American Broadcasting Company offered time, and a foundation offered the money to pay for the first four hour-long telecasts.

These telecasts on Saturday, June 1, and each following Saturday (seventeen in all) from the country's best-known arena were a revelation to America. As a television ministry, it was a thousand times more effective than the Graham Team's studio program of earlier years, for the crowd in the Garden created a strong sense of participation for the viewer, who was now eavesdropping on an event not watching a contrived half hour of song and talk.

After the first telecast, over 25,000 letters came in to encourage or thank Billy Graham, or to tell of decisions made for Christ while viewing. Each succeeding Saturday widened and deepened the influence of the television crusade. In Chicago at Polk Brothers' display of TV sets at the Chicagoland Fair, so many people watched those sets that happened to be tuned in to the crusade and ignored the others that the sales representatives went down the long line and turned all sets to the crusade. In Buffalo, the Council of

Churches reported that criticism of the New York crusade had been swept away and that church attendance had reached an unprecedented figure for this time of year.

The first television crusade provided a turning point in the Graham Team's ministry. More than 1.5 million letters were sent to Billy in three months. He had been a household name for some years, but now his message came right into homes across the nation. By the end of this first television crusade, no less than 30,000 Americans had written in to state definite decisions made for Christ during or after the telecasts; and by the network's assessment of the normal proportion of letter-writers to viewers, the total number of decisions was probably considerably more.

From then on, part of each crusade was televised across the nation, generally by videotape shown several weeks or months later.

Having extended beyond the original six weeks, the executive committee booked Yankee Stadium, home of the New York Yankees baseball team, for the closing rally on July 26. The temperature inside the stadium that day was 105 degrees. More than 100,000 people attended, with more thousands outside the gates, listening by loudspeaker.

Billy and the committee had already decided, after much prayer and an all-morning discussion, to extend again until August 10. Some were afraid of an anticlimax. Billy replied that he could find no scriptural basis for worrying about that. Christ's entry into Jerusalem was a great climax; His death the following Friday was from a human viewpoint "a great anticlimax, yet it proved to be the turning point of history."

"Mr. Graham anticipated," wrote his secretary, Luverne Gustavson, on July 16, "a terrible drop in attendance this week, with no large delegations booked, but it's been amazingly full! And hundreds still come forward. There is a 'deeper' tone to the whole services, it seems. And Mr. Graham's messages are largely to Christians, so a lot of the early converts are getting established in the Christian life. His subjects on prayer and the Holy Spirit have been exceptionally good."

Billy was exhausted. He had been preaching ten weeks nightly without a break. He now cut out other engagements, spent most of the day in bed, sometimes would almost cling to the pulpit. "I had nothing to give; I had exhausted my mind. Yet I'm sure that everyone would agree that the preaching had far more power. It was God taking sheer weakness—it's when I get out of the way and say, 'God, you have to do it.' I sat on the platform many nights with nothing to say, nothing. Just sat there. And I knew that in a few minutes I'd have to get up and preach, and I'd just say, 'Oh, God, I can't do it. I cannot do it.' And yet, I would stand up and all of a sudden it would begin to come—just God giving it, that's all." The crusade cost him physically even more than London.

On August 10, they extended for the third and last time. "Not even the most vocal critics," Billy wrote on August 26, "can now say that it was publicity, organization, or showmanship. There is an element of the Spirit of God that is beyond analysis and rationalization."

The crusade ended after sixteen weeks with a rally in Times Square on the evening of Sunday, September 1. The crowds stretched shoulder to shoulder down Broadway as far as the eye could see, and spilled into the cross streets, their singing echoing beneath the commercial buildings, hotels, and movie theaters. The "crossroads of the world" became a great cathedral. The congregation was Billy's largest until that time, though sixteen years later in Korea, he would address more than a million people face-to-face.

The Protestant Council of New York was in no doubt that the crusade had fulfilled its purpose. Some six months after the close, its executive secretary, Dan Potter, wrote to Billy that the four objectives had been "met in a miraculous way: to win men to Christ; to make the city God-conscious; to strengthen the churches; to make the city conscious of moral, spiritual, and social responsibilities."

On May 15, 1958, one year to the day after the opening of the crusade, the Protestant Council held a united rally at Madison Square Garden. Billy sent greetings on tape from the San Francisco crusade. When the associate evangelist who was present asked converts of the previous year's crusade to stand, it seemed almost half of the 17,500 present were on their feet.

A New York minister wrote to Billy: "The real results of the crusade are not in statistical form or in ways that can be measured. You cannot tell what the crusade did for the morale of us ministers, the new confidence it gave us, the motivation it supplies for the preaching of the Bible and Christ crucified."

10

$\mathcal{U}$NDER THE $\mathcal{S}$OUTHERN $\mathcal{C}$ROSS

Australia did not seem to Billy Graham the likely scene of a crusade that would move a nation. Its population was less than that of New York City and scattered over a land mass the size of the United States without Alaska. A vast majority lived on the southeastern seaboard, especially around Sydney and Melbourne, but that was not immediately significant to the team. The Australians, with an expanding economy, an exceptional emphasis on sport and the outdoor life, and a worldwide reputation for independence and bluntness of speech, had not previously proved receptive to evangelists, especially those from abroad.

The forty-year-old Billy came at the official invitation of the major denominations in each state, and in New Zealand, for a crusade during the late summer and autumn, February to May, 1959. Billy sent Jerry Beavan to Sydney a year earlier to prepare. Beavan soon saw that by landline relays, tape recordings, and the buying of time on radio and television, together with a full use of Operation Andrew, most of the people of Australia might be touched. "I really believe that we are right on the verge of a national spiritual awakening here in Australia," he wrote. "There are so many evidences that God is doing an unusual thing that we are constantly overwhelmed by his blessing... There is more prayer right now in Sydney than there was in New York City at the height of that crusade."

The first crusade was to be at Melbourne—cultured, wealthy, conservative. It was a quietly self-confident city that might graciously allow Billy a hearing, and little more, although the crusade chairman was Dean of the Anglican Cathedral and the vice-chairman was President-General of the Methodist Conference. For a director, Billy sent Walter H. Smyth, a minister from Philadelphia. Smyth had worked with him in Youth for Christ and subsequently in his film distribution office, and would take an increasingly important part in the Billy Graham ministry as International Director in the years ahead. Melbourne loved Walter for his "brotherly and cooperative spirit," his tact and efficiency and calmness in crisis.

Early in 1959, with Australia reaching a peak of preparation, Billy was at a conference in Dallas when he began to suffer severe pain and restricted sight in his left eye. The blockage was caused by overstrain (he might have had a blood clot) for he had been carrying too heavy a speaking schedule, along with all the problems caused by growth of the Association. He was ordered a complete rest in the sun in Hawaii. Melbourne was postponed by a week and Sydney shortened by a week. Billy was ordered to do little more than the evening preaching, and to swim or play a short round of golf on most days.

The Australian crusade opened on February 15, 1959, at Melbourne. Despite Australian zeal, the Americans expected a small crusade, and autumn weather being chancy, had chosen the largest indoor arena (now the Festival Hall) out in West Melbourne, which seated only 7,500, increased by a temporary annex for closed circuit television to 10,000. But on the opening Sunday afternoon, the arena could not contain the crowds. Billy went outside and addressed, in a sudden rainstorm, an overflow crowd estimated by the police at 5,000.

After five days, the crusade moved to a new open-air auditorium inaugurated the previous week, the Sidney Myer Music Bowl in King's Domain, across the Yarra River in the center of the city. Its unusually shaped aluminum roof covered only the platform and some 2,000 seats, but the Bowl was so designed that a great audience could sit on the grass slopes and look down to the platform, and thousands more could stand behind in a wide arc. The acoustics and amplification were perfect: The fringes of the crowd, though unable to see, could hear every word of song and sermon. Melbourne spilled out to King's Domain in such numbers that the team and committee marveled at the smallness of the faith that had been content to book the indoor arena.

"When Billy gave the invitation," wrote Grady Wilson the next morning, "immediately they began streaming down the aisles from all directions. There were more than 3,000 that came forward, and finally Billy threw up his hands and said, 'Stop, ladies and gentlemen, there is no more room. If you want to give your life to Christ, go home and drop me a letter in the mail, and I will send you follow-up literature that will help you in your Christian life.' It has been simply fantastic what God the Holy Ghost has done here."

As hundreds of that 3,000 crowded onto the platform, a hard-bitten police inspector complained: "That platform won't stand the weight, there'll be a collapse." The inspector, who had previously indicated that the whole crusade was both nonsense and a nuisance, murmured in awed tones: "There is something here I don't understand. There is something here with depth that is beyond me. It can only be God at work." When numbers at the Myer Bowl on Sunday topped 60,000, all Australia read the headlines' news of the amazing turnout.

The Music Bowl was a perfect place for the nonchurchgoer. A solicitor told a lawyer on the committee, "I would be uncomfortable in a church, but people like me find it very easy to go along and listen to Billy in these surroundings. Everything is so natural. This is how I think Christ must have preached when he was talking to the people of his day." Even drinkers outside a hotel called to Billy as he passed, "Good on you, Billy, we're for you!"

Billy's left eye troubled him a little, but he made a complete recovery. The entire team warmed to the friendliness of the Australians, as the Australians to theirs. Cliff and Bev won a large place in the affections of a nation that loves to sing. "They created a wonderful atmosphere in the early stages of each meeting," runs the memory of a businessman convert, "and that atmosphere helped us to realize fully the joy and love of Christianity."

In the third week, the Myer Music Bowl had to be vacated because of Melbourne's Moomba Festival. The crusade moved to the Agricultural Showgrounds, far from the city center and the residential suburbs—near freight yards, power stations, and a slaughter house. This third move, to uncongenial surroundings with bad acoustics, did not prove to be a disadvantage, and the crusade continued to be the main topic in Melbourne.

Then came the torrential rain of March 2. On March 3, a youth night, the rain was worse, if possible, yet about 25,000 attended. The platform was not covered, so Billy's tie-microphone stopped working and he preached crouching over a low microphone on the dais. Most of the people were in the stands, but those who came forward had to plough through the mud in the open, 1,200 of them.

Meanwhile, at Myer Music Bowl, the rain washed away the loose earth on the slopes and poured down to flood what had been the counseling area. Had the crusade stayed, it would have been drowned!

On Sunday, March 15, the final meeting took place at the Melbourne Cricket Ground, then one of the largest and best designed stadiums in the world. Long before the arrival of the governor of Victoria, Sir Dallas Brooks, the stands were full and people were still crowding into the gates. The secretary of the Melbourne Cricket Club made history by allowing thousands to sit on the turf and by allowing women and children to enter the members' stand.

The governor read the Twenty-third Psalm and Billy, before his address, gave out a special message from President Eisenhower. Billy was overwhelmed by the size of the crowd, greater even than that of Wembley in 1954. Luverne Gustavson, far back in one of the stands, echoed the thoughts of the team when she wrote that evening: "It was a stirring sight to see so many people gathered so reverently for a Gospel service. Then at the end of the service when the congregation joined to sing 'God Be with You Till We Meet Again,' my throat got all lumpy. For certainly most of these people would never meet again until in the Presence of Christ."

More than 4,000 inquirers came forward at the invitation. With the counselors beside them, it was an amazing sight in itself. Counseling was held up briefly when "God Save the Queen" was played at the departure of the Queen's representative.

Even more than the governor's presence, another action seemed to spotlight Melbourne's reaction to the crusade. Close behind the Cricket Ground lies a main suburban railway. Normally, red trains and green trains clatter noisily at frequent intervals. That afternoon they were strangely quiet. The head of Victoria Railways had personally ordered trains to proceed slowly in the vicinity during the service.

Seven weeks after the Graham Team had left Melbourne, the Chief Justice of Victoria, Lieutenant-General Sir Edmund Herring, echoed in a private letter to Billy the public comments of churchmen: "Your crusade here," he wrote, "has had tremendous repercussions. All the churches have new recruits to look after, and all I have been in touch with are doing everything they can to make them welcome and keep them in the fold. But, quite apart from the number of people who have either been brought into the churches or brought back to them, we all owe you a debt for sweetening our own lives and making the great bulk of the people who are, sad to say, outside the Christian World, pause and think for a minute of where they stand." In 1964, Herring could strongly endorse his 1959 letter. "I would say that in all sorts of ways and all sorts of places the influence of Billy Graham is still felt here." And in 1969, in his second Melbourne crusade, Billy could see this for himself.

After rallies in Tasmania and crusades in New Zealand—and a week's rest on Queensland beaches—Billy went to Sydney for four weeks for a crusade that was firmly consolidated as part of the continuing mission of the church.

Virtually the entire Protestant Church community was officially committed to support, and many individual churches and parishes shaped their programs around the crusade. Counseling classes enrolled more than double the number of people that enrolled in New York, with its far greater population. (This though was dwarfed by Los Angeles in 1963, which enrolled 23,000.) Of the 6,000 people selected as counselors or advisers, over half were Anglicans from 160 parishes. Sydney also taught the Graham Team the new concept of a pre-crusade citywide visitation—every home in the entire city was visited with an invitation to attend.

Thousands of small prayer meetings in homes and the press coverage from the Melbourne crusade raised expectancy. The Sydney press had been Billy's ally ever since his first press conference on his way to Melbourne, and it covered the crusade as no other event since the Queen's visit.

On the first day, 50,000 people came to the Agricultural Showground. Few of the committee had quite expected their "city of happy pagans" to show much response, yet nearly 1,000 came forward, and so it continued day after day. From the platform it was "always deeply moving," wrote Archbishop Marcus Loane, "to watch the solemn audience suddenly break up when the invitation was given, like a giant human anthill stirred to life, as thousands rose from their seats in the arena or in the farthest stands to go forward." This movement was essentially an individual action: one here, another there, pushing past the row of friends or strangers to the aisle; then, at the platform (though a host of inquirers and counselors were all around) the convert conscious, as was often testified afterward, of no other people around. The prayer of committal would be repeated as if alone with God.

More than once, heavy rain turned the Showground into a quagmire. Roy Gustafson, Billy's old friend of Florida days, had gone to Australia as his guest, "with some big question marks. Just because numbers are large is no proof that God is in it. Goliath was big...." On the first Friday at Sydney, rain fell intermittently during the service. At the invitation, said Gustafson, "the rain came down like a tropical storm. you couldn't even see the people in the stands. They couldn't see the platform. And Billy started the appeal. I said to myself, 'He must be crazy. No one will come tonight.' But 1,700 people came, and stood in water and mud up to their ankles. I remember a counselor drenched to the skin, with half a dozen people under an umbrella, and he in the middle standing with a Bible. Water was coming through in a fine mist and ruining the Bible, but he was pointing the half dozen to the Savior. That night I was absolutely convinced that God had laid his hand on Billy."

On May 10, 1959, at the final service, 150,000 people were present: 80,000 in the Showground and 70,000 in the adjoining Cricket Ground, linked by amplifiers. A further one million Australians listened either by landline or by the live radio broadcast. There was an exciting touch when the two great choirs, with Bev Shea, sang "How Great Thou Art" in alternate verses, one from the Showground, the next from the Cricket Ground. Billy preached on "The Broad and the Narrow Way," and as the inquirers streamed forward Billy repeated, "What a sight! What a sight to see these hundreds coming through the rain. You who are in the Cricket Ground, you come forward too. Come and stand around the fences, and you who are listening to the landline relays, come and stand at the front of the auditorium where you are." A total of 5,683 people made decisions that day. "The thanksgiving prayer in the follow-up room," wrote the chairman of the follow-up committee, "when all the cards had come in and were being processed, was unforgettable."

The Sydney crusade and the associate crusades, with Billy traveling the continent to conclude each, stirred all of Australia. As one leading minister put it succinctly, "The whole country was rocked by the Graham phenomenon." Owing to Australia's unique distribution of population, probably 50 percent heard Billy Graham in person or through landlines, and almost all the rest heard him at least once on radio or by television.

Australia had never previously known a nationwide religious revival. The total figure of those who signified a committal to Christ in the crusade exceeded 130,000—no less than 1.24 percent of the population. As the Melbourne crusade secretary commented, "This must represent such a flood of new life and power into our whole religious force, which will surely go on to challenge the ungodliness and immorality about us." For the next ten years, half of the members of the theological colleges were fruit of the crusade, directly or indirectly, as converts or those who came to full consecration. Missionary societies of all denominations received scores of recruits.

Melbourne, and Sydney even more, proved how effective a crusade can be when integrated fully into the continuing work of the churches. Whereas in New York, a year after the 1957 crusade, less than half the inquirers were found to have been contacted, the Australian churches shepherded their converts by every means available, and saw the majority become strong in faith. As the perspective of the years lengthened, 1959 stood out as a landmark date.

For Billy and the team, 1959 ended their first ten years since Los Angeles with the assurance that in the decades ahead they "would see greater things than these."

Part Two

1960–1976

II

REACHING OUT

BILLY AND RUTH'S DECISION THAT RUTH SHOULD GIVE PRIORITY to the children, at the cost of frequent separations, brought its reward: Their two sons and three daughters enjoyed a happy, high-spirited family life, despite their father's frequent absences and the pressures of his fame.

"Because of their example," writes the eldest, Gigi, "I respected them and listened to their advice. I saw Daddy live what he preached. I saw them making Christ their life, not just their religion."

"I was able to see Christ in my parents," says the youngest, Ned. "Their love *and prayer* have guided me all my life, including my own commitment to Christ."

Franklin comments: "History has shown that many public figures live two lives: one for the camera, the other behind closed doors. Not so with Mom and Dad. Their lives are the same before the public as they are behind closed doors."

Each of the children, in his or her time and way, dedicated their lives to Christian service.

Working from a supremely happy home, Billy Graham's ministry expanded and deepened during the 1960s and 1970s. Supported by his family, his team, and the men and women of the Association offices, Billy could seize his ever-widening opportunities to bring Christ's message to millions.

The years were marked by great crusades: London again at Earl's Court; New York again at the new Madison Square Garden;

a television linkup across Europe from Dortmund, West Germany; scores of cities in North America; many capitals of the world; and some remote areas such as Nagaland.

Simultaneously, Billy was creating new openings. As Ruth says, he "is constantly thinking how best, in the short time we have left, to present the world with the claims of Christ and the hope that is to be found in the everlasting Gospel. Big thoughts. Big plans. He carries the world in his heart, as it were."

World Wide Pictures, the motion picture arm of the Association, carried the Christian message across the continents through feature films. In America, long before the rise of the "electronic church," Billy Graham crusades were shown regularly on television. The telecasts enormously increased the scope and results of Billy's evangelistic ministry. Some of them were later edited into films for showing in theaters and halls, while the films of his crusades in distant parts were shown on television with great effect.

In 1960 Billy founded *Decision* magazine. Four years earlier, with his father-in-law, Nelson Bell, he had founded *Christianity Today* to be a "strong, hard hitting, intellectual magazine" to propound the evangelical view. Many friends wanted Billy to make it a house organ of his association, but he decided against, and the independence of the magazine helped it to become a strong factor in the evangelical resurgence. A few years later, he invited Dr. Sherwood Eliot Wirt, a minister in Oakland, California, who had been a journalist before ordination and had written an excellent book about the San Francisco crusade of 1958, to create an illustrated color magazine for popular readership. It should promote the Gospel and discipleship and bring news of the crusades and other Billy Graham ministries so readers would support them by prayer.

While George Wilson and the Association office in Minneapolis prepared their expansion into major magazine publishing, Woody Wirt was lent to *Christianity Today*. "This was good experience in editing, but totally different productionwise from what I would meet. For example, *CT* used no pictures. So when Billy gave me the green light at a team meeting in Montreux in August 1960, and told me to go back to Minneapolis and put out *Decision*, I really had to start from scratch. It was on-the-job training. I had written for magazines, but knew nothing about producing one. I was a complete and total ignoramus! The one thing I did know was good writing from poor, and I determined that *Decision* should have no mediocre material.

"I visited New York and talked to religion editors of various media. I remember old Dr. Bradbury, the editor of the Baptist *Watchman—Examiner*, whom I visited in his funny little office high in an old building in Manhattan. I asked him what he thought *Decision* should be like and he said, 'Mr. Wirt, there is a hiatus in the field of Christian publishing. We used to emphasize Christ and his work and the Holy Spirit, and what it means to walk with God. Our magazines don't do that any more and it's a pity.' I thought, *By the grace of God, that's the kind of magazine I want to put out.*

"So instead of talking about the ramifications of the Christian faith, *Decision* talked about the faith itself, its source, its meaning, its significance. We talked about grace, and faith, and the Cross, and the Bible, and especially about Jesus. We tried in every issue to show how people could be saved. And I soon struck a principle of balance."

Each issue would include a sermon by Billy Graham, stories from his latest crusade, and a focus on prayer for the next. In another popular feature, men and women told how they had found Christ through the Graham ministries and of how their lives had changed: *Decision* selected a few representative stories each month from the flood of letters that poured unsolicited into Minneapolis. They were selected to help others, not to glorify Billy.

The balance would be made up with a Bible study, articles for youth and for women, articles about history or biography, and feature the missionary call. "I also went for the light touch and for poetry. Russ Busby's photos and Bob Blewett's paintings made a great contribution. In time we assimilated a fine staff and the production of the magazine became a thrilling experience. We had wonderful support from Billy, from the team, and from the staff and employees at the Minneapolis office. As for the readers, it was simply amazing to see the subscriptions come in every day by the hundreds. We seldom got a critical letter."

Decision carried no advertisements, yet paid its way from the start. Within nine years the circulation in North America had reached four million. Before its twentieth year, *Decision* in its different editions and in six languages had become monthly reading in five continents. Sherwood Wirt and, after his retirement, his successors, Roger Palms for many years and then Kersten Beckstrom and Bob Paulson, have kept it a force for Christ across the world.

Billy was also quick to accept and absorb the suggestions of others. The late Lowell Berry, an industrialist of San Francisco whose life had been blessed by the crusade of 1958, suggested that a school of evangelism should be held during a crusade. In the fourteen years after the first school held during the Chicago crusade of 1962, Berry gave half a million dollars in scholarships.

The schools have become one of the most significant segments of the Billy Graham ministry.[4] They have been an incalculable influence on pastors and students. For an example, the school held during the Rio de Janeiro crusade of 1974 drew 3,500 men and women to Rio. They came from Amazon rain forests to the cool southern mountains, from the savannas to new Brasilia and abundant Sao Paulo, traveling by country bus along earth roads and then by swift modern buses along the network of highways that link the enormous country. From Recife, with its glorious beaches, a convoy of four buses included most of the Baptist seminary and the women's college for Christian education, both drawing their students from throughout the northeast. They traveled night and day for forty-two hours, to hear "a great and famous preacher," to "learn his methods," and to "share in the work of the crusade."

The Brazilians appreciated every lecture, but the seminars were the high spots. These gave time to talk and discover one another, for most of them knew little or nothing of Christians in other denominations. The school of evangelism broke down those barriers throughout Brazil, just as the crusade preparations had broken barriers in Greater Rio. The atmosphere of the school, its spirituality and the seriousness with which it faced the problems of evangelism, heartened pastors and laity, especially the young.

Billy Graham and the crusade itself formed the focal points. When Billy addressed the school, his evangelistic emphasis and his appeal for a deep spiritual life left a strong impression. A pastor in the rolling uplands of Minas Gerais, living a four hours' bus ride from the regional city and a forty minutes' walk from the bus stop, summed up the school of evangelism: "It all really boils down to one thing: I got out of the school of evangelism a passion for souls."

The pastors from the interior, like those of Rio who had prepared the crusade, were heartened and humbled when they attended the huge stadium services, especially the final Sunday afternoon with its extraordinary atmosphere of joy. They watched in awe the 225,000 people who had gathered to hear Billy, for the total of non-Catholics in Rio in 1974 numbered less than 100,000. As the service began, they heard the hammering on the gates by those who could not get in.

And when they returned home, they were able at once to put into practice what they had learned, for the whole service had been televised live. The television company estimated that 25,000,000 people had watched and heard Billy's sermon.

12

THE RECONCILER

IN SEPTEMBER 1963, A BAPTIST CHURCH IN A BLACK AREA OF BIRM-
ingham, Alabama, was destroyed by bombs that caused the
deaths of four children. It was one more serious incident in the
racial tension of those years in the southern states of America.

The next Easter day, 1964, Billy Graham brought his team,
which had been racially integrated for seven years, for an evangelistic rally in Birmingham's main stadium, where the segregation
between blacks and whites, then customary, was abandoned for the
day. Bev Shea recalls the fear of many in the city that such a move
would provoke violence, but the community leaders believed that
Billy could have a deeper impact than anyone else.

The crowd of over 30,000, estimated to be equally black and
white, went out of its way to be friendly to one another. Billy
preached a straight address of love, repentance, and faith, and the
national press reporters were stunned at the response, as blacks and
whites streamed forward at the invitation.

Billy was able to promote racial conciliation because he had
been among the first to do so, and had worked consistently for the
end of segregation in the south. As a southern boy he had taken it
for granted. "It rarely occurred to me in my childhood to think
about the difficulties, problems, and oppressions of black people.
In high school, I began to question some of the practices, but it was
not until I'd actually committed my life to Christ that I began to
think more deeply about it." At Wheaton, which had been founded
as an antislavery school, Billy notes, It was "very strong in its social

conscience, especially on the race question, [and] I began to realize for the first time that if I were a Christian, I had to take a stand."

More than forty years later, at the Tacoma crusade of 1983, a black woman who came from the south told the local newspaper about her childhood memory of the young unknown Billy Graham. He was to be the preacher at a tent revival during his vacation from Wheaton. She was with her mother and the other colored people (as they were then known) at the back, segregated behind the customary rope. While they waited, the child of her mother's white employers came down to play with her, and they strayed from the rope as they played. A white woman stopped her. "She was propelling me towards the back of the tent," recalls the Tacoma resident, when a large hand settled on her shoulder. It was Billy Graham.

"You're going the wrong way, sister," he said. "She belongs down front—all the children belong down front so God can smile on them."

"He gently loosened me from the woman's grip and led both of us children to the front of the tent. Then he had all the children, colored and white, gathered at the front of the tent. The segregation rope was removed, because Billy Graham refused to preach to a segregated audience."

When he first began crusades in the South in 1950, Billy accepted segregation in seating but not among those who came forward: "There's no racial distinction here," he would say from the podium. "The ground is level at the foot of the Cross." At a southern crusade in 1952, he personally pulled down the ropes. "That was among my first acts of conscience on the race question. I determined from then on I would never preach to another segregated audience."

The Chattanooga crusade of 1953, more than a year before the Supreme Court decision of 1954, was fully integrated, and every crusade afterward.

In 1956, after a private talk with President Eisenhower, Billy went quietly to work among religious leaders of both races in the south, encouraging them individually to take a stronger stand for desegregation and yet to demonstrate charity and patience. During the following years, sometimes at personal risk, he held integrated meetings of reconciliation in cities where there had been racial conflict or violence. President Johnson wrote to him: "You are doing a brave and fine thing for your country in your courageous effort to contribute to the understanding and brotherhood of the Americans in the South."

Through writing and speaking, Billy supported civil rights reform, but he would not join freedom marches, convinced that he could contribute a better way. He was abused by both sides in the conflict.

Martin Luther King understood and appreciated Billy Graham's work. In 1957 Billy invited King to brief the team. During the New York crusade, King addressed them twice privately and gave the prayer one evening. In later years, the two men twice held long discussions, and in 1960, at the world Baptist conference in Rio de Janeiro, Billy gave a dinner in Martin Luther King's honor, inviting Southern Baptist leaders, some of whom were uncomfortable eating with King, since restaurants, toilets, hotels, and most churches, were segregated in the South at that time. In his speech at the dinner, King said that his work for civil rights would be much harder were it not for the Billy Graham crusades.

Billy was certain that the race problem was fundamentally moral and spiritual. He believed that forced changes on either side would deepen prejudice. "But if you preach the love of Christ and the transforming power of Christ, there is not only a spiritual change but a psychological and moral change. The man who receives Christ forgets all about race when he is giving his life to Christ."

An outstanding example of change was Jimmy Karam of Little Rock, Arkansas, who had become notorious in the nation as a violent leader of those who resisted federal attempts to impose integration in the schools. A lapsed Catholic and married to a Baptist, Karam was a successful businessman and political boss and a self-proclaimed "real rough, tough fellow." On a visit to New York in 1957, Karam was taken against his will by Governor Faubus to the Billy Graham crusade. He heard Billy say that it made no difference what sort of life you had lived. Christ had died for your sins and risen from the dead; therefore, God can wipe the slate clean if you will believe.

As Karam recalls, "If Billy Graham had said that night, 'Now, Jimmy, you have got to quit drinking; you have got to quit gambling and running around and lying,' I would have said, 'Forget it. I have been trying to quit. There is no way.' I had tried all of my life to live a decent life. But when I accepted Jesus Christ into my life, he took away drinking, smoking, gambling, running around, and all the things I couldn't do for myself. He did it just like that. That is what is so wonderful about Christ. That is what is so wonderful about Billy Graham's ministry. I don't care how many kings or queens he had been with, Billy Graham has saved lives such as mine all over the world. And that is what he lives for; he lives to see lost people find salvation through Christ and then to help us grow in Christ."

Jimmy Karam's family soon saw that he had stopped swearing, but his reputation was so terrible that his daughter's pastor declined to waste time counseling him. Then the pastor came, saw his sincerity, and helped him to consolidate the decision. Karam quickly became a force for racial conciliation in the south and for evangelism. "My whole life changed. I only wanted to tell other people about Christ. Every talk I make is my testimony of what my life was before Christ and what it now is with Christ." Being of Lebanese origin, he could speak with authority about the tensions between Arabs and Jews, between whites and blacks, which only Christ can give strength to resolve.

Karam and his pastor, W. O. Vaught, wanted to bring Billy to Little Rock. Local conditions made this impossible for two years. Then a week that began with yet another bombing, ended with meetings in War Memorial Stadium, which led Vaught, the crusade chairman, to write to Billy: "There has been universal agreement in all the churches and out across the city that your visit here was one of the finest things that ever happened in the history of Little Rock. So very many people have changed their attitude, so many people have washed their hearts of hatred and bitterness, and many made decisions who had never expected to make such decisions."

Many years later, when Martin Luther King was dead but violence and discrimination had disappeared from the southern states, Senator Daniel Moynihan summed it up well in a private letter to Billy: "You and Rev. King, more than any two men—and, surely, with God's help—brought your own South out of that long night of racial fear and hate."

But Billy was not concerned for only his own country. He worked for racial reconciliation in the Middle East and wherever he had opportunity. Nowhere was this more evident than in South Africa. He refused to conduct a crusade or rally unless apartheid conditions were lifted.

The opportunity came at last in 1973 through the work of Michael Cassidy, a South African brought to Christ at Cambridge University through a friend who had been converted at Harringay. Billy's 1955 mission at Cambridge followed soon afterward, and Michael had a new hero. At the New York crusade in 1957, he dedicated his life to mass evangelism in Africa. He founded Africa Enterprise.

By 1973 Cassidy was able to promote an interracial, integrated congress of evangelism at Durban, which Billy Graham addressed. At King's Park rugby stadium in Durban on the Sunday afternoon of the congress, and at Wanderer's cricket ground in Johannesburg a week later, Billy preached to completely integrated audiences.

At Durban, so quiet and good-natured was the crowd that the police dogs, which were usually needed to separate brawlers when different races came in big numbers to a stadium, were soon returned to the vans. The police kept out of sight. Apartheid had even been lifted from the restrooms. The friendliness of the races, their discovery of each other as being equally first-class citizens, made a startling impact on Durban, especially because of the immense size of the rally. Even opponents recognized that only Billy Graham could have brought it together in the South Africa of 1973.

"The sight of black and white South Africa together in that field," said a black bishop, "singing and praying to the one God, was a foretaste of what future generations in this land are certain to enjoy if we today will be faithful."

At Johannesburg, where the sermon was carried live to the whole nation by South African radio, the conclusion of Billy's sermon brought an immediate response. In the cricket ground, what at first seemed only a sprinkle of individuals soon became a slow floodtide of humanity. The platform where Billy stood waiting, chin on hand in prayer, had been set in the center of a counseling circle fifty yards wide, reached by aisles kept open between the massed listeners sitting on the turf in front of the packed-out stands. The inquirers, pressing forward, filled the counseling space, yet still came down the aisles in a great flow of all colors of face and clothing.

Less than 3,000 trained counselors helped more than 4,000 people who had streamed to the front. People from every race in South Africa mingled. The fear that lies at the root of apartheid was lost at the foot of the Cross.[5] Billy Graham's ministry in South Africa is recognized as one of the many significant contributions to the ending of apartheid and the coming of majority role twenty years later. Nelson Mandela himself, as he told Michael Cassidy in 1993, had been "much touched" by a Billy Graham telecast while in prison and had sought to tell Billy personally during a visit to America, but Billy had been in the hospital having an operation on his foot.

13

SCENES FROM WEST AND EAST

IN AUGUST 1963, BILLY GRAHAM HELD A CRUSADE IN LOS ANGE-les, where he had sprung to fame fourteen years before. Instead of the circus-style tent of 1949, the team had the Los Angeles Coliseum, America's largest stadium used primarily for football and track meets—a vast oval with the tiers rising from ground level.

On one youth night, the number who came forward (3,216) did not fall much short of the aggregate of decisions recorded in the entire eight weeks of Los Angeles 1949. Despite the huge crowds, the reverent dignity was unforgettable. "I can't get over it," exclaimed the comedian Jack Benny. "These people are so quiet! I have never seen anything like it."

At the final service, 134,254 persons passed through the turnstiles, leaving an estimated 20,000 outside—the highest number recorded for any event at the coliseum. The stadium later erected a bronze plaque recording the occasion, bearing in bas-relief Billy's head and an impression of the scene.

After Cliff had led the choir and people in song and Bev Shea had brought all to a quiet expectancy by his solo before the sermon, Billy Graham once again set forth the essentials of the Christian Gospel. Then he said, "I'm going to ask you to do something tough and hard. I'm going to ask you to get up out of your seat, hundreds of you, get up out of your seat, and come out on this field and stand here reverently. Say tonight, 'I do want Christ to forgive me; I want a new life; I want to live clean and wholesome for Christ; I want him to be my Lord and my Master.' God has spoken to you. You get up and come—we're going to wait right now—quickly—hundreds of you from everywhere."

And not another word. He stood back, arms folded, head bent in prayer. At once the flow began. As in Sydney or Chicago or scores of cities throughout the world, it looked from the platform like a mass movement. But far up in the stadium it was one here, another there—a deliberate, costly choice, down the aisles and onto the grass. Billy stood motionless, a distant figure barely discernible above the sea of people, young and old, waiting until the tide ceased to flow and he could address them briefly before giving the benediction and the counseling began.

On the platform one night sat the German theologian, Professor Helmut Thielicke of Hamburg, who had come frankly critical: "[I] saw it all happen without pressure and emotionalism (contrary to the reports which I had received up until now). . . . I saw them all coming towards us, I saw their assembled, moved and honestly decided faces, I saw their searching and their meditativeness. I confess that this moved me to the very limits. Above all there were two young men—a white and a black—who stood at the front and about whom one felt that they were standing at that moment on Mount Horeb and looking from afar into a land they had longed for. I shall never forget those faces. It became lightning clear that men *want* to make a decision. . . .

"The consideration that many do not remain true to their hour of decision can contain no truly serious objection; the salt of this hour will be something they will taste in every loaf of bread and cake which they are to bake in their later life. *Once* in their life they have perceived what it is like to enter the realm of discipleship. And if only this memory accompanies them, then that is already a great deal. But it would certainly be more than a mere memory. It will remain an appeal to them, and in this sense it will maintain its character *indelibilis.*"

Billy and the team were determined to do all that they could to lessen the number of those who did not "remain true to their hour of decision." Training and follow-up were useless without prayer, but with prayer and profound trust in the Holy Spirit the team continually refined, improved, and adapted the methods they offered to the churches. Thus, as the decades passed, a crusade could handle numbers that would have been unbelievable in the earlier years.

The crusade at Seoul in the Republic of Korea in 1973 dwarfed the numbers recorded at Los Angeles ten years earlier. In the wide Han River, which marks the western edges of downtown Seoul, lies the open space of Yoido island where Samuel Moffett, the first missionary, had landed in 1883 and was stoned. One of the stone-throwers became a convert and the first to go as a missionary to his own people. Yoido is linked to each bank by bridges carrying the main road to the airport. The island's chief feature is the "May 16" People's Plaza, a long narrow paved runway, approximately one mile by two hundred yards, formerly the famous "Quay 16" landing ground of the Korean War. This was the place secured for the crusade.

About 300,000 people gathered for the first service. The ground had been grid-marked for crowd control, allowing almost exact statistics. As the team and staff members looked from the platform at the crowd stretching away in both directions of the long plaza, some wept openly as they felt "the waves of anticipation and joy and excitement pouring up" from that huge crowd down below. Long-serving missionaries like Sam Moffett, son of that first missionary, had been expecting a multitude, yet he was "stunned by the emotional impact of that many people on that island." Billy had often said that statistics are totally meaningless in the sight of God, but no preacher could fail to be moved when he walked onto the platform and saw such a crowd under the arc lights. Ruth wrote to her family, "It is one of those things impossible to take in."

Throughout the crusade, great numbers of Koreans spent all night in prayer on the plaza, while others prayed in the churches and pastors stoked the fires. "I continued," recalls one, "to emphasize three things in my church. First, prayer. Second, attendance by all members at the crusade. Third, I encouraged them to take their unsaved friends." The crusade became the talk of the city from cabinet minister to waitress, from shop assistant to barber. It was a chief topic on talk shows and the news. Friday was Army Night and Saturday, Youth Night. Christians, excited at the huge numbers attending, began to aim at no less than a million for the closing service on Sunday afternoon. That would be a resounding witness to both parts of the divided nation. At the committee's request, Billy Graham publicly suggested that, for the glory of God, it would be wonderful to have a million to hear the Gospel face-to-face.

Billy was determined that it should be for God's glory, not the team's. As one missionary commented, "Here were men and women who were really committed to the things of God. It became very obvious to me why he was blessing their ministry so richly: it was because they had no illusions but that it was all his. They seemed very careful from Mr. Graham on down, to protect that aspect and not to get their eyes off Jesus—lest, like Peter, they sink into the waves."

Sunday, June 3, 1973, turned warm with only passing clouds. Two hours before the service time at 3 P.M., Billy and his interpreter, Dr. Billy Kim, joined the stream flowing toward Yoido.

When Billy Graham mounted the platform, a solid block of humanity quietly awaited him. Every section, every aisle between, and away to edges of the plaza hitherto unused, sat an unbroken mass of people, who throughout that service, unless singing, stayed incredibly quiet. In Kim's experience of Korean crowds, none had been so still. Even children seemed neither to fidget nor cry. Statistically, there should have been hundreds of faintings, dozens of heart attacks, or other medical emergencies, yet the first-aid posts dealt with a mere 117 minor cases. Dissidents or protesters or cranks might have abounded, yet only one mental case made a brief commotion close to the platform.

The grid chart registered the figure of 1,120,000 present. Korean Christians and the team alike felt that organization, publicity, and a famous preacher could not have drawn that crowd and kept it so reverent. "It had to be the Holy Spirit." Many had waited all night and then through a hot morning. One bedridden old lady, nearing death and forbidden by her family to go, crawled out of her bedroom window and dragged herself to the plaza.

For all who took part, that final crusade service is a dreamlike memory: the solemn responsibility of ministering to such a multitude, the visual impact of so many mortals in one place.

Billy Graham knew he had a special responsibility when he came to the invitation at the close of his sermon. With a million present, it would have been easy to trigger a mass reaction. He therefore made his invitation harder than usual. "If you're willing to *forsake all other gods,* stand up." There was a hush upon the audience at first. Then one here and one there arose, until thousands were standing. Billy led them in the prayer of accepting Christ. He gave them his brief word on the duties and responsibilities of a Christian. Then he said, "Counselors with your material, make your way back to those people who are standing." Over 12,000 cards came in that day. Thousands more followed by mail from people contacted without time for proper counseling. And, as the future showed, a great many made genuine commitments who never were reached by a counselor at the plaza.

The million did not move during the counseling. Many prayed as they sat. Thousands upon thousands began to sing. Then a helicopter rose from behind the platform. Dr. Han, the chairman, put up his hand for silence. He explained that Billy Graham was leaving Korea that afternoon, and he could not say goodbye personally to everybody, but his helicopter would circle in farewell over the plaza.

At Dr. Han's word, the entire million and more stood and waved their hymn sheets or newspapers or whatever they carried. It was unbelievably poignant. Billy found the breathtaking view of this waving multitude indescribable: "The only comment I have is, Thanksgiving to God for all he did!" [6]

14

$\mathcal{T}$RUE $\mathcal{F}$RIENDSHIP

A MERICA WAS IN UPROAR OVER WATERGATE IN THE SPRING OF 1973.

When Billy Graham returned to North Carolina for the Charlotte crusade between his work in South Africa and that in Korea, he was pressed to comment on television and in print. His views were widely quoted.

"Of course, I have been mystified and confused and sick about the whole thing as I think every American is," he said. He called for punishment of the guilty and replacement of "everybody connected with Watergate," but deplored trial by the media and by rumor, and leaks of confidential evidence. He saw the scandal as "a symptom of the deeper moral crisis." He stated, "The time is overdue for Americans to engage in some deep soul-searching about the underpinnings of our society and our goals as a nation." No political party could claim to be "Mr. Clean."

Billy did not then think that President Nixon had known about Watergate, believing that "his moral and ethical principles wouldn't allow him to do anything illegal like that." He had known him for a long time and "he has a very strong sense of integrity."

Richard Nixon and Billy Graham had in fact been friends for over twenty years. "The friendship is well rooted," wrote Nixon's daughter, Julie Nixon Eisenhower, in 1975, "and stems from the days when my grandmother first began to follow the ministry of Dr. Graham. I am sure that part of my father's feeling that he can trust Billy Graham as a man of God stems from his knowledge that Nana believed with all her heart in the Graham mission."

The friendship grew deeper during the years when Nixon was vice-president (President Eisenhower had great affection for Billy) and in the Kennedy-Johnson period.[7] In December 1967, Nixon begged Billy, who was convalescent after pneumonia, to join him in Florida where he had gone alone to decide whether to seek the Republican nomination for 1968. As they walked the sands together, Billy glimpsed Nixon's fear of the pain and trouble the presidency would bring; but the 1970s would be dangerous for America and the world, and Nixon believed he could help. Billy's counsel was a strong factor in Nixon's decision to run.

Billy was not partisan. Lyndon Baines Johnson trusted him and was the first to attend a Graham crusade while president. After laying down office, LBJ recalled in a letter to Billy "those lonely occasions at the White House when your prayers and your friendship helped to sustain a president in an hour of trial.... No one will ever know how you helped to lighten my load or how much warmth you brought into our house. But I know." Mrs. Lady Bird Johnson shared with the present writer her feelings of affection for Billy and Ruth Graham. "I know how much Lyndon treasured Dr. Graham's counsel. He found solace in him both as a religious adviser and a friend in good times and in times of trial and anguish. My appreciation for them has grown through the years—for the ways in which they have touched and enriched our lives and the lives of people the world over."

In the election of 1968, when Nixon realized that he had won by a small margin, he invited Billy to his hotel suite, called his family together, and asked Billy to lead them in a prayer before he went down to meet the press. Billy thought this rather significant because the president-elect of Quaker background had been reluctant to talk openly about his personal faith—though Billy believed it to be deep.

When forming the new administration, Nixon asked Billy what job he would like. Billy replied, "You could not offer me a job as an ambassador, or a cabinet post, that I would give a second thought to. When God called me to preach, it was for life." Nixon said, "I knew you would say that, and I respect you for it." The press built up Billy as if he and his ideals were a major influence behind the Nixon White House. His influence in fact counted for less than was popularly supposed. He was one of a wide range of clergy asked to preach. He saw President Nixon on fewer occasions privately than he had President Johnson and knew less of what went on. The Grahams were led to believe that some of the White House staff were anxious to restrict and frustrate any influence he might have.

Nevertheless, the two men remained friends in spite of the inevitably changed relationship when a private citizen becomes president. Like millions of Americans, Billy Graham's feelings toward the Nixon of 1969–71 were positive.

Nixon attended the Knoxville crusade in 1970, and his presence provoked antiwar protests. When Charlotte honored Billy Graham in 1971, President Nixon, then at a peak of achievement nationally and internationally, "gave one of the finest non-political addresses I've ever heard," wrote the day's organizer, who added: "The President spoke without notes and quite obviously from the heart in a moving tribute to Billy." In January 1973, during celebrations following the second inaugural after Nixon's landslide victory, Billy noticed a slight change in the president. "I could tell by his eyes that he was under some severe strain. At that time I had no idea what was about to come, nor did any of his other friends."

The emerging Watergate scandal dismayed and shocked Billy.

During the summer of his return from Korea, he found the political situation "so discouraging" that it had almost made him "physically sick." He wrote: "While I cannot defend the Nixon administration's wrongdoing, I am disturbed by the 'overkill.'"

Billy believed that America harmed itself by a double standard that condoned lawbreaking by men with more popular causes.

Billy was attacked by those who held that "though supposedly a 'moral leader,' he failed to cut bait with the immorality of the White House until it was too late and any criticism of Nixon would seem to be like kicking a friend when he was down." Many who admired Billy were puzzled by his refusal to condemn; at the same time he was being urged by those who stood by Nixon to rally publicly to his defense. "He was criticized severely," one of Billy's oldest friends recalls, "but once again it was his love for a friend he was seeking to help, in his onerous task as president—a friend, rightly or wrongly, who was going through a tough time."

Billy, however, was unable to get through to the president. During the 1972 campaign, a White House staffer had suggested a debate between an opposition candidate and Billy. The president killed the idea: "No, it may hurt his ministry."

"That was his general attitude throughout my years of friendship," comments Billy, who believed that was the reason Nixon deliberately kept aloof as the crisis deepened. "I tried to get in touch with him a number of times, to assure him of my prayers and urge him to seek the Lord's guidance in a very difficult situation.... Mr. Nixon was a personal friend and at no time did I consider him as a parishioner. I seriously doubt if he looked upon me as his pastor, though having a pastor's heart (even though I am an evangelist) my feelings could not help but go out to him in his times of suffering and sorrow. There was little I could do for him except pray."

In December, he was invited to preach at the White House, and they had a long private talk. While in Washington, Billy recorded a candid and perceptive discussion of his views that *Christianity Today* published in January 1974. The two men met once and talked on the telephone twice in the six weeks following publication. "I am sure," wrote Billy, "that he understands that we cannot condone the things that are wrong, even though we love him as a friend and respect him as a world leader. At the same time I am well aware of the forces that are arrayed against him. I am convinced that he will survive."

Then, in May 1974, came the Watergate tapes. They revealed a man who was a stranger to Billy. It seemed almost as if there were two personalities in one skin: the man he had known and the totally different man of the tapes. Billy repudiates the view that Nixon fraudulently hid his character to maintain their friendship.

"The whole situation," says Ruth Graham, "was the hardest thing that Bill has ever gone through personally." With great reluctance, Billy issued a statement condemning the blasphemies and repudiating the behavior, but refusing to forsake Nixon, for which he was heavily criticized.

Billy was heavily criticized again thirty years later when a further batch of tapes was released that included a conversation between Nixon; his chief of staff, H. R. Haldeman; and Billy Graham in the Oval Office following the Prayer Breakfast of February 1, 1972. Billy had scores of informal chats with the president in which they "discussed every conceivable subject." Billy had no idea that Nixon was abusing the privacy of friendship by running a voice-activated recorder so unpremeditated and quickly forgotten remarks were preserved to haunt him long after Nixon was dead.

A casual comment by Haldeman leads Nixon to affirm that most of the writers in the media and Hollywood are Jewish: "This does not mean," comments Nixon, "that all the Jews are bad," but that most are left-wing radicals who want "peace at any price except where support for Israel is concerned. The best Jews are actually the Israeli Jews."

Billy agrees, and when Nixon says that a "powerful bloc" of Jews confronts him in the media, Billy adds, "And they're the ones putting out the pornographic stuff." At one point in the conversation Billy says: "This stranglehold has got to be broken or the country's going down the drain."

"You believe that?" asked Nixon. "Oh, boy, so do I. I can't ever say that but I believe it."

"No, but if you get elected a second time, then we might be able to do something," Billy replies. He mentions that many Jews in the media are great friends of his. "They swarm around me and are friendly to me. Because they know I am friendly to Israel and so forth. They don't know how I really feel about what they're doing to this country. And I have no power, no way to handle them, but I would stand up if under proper circumstances."

"You must not let them know," says Nixon.

Thirty years later, Billy was appalled when he read and heard his remarks of 1972. He issued an apology immediately on March 1, 2002: "Although I have no memory of the occasion, I deeply regret comments I apparently made in an Oval Office conversation with President Nixon and Mr. Haldeman some thirty years ago. They do not reflect my views, and I sincerely apologize for any offense caused by the remarks. Throughout my ministry I have sought to build bridges between Jews and Christians. I will continue to strongly support all future efforts to advance understanding and mutual respect between our communities."

The media was already in an uproar, some of the commentators even suggesting that "the American icon, the closest we have to a spiritual leader of America" had hidden anti-Semitic views, that his long recognized support for persecuted Jews in Communist countries had been a charade. Those who opposed Billy's ministry, yet had long been silenced by the nation's respect and affection, were pleased to have a means of attack. But many who admired him were puzzled and grieved, while others sought to explain or condone.

A letter in the *New York Times,* however, put the matter in perspective. The widow of Rabbi Marc Tanenbaum of the American Jewish Committee, told how Billy would always telephone before a mission in a Soviet-bloc country to ask if he could do anything for the Jews; and how he had "worked behind the scenes to extricate a number of Jews" from the Soviet Union; and that his phone call to Nixon during the 1973 war convinced the president to decide to send military airlift assistance to Israel. She ended her letter: "Were he alive today, I believe my husband would have come to his good friend's defense."

But Billy did not wish for any defense. In the course of a long statement on March 16, 2002, he said, "I cannot imagine what caused me to make those comments, which I totally repudiate. Whatever the reason, I was wrong for not disagreeing with the President, and I sincerely apologize to anyone I have offended.

"I don't ever recall having those feelings about any group, especially the Jews, and I certainly do not have them now. My remarks did not reflect my love for the Jewish people. I humbly ask the Jewish community to reflect on my actions on behalf of Jews over the years that contradict my words in the Oval Office that day.

"In the Bible we read, 'Above all else, guard your heart; for it is the wellspring of life. Put away perversity from your mouth; keep corrupt talk from your lips' [Proverbs 4:23–24]. That is true for me as much as anyone else. Every day I have to renew my heart before God and ask for his grace and strength."

Reflecting, as an old man, he realized, "Much of my life has been a pilgrimage—constantly learning, changing, growing, and maturing. I have come to see in deeper ways some of the implications of my faith and message, not the least of which is in the area of human rights and racial and ethnic understanding.

"Racial prejudice, anti-Semitism, or hatred of anyone with different beliefs has no place in the human mind or heart. I urge everyone to examine themselves and renew their own hearts before God. Only the supernatural love of God through changed lives can solve the problems that we face in our world. . . ."

He ended: "I take daily comfort in the psalmist's words in the Old Testament: 'The Lord is merciful and gracious, slow to anger, and plenteous in mercy' [Psalm 103:8]. Every year during their High Holy Days, the Jewish community reminds us all of our need for repentance and forgiveness. God's mercy and grace gives me hope—for myself, and for our world."

When the Watergate scandal reached its climax, in August 1974, Billy was in Europe for his long prepared Lausanne Congress, and then in the hospital with an infected jawbone. Thus he was spared the deepest agonies of the president's personal friends. After the resignation, Billy's efforts to speak personally or on the telephone were rebuffed until a telephone conversation in November.

In March 1975, shortly before the Albuquerque crusade, Billy Graham was invited to San Clemente. "The purpose of the visit," writes Julie Eisenhower, "was simply to reassure both of my parents of his complete love and faith in them. The lack of hypocrisy and absence of a 'holier than thou' attitude had always impressed me tremendously. Dr. Graham's capacity for friendship and his eagerness to love make him stand apart from other men." Their renewed and deepened friendship helped Richard Nixon's recovery and his rehabilitation as an honored elder statesman in the years before his death.

Thus Watergate was a deep shadow and disappointment to Billy but highlighted his compassion and integrity. "A real friend," commented George Cornell of the Associated Press, "remains one in a pinch, particularly so then; and any friendship is hollow and a sham if it doesn't stand up under pressure, when trouble comes. Personally, my hat is off to Graham for continuing to be a friend when being so was rough and when expediency was against it. A weaker character would turn tail when a friend starts going under, afraid of getting bruised himself in the downfall."

The crusades that followed showed Billy Graham's strength to be undiminished. And Watergate must be seen in perspective. It finished and was past just as Billy reached a new plateau. Through the Lausanne Congress on World Evangelization and all that followed, he was beginning a world ministry on a wider scale than ever before.

15

LAUSANNE

ON JULY 16, 1974, NEARLY 4,000 PEOPLE FROM MORE THAN 150 nations gathered in the Palais de Beaulieu at Lausanne, Switzerland. The opening fanfare rang through the convention hall, hung with banners that displayed in six languages the motto of the congress: "Let the Earth Hear His Voice."

The climax of the first evening was a major address from Billy Graham, who knew the urgency of the hour. He believed in the possibility of world evangelization by the end of the twentieth century. He could help Christ's church on earth recover in the century's last quarter, the thrust and passion that had been lost. In the opinion of Christian world leaders who heard it, his speech "raised high the banner of true evangelical, biblical Christianity. It made very clear the issues of our day, and what Lausanne was and where it was going. Everyone was thrilled with this bold, forthright declaration of contemporary evangelical truth."

Immediately after his address, Billy and Bishop Jack Dain, the congress executive chairman, switched on the "Population Clock." Placed in a huge illuminated map of the world, the clock counted up the net number of people being born. A few moments later the figure had reached 25. By 9:55 that evening it showed 163,569. When formally switched off, it had registered that over 1,800,000 people in need of the Christian Gospel had been born since the congress began.

The Lausanne Congress had grown from a seed planted by Billy sixteen years earlier when he had brought a small group to another

Swiss resort to discuss the urgency and issues of world evangelization. From that had come a world congress in Berlin in 1966. The
Emperor Haile Selassie of Ethiopia opened it with a resounding call:
"O Christians, let us arise and, with spiritual zeal and earnestness
which characterized the apostles and the early Christians, let us
labor to lead our brothers and sisters to our Savior Jesus Christ who
only can give life in its fullest sense." A few years later, overthrown
by a Marxist coup, he was put in prison and died.

The 1,200 delegates reflected the pattern of the times, the
majority being born in the West although many served developing
nations. The congress demonstrated that those who accepted the
authority of Scripture and believed in leading others to the living
Christ were far greater in numbers, learning, and influence than
had been supposed. To the Church as a whole, absorbed in concern for restructuring society, building unity, or redefining belief,
Berlin brought an urgent, considered appeal "to return to a
dynamic zeal for world evangelism."

Berlin gave rise to regional congresses that had immense effect
throughout the world. They were financed by the BGEA but Billy
kept away, as he said, "for fear that they would think I was in a
dominant role."

By January 1970, Billy had seen the need for a second world
congress to discuss and carry forward all the implications of
Christ's Great Commission to his disciples. Billy moved slowly.
Once the decision was made, the preparation was thorough, and
thus the Lausanne Congress of July 1974 made an immediate decisive impact on those who attended.

From the outset the participants sensed that it ushered in a new
epoch. The division between missionary-sending and missionary-
receiving nations had gone. Whites were outnumbered, and skin
color was insignificant in this totally interracial congress "magnif-
icently obsessed" with reaching the unreached in a spirit of love.

The Third World was not looking in on the deliberations of the
West, as at Berlin, but giving counsel and inspiration equally:

A person's contribution, not background, counted. Those who lived in spiritual backwaters like Britain and Western Europe were surprised to find how fast Christianity grew elsewhere. A Bolivian bishop wrote afterward to Billy: "My countrymen and I had not only received inspiration and challenge and a large amount of materials for our task today, but also the evidence of the amazing renewal of the churches of Christ around the world."

The participants found that this congress was molded by their own hard work and deliberations. Unlike many international church conferences, no secretariat sought to impose theologies or conclusions, nor did they need to wrest its direction from the hands of any dominant faction. Lausanne achieved a fusion of minds, hearts, and goals because it was not afraid of tensions.

In no area was participation more evident than in the creation of the Lausanne Covenant, a term chosen deliberately. "We wanted to do more than find an agreed formula of words: we were determined not just to declare something but to do something, namely to commit ourselves to the task of world evangelization." The long, closely argued Lausanne Covenant was an authentic act of those gathered there. Therefore, it was taken seriously and studied carefully at Geneva, Lambeth, Rome, and throughout the Christian world. Evangelicals were soon acting on it, as Billy commented four months later: "It seems that God inspired a historic document that could well be a theological watershed for evangelicals for generations to come."

The congress also set up the Lausanne Continuation Committee. In the years that followed, this sponsored workshops and conferences on matters of great movement and research. It also forged new methods and understandings for the fulfilling of the Lausanne Covenant and the Great Commission from which it was derived.

For most of the eight days at the Palais de Beaulieu, Billy Graham stayed in the background. Bishop Dain recalled, "He was always available for consultation, guidance, and advice without ever seeking to intrude his role into that of the congress itself. He was the honorary chairman, and yet he was very, very rarely seen on the platform. In itself this is a remarkable tribute to a man of God who has wielded, under God, such power and influence and yet who quite deliberately chose to adopt that minor-key role."

More than 600 people requested interviews. As Billy recalls, "I was absolutely swamped with unscheduled meetings and scores of appointments that kept me going from about 7 A.M. till 11 P.M. every day." This included press and television interviews. Many participants had arrived with authority from their countrymen to beg Billy to hold a crusade in their lands, like the president of the Supreme Court of Cambodia, who had been converted from Buddhism by reading Billy's book, *Peace with God.* The following spring, after the Khmer Rouge takeover, he and other prominent men were taken to a stadium and shot.

The congress concluded with a great service of Holy Communion. The preacher administering Communion, Anglican Bishop Festo Kivengere from Uganda, was caught up in the realization that the Cross of Christ "was the only possible answer" to what had been discussed. His powerful sermon and the distribution of the bread and wine to more than 4,000 people took far longer than intended. Billy, as he rose at last to give the closing address, "The King Is Coming," felt himself somewhat an anticlimax, though no one shared that feeling. He was suffering much from an infected jaw. He recalls, "While I was speaking, it was difficult to keep my mind on the message because of the pain. I was afraid to take a pain killer for fear I would not be alert." Since it was already late in the morning, he shortened his address.

Billy stressed the urgency to evangelize because of the certainty of Christ's return, and in calling for rededication and recommitment, he did not hesitate to confess his own need. "You know what God has been saying to you these past ten days. I know what he has convicted me of, and what I must do." This public remark, which in fact referred to his private determination to cut out any lingering desire to play a political role in his own country, made a strong impression, especially on those from the Third World. "Dr. Graham confessing his own weaknesses—we thought we were the only ones that had problems like that. This was the most moving message for us!"

Closing his address, Billy touched on eight characteristics needed in a man or woman who would be an instrument that God can use. He ended: "The problems with which we wrestle as we go back to our places of service are in many cases not intellectual. They lie deep down within the will. Are we willing to deny self and to take up the Cross and follow the Lord? Are you willing? Am I willing? . . . The King is coming!"

Lausanne 1974 had become a date in Billy Graham's life comparable to 1949 and 1954. The Los Angeles campaign in the tent at the corner of Washington and Hill Streets in 1949 had made him a national figure. Five years later, the Greater London crusade of 1954 had brought him world fame. Twenty years after London, Lausanne showed him to be far more than an evangelist: He was a world Christian statesman, a catalyst who could bring individuals and movements to a fusion that set them on a new path for the glory of God.[8]

*P*ART THREE

1977–1983

16

BILLY AT SIXTY

FACING YET ANOTHER CRUSADE, WHETHER IN NORTH AMERICA or some distant continent, Billy would complain to Ruth that he cannot possibly get through the heavy list of press conferences, ministers' meetings, and the school of evangelism; countless interviews, perhaps businessmen's or governor's prayer breakfasts; and every night to preach to a huge stadium audience, knowing he will be heard and viewed by millions on TV. Afterward, he would enthusiastically state that the crusade had been the greatest opportunity ever. Together with dislike of dark and rainy days and his worrying about the weather (with some reason, in view of the number of rain-drenched, windswept stadiums he has preached in), his groans disclosed the human side.

And so did the anticlimax. He once wrote: "I have often gone on three- to six-month crusades abroad in the midst of a whirlwind of activity. I jet home to the quietness of this mountain and for the first few days I hardly know what to do with myself. There even come times of depression. However, that all soon passes."

Difficulty of adjustment, pressures when on tour, and unceasing responsibilities contributed to Billy's tendency for insomnia. In bed by eleven or twelve, he was always a light sleeper, often waking in the night or very early, when his mind became alert at once.

That at least gave more opportunity to nourish the devotional life. When Ruth, an even earlier riser, returns to the bedroom with the mail, she finds him sitting on the bed reading the Bible. She says, "He reads long passages of it at a time. He's always at it, but it isn't as if 'From 7:00 to 7:30 this morning I have Bible reading.' That's not Bill's nature, he's not that organized a person. But he does read the Bible continually, and every day, and large portions of it." Away from home, the pressure of a tight schedule offers Billy less opportunity, but he says, "I take time each day in the morning and evening to read passages of Scripture and ask the Lord to speak to me through them—apart from any preparations of sermon material."

Although he once gave away more than a million copies of *The Living Bible* to those who wrote in after a telecast, he always preaches from the *King James Version*. By his sixtieth birthday, he had used up at least thirty-five copies of the Bible, but wishes he had one copy with all his own annotations. Instead, he has many translations partially marked up. He makes notes on scratches of paper, transferring his thoughts and ideas to a Dictaphone to be typed up, rather than writing everything in his Bible.

As for prayer, Billy says, "I have learned, I believe, to 'pray without ceasing.' I find myself constantly in prayer and fellowship with God, even while I am talking to other people or doing other things." Billy has friends in almost every country in the world, and news of crisis or violence will instinctively focus him on individuals. His prayers go especially to countries once open to the Gospel and, known from his personal visits there, where Christians suffer persecution.

Billy prepares sermons and speeches with exceptional thoroughness. A voracious reader, especially of biography, history, and current affairs, he cultivated a nearly photographic memory for the printed word and could assimilate a page swiftly, whether newspaper (subscriber to many) or book. Ruth extends his range, being an even more dedicated bookworm, distilling for him her browsing in C. S. Lewis, Alexander Solzhenitsyn, Blaise Pascal, G. K. Chesterton, George MacDonald, and much more: poetry, literature, theology, Bible studies, and other areas. As they lay in bed at night, she would tell him what she was reading during the day.

The humorous stories with which he delighted audiences before turning to serious matters were often provided by Grady Wilson who found that Billy, for all his great sense of humor, could be slow to catch the point. In addition, two or three of his staff, including associate evangelists, produce facts, stories, news items, statistics, and so on. Billy then turns this raw material into his own product, dictating, rewriting, digesting. He likes the quip that to borrow from one writer is plagiarism, but from many writers is research—saying that in this sense, he is a great researcher.

Billy could use an assistant's words in articles or his newspaper column, but he says, "I have never been able to find anyone who could write for me in speaking. The sentences must be extremely brief, paragraphs brief and extremely simple. The average American has a working vocabulary of 600 words; the average clergyman has a vocabulary of 5,000 words. As I have grown older I have had to study to be simple."

And he wished he had studied more. As the years passed, the tension tightened between his desire to use the ever-increasing opportunities and his desire to hide away and study, for although not an academic mind he had shown himself, in the words of the distinguished journalist George Cornell, "a highly sophisticated, sensitive, and imaginative thinker" who had made Christianity simple for millions without cheapening it.

Sermon preparation and the writing of his books (including several best-sellers) happened mostly at home in Montreat. Although he would often work on a new book while on vacation in some warm climate, his home and family formed the human bedrock of his ministry and his life. The family of two sons and three daughters had been completed by the birth of Nelson Edman (Ned) Graham in 1958.

The Graham home was not elegant or pretentious and was a veritable Noah's Ark. Together with the Great Pyrenees sheep dog, Belshazzar, and afterward Heidi the St. Bernard and successors, they had sheep, flying squirrels, rabbits, even a skunk, a horse, a mule, and a pony. A goat named Khrushchev could be smelled a mile away, until they had to get rid of him. "We took him in the jeep," recalls Anne, "and drove and drove until we felt we had confused him enough that he would never come back home. We let him off. And as we were driving up the driveway, there he was, welcoming us with sort of a knowing grin, much to the glee of all of us children."

For Billy, each of his five children was his favorite. He treated them according to their characters, playing ball or teaching the boys to shoot; teasing Gigi, playing rough with Bunny, being very loving with Anne. "He was always loving and affectionate with each of us—always hugging us girls. Even if he were just taking us shopping, or to a meeting or to church, he would hold our hands and walk beside us, as proud as though we were sweethearts instead of daughters." When they grew older, he still held their hands but would introduce them to everyone from bellhops to presidents.

Even though Billy was away from his children for long periods of time and they missed him dreadfully, their childhood memories are dominated by the fun of his presence rather than by resentment at his absence. They ascribe this to the sterling character of their mother.

Ruth missed her Bill even more than the children, but she never wept in front of them or complained. "She stamped on our minds at a very early age that he was going for Jesus' sake, to tell others the good news of the Gospel of Jesus Christ, and we never questioned his having to go." She would deliberately distract them so he slipped away without fuss, and soon they could count the days to his return. Ruth had a special gift for making the household revolve around Billy even in his absence: He was head of the household. Looking back on those days, the children are sure too that the extraordinary sense of his presence when not physically there should be attributed to his faithful, constant prayers.

The children respected their parents and listened to their advice. "I saw Daddy live what he preached," said Gigi. "I saw them making Christ their life, not just their religion." The Grahams brought up their children to have a deep sense of right and wrong, a sensitive conscience, and an instinct of courtesy and thoughtfulness toward others. They taught them how to make decisions regardless of public opinion.

The Grahams never were disapproving parents but understanding and forgiving, not least during Franklin's wild years of rebellion so vividly described in his autobiography *Rebel with a Cause*. Their prayers were answered, shortly after his twenty-second birthday: "I put my cigarette out," he writes, "and got down on my knees beside my bed. I'm not sure what I prayed, but I know that I poured my heart out to God and confessed my sin. I told Him I was sorry and that if He would take the pieces of my life and somehow put them back together, I was His. I wanted to live my life for Him from that day forward. I asked Him to forgive me and cleanse me, and I invited Him by faith to come into my life. . . . The rebel had found the cause."[9]

Away from home, one of the greatest prices Billy Graham had to pay was an instant recognition by so many Americans and foreigners: "It is impossible for me to go out for a quiet meal with my wife or family, to stroll down a street, to walk in a park. Always being recognized gives me a great opportunity to witness, but it is also physically draining." He will not tell a lie when asked point-blank if he is Billy Graham, but he can often sidestep gracefully because a face seen on television, or from a seat in a stadium, never looks quite identical with a face met unexpectedly at close quarters. A man followed him into the restroom of a Howard Johnson restaurant in Charlotte. "You look so much like Billy Graham," he said. "Have you ever been told that before?"

"Oh, yes, people always tell me I look like him," Billy replied.

The man said, "Well, after seeing you close up, I realize that you are not."

But Billy loved to tell of the man in an elevator who stared, then asked, "Are you Billy Graham?" When Billy said yes, the man exclaimed, "What an anticlimax!"

And once in a British railway dining car, when he was traveling with Grady to the Keswick Convention centenary, he ordered cider, the west country's strong drink, in the belief that it was non-alcoholic like American sweet cider. The Scottish waitress said, "I had thought you were Billy Graham, but as you are drinking that, you can't be!"

If he ate in public, people would come up to greet him or question him or for an autograph. As Gigi recalls, I had "never seen him rude to anyone when the line has been ten or twelve long for autographs during one meal. With all the hectic schedule and the pressures during a crusade, I have only seen him be gracious and Christlike." Very occasionally he might be sharp with one of his staff, a sign that he was really overtired.

Billy never found it easy to discriminate between claims on his time. He grew increasingly impatient with administrative responsibilities, yet he knew they were a key to wider usefulness. The unceasing flow of invitations to speak, many offering superb opportunities for a clergyman's ministry, often in a secular setting; the unceasing flood of requests for appointments, at home or wherever he went; the hours or days needed for travel, could have been crushing. As Billy explained, "The spirit is willing but the calendar is limited and the body is weak.... I would appreciate your prayers that the Holy Spirit will teach me how to give priority to the right things and the courage to say no to the rest."

If he tied himself down with too many engagements, he could not seize sudden strategic openings. "I want to be flexible, so I can change plans at the last minute if necessary, to go and do what I believe the Holy Spirit would have me do—like Philip, preaching in great evangelistic meetings in Samaria, who was suddenly whisked away by an angel to talk to one man, the Ethiopian nobleman—which was not in his date book!" Such flexibility is a part of his nature.

Walter Smyth, in their long experience together, became very conscious of this, as he said, "Somehow, out of all these changes which from the human standpoint seem sometimes a bit distracting, eventually comes God's plan. I think it's because God knows Billy better than we do, and has made him the way he is. I've seen again and again where I thought: Goodness! Not another change! And yet it was the very thing needful." And as Grady used to joke, "Billy must have a very clean mind. He is always changing it!"

Yet Billy Graham's ministry was not powered by a fit man's energy. For years he had a succession of physical problems that, as Billy stated, "from time to time have either weakened me or have been irritating enough to humble me." He learned gradually to live more within the limitations of his strength so his health became better in his later fifties, with occasional setbacks, than five years earlier, until the onset of a Parkinson's-related disease in the late 1980s.

Billy exercised more than when younger. He almost abandoned golf but jogged regularly. At Montreat he measured the only level stretch of his mountain drive: back and forth ten times is a mile. When in Honolulu for a convention address, he measured a stretch between two points in a parking lot and faithfully jogged a mile before going on to visit his radio station. His practice around the world was similar. With a moderate appetite, he enjoys fresh vegetables and salads, fish and chicken. He loves olives but rarely eats dessert. For breakfast he likes an egg (eating only the white), orange juice, and coffee.

Billy's nature is essentially a happy one with a great sense of humor, but he adds to his burdens by the intensity of his absorption in the ministry. He inherited his mother's intensity (his father was more relaxed, with a dry sense of humor) and deeply feels the moral decline of his country, the sufferings of persecuted Christians, the shortness of time before free speech and free worship may be extinguished in yet another part of the world. Friends and relatives find him relaxed, delighted to learn how they are, and thinking of ways to help them. "And then after a little bit," said one relative wistfully, "you've lost him." He will be off on some aspect of the ministry or a book he has read, or will fall silent, his mind back on a problem or winging far away to an associate who is engaged in a spiritual battle. Even at Christmas, after enjoying every minute's chat and playing with the grandchildren, he would suddenly disappear to his desk, to rejoin later in the evening before slipping away again.

Billy's manners are those of the Old South, with no sense of self-importance. Coming off a train with Grady, he once saw two nuns burdened down with bags and carried the bags to their car. Billy learned early to live with praise and criticism. Billy comments that "it is sometimes a conscious battle" to accept graciously a violently unfair verbal assault, but "most often it is just my natural way. I have really never been a fighter at heart and do not like to engage in sharp answers. I believe that a soft answer turneth away wrath." Although, as Ruth remarks, "Sometimes a soft answer makes them furious!" Anne could not remember, whenever he shared his experiences, "one single time that he criticized someone or made a disparaging remark about any particular person. Even those who were outright in their hatred of him, when we asked him about it, he would just say that perhaps they needed our love and prayers more than others."

On the other hand, states Billy, "Everybody needs some friends around him who will say, You are *wrong!* And that includes me. I really value the friendship of people who'll just tell it to me like it is, even though I may try to defend my position for a while." Many of the developments and changes over the years in the crusade ministry and in Billy's personal attitudes followed public or private criticism.

Although he preaches to vast crowds, Billy loves to be with individuals and to minister to them. Long before he was sixty, he had found that he had unique opportunities to bring spiritual help to presidents, Cabinet members, and governors; to ambassadors and heads of state around the world; and to those at the top of their professions.

Eminence, however, is not a necessary passport to Billy's concern. A Tennessee pastor, whose marriage had been saved after his wife was led to Christ by Billy, wrote to him many years later, "You have always acted as though every little Christian was as important in your sight as in the sight of Christ."

17

INTO EASTERN EUROPE

A REMARKABLE SIX YEARS BEGAN FOR BILLY GRAHAM IN SEPtember 1977 with his breakthrough into an expanding ministry in Eastern European Communist countries. Simultaneously, more and more opportunities came in other parts of the world and in the United States. The period ended with his great conference of itinerant evangelists in the summer of 1983, which was not so much a climax as the opening of the next phase. His objectives were being fulfilled: to proclaim the Gospel of Christ to as many people as possible, to build bridges of understanding between the peoples of the world, and to work for true peace between the nations.

On September 3, 1977, however, Billy, Ruth, Cliff, and a small team met in a hotel in Vienna with considerable apprehension. They had been invited to Hungary. They knew that any hope of further ministry in the Socialist countries of Eastern Europe, and in the Soviet Union itself, hinged on that one week's visit.[10]

For twenty years, Billy had cherished a hope of preaching in Hungary. The invitation of 1977 came suddenly after five years of patient diplomacy by Walter Smyth and a Hungarian-American physician, surgeon, and pastor, the late Alexander S. Haraszti of Atlanta; and as the result of the determination of a Hungarian Free churchman, the late Sandor Palotay, a hunchback with a complex character who was president of the Council of Free Churches and unpopular with many Christians but devoted to their cause. He had recognized Billy's genius from afar, and risked position and career to bring him to Hungary.

Billy Graham was also at risk. The Socialist countries of Eastern Europe formed the one large area of humanity, other than mainland China, where he had never preached. He knew that some of his countrymen would accuse him of compromise with Communism, yet he could not refuse to minister to men and women because they lived under a different political ideology; most had no choice.

Billy's first main engagement in Hungary was to preach in the open air on Sunday afternoon in the grounds of the Baptist Youth camp above the Danube, sixteen miles north of Budapest. To conform with the State's rules governing religious liberty, the meeting had to be on church property, with no announcement in the press. "We were told that perhaps 3,000 persons were expected," recorded Billy in his diary. "To reach the camp, we drove up a steep dirt road for a mile or two. All along the road were people walking to the camp: old, young, some with their best Sunday finery, some peasant women in black stockings, black full skirts, and shawls." Special public buses and streetcars had carried loads of people every two minutes to a place close to the dirt road. No police were in sight except to direct the heavy traffic.

Hungary's Protestants and Catholics had pushed aside denominational lines. News of the meeting had spread by word of mouth, and believers spent hours on long distance telephone calls. By train, plane, or car, a thousand people came from nearby Czechoslovakia; others came from Poland, Rumania, Bulgaria; a top-level Baptist delegation came from Moscow; thousands upon thousands arrived from all parts of Hungary, many bringing nonbelievers.

About half the audience may have been under twenty-five, although the turnout of all ages surprised the authorities. The police estimated that 30,000 or more squeezed into the twelve-acre campsite, and even beyond its fences, under the poplar and locust trees. It was Hungary's largest gathering for a preaching service since World War II, which made it an hour of great encouragement to Protestants and Catholics, young and old. As Billy and Ruth walked to their places, they received prolonged applause.

"The choir was glorious," continued Billy. "The Hungarians love music and sing beautifully. A simple platform of split poles had been constructed, and when I began to preach, the sun beat down unmercifully. A plump lady with a big smile slipped onto the platform and handed Ruth an umbrella for shade. I preached on John 3:16, outlining as clearly as possible the fact of God's love for us, regardless of our backgrounds." Impeccably translated by Dr. Haraszti, Billy began by referring to his hope of building bridges between peoples. "I come from a different social system," he said, "but we are bound together as brothers and sisters in Christ." He then turned to his Bible and read his text, commenting that no matter what system you live in, God loves you.

His homely illustrations amused and warmed the crowd, and he preached Christ plainly, for a verdict, just as in Nagaland, Korea, South Africa, and in North and South America. "At the end of the sermon," continues Billy, "I asked people to raise their hands if they sincerely wanted to commit themselves to Christ, and thousands showed their hands all over the hillside." Many were young people from Christian homes, taking courage from the crowd to make an open commitment to Christ, which they knew could harm their careers; thus a Lutheran pastor's son, winner of four gold medals in the Olympic pentathlon, was quietly dropped from the team when it was known that he had consecrated his life at this meeting and would train to be a pastor.

The Grahams were taken to lunch in company with church leaders at Hotel Sylvanus, which overlooked the Danube and the castle-clad mountains beyond, and returned to Budapest by leisure riverboat, watching picturesque villages, churches, and farms slip by. It was dusk when they came upon the splendid view of central Budapest, with the floodlit parliament house on the left bank and the royal palace and St. Mathias Cathedral high on Castle Hill on the right.

They went immediately to Sun Street Baptist Church. Billy recalls: "As we neared the church we could see the courtyard and the street packed with people who could not get inside. Loud-speakers carried the service to those outside and to several other churches, which were also filled. The service was long, and the crowded church hot, but the people were attentive, hungry for the Gospel. . . . I was tired after a long day, but God gave me strength as I spoke about the meaning of faith in Christ.

"At the end of the service there were soft sounds all over the church, as if people were clicking their tongues. We were told later that it was from dozens of tape recorders being turned off." Tapes were copied, recopied, and sent all over Hungary and other Eastern bloc lands. Thus Billy's voice and Haraszti's translation became familiar to thousands who had not attended that service.

Many Party officials and factory managers had come out of curiosity but some with sincere interest. As Billy traveled throughout Hungary in the next week, preaching to overflow crowds in small Baptist churches, the Hungarian people were kept from knowing much about it, though again and again Billy had evidence of the encouragement that his visit brought to believers, open and secret. If the country as a whole could not be reached, those who mattered in the state and church were captivated. The secretary of state for church affairs, Imre Miklos, officially an atheist, became Billy's warm friend.

The two leading Protestant bishops, Kaldy of the Lutherans and Bartha of the Reformed, had been openly critical of Billy Graham and had refused the use of their church buildings, which would have held far more than those where the indoor meetings took place. Both bishops, out of courtesy, shared platforms with Billy. Talking to him informally and listening to his addresses swept away their mistaken belief that he was naïve, narrow, and unconcerned with the social role of the church. "I was deeply impressed," recalled Bartha a year later, "by his warmth, his Christian spirit, his honesty, and his humility in saying, 'I have come to learn.' I took him to my heart." Both recognized Billy's integrity that he would not say one thing to their faces but another when he returned to the West. For one of the bishops, the visit was the beginning of a new flowering of his faith.

The coming of Billy Graham to Hungary proved to be a significant event in the improvement of relations between the atheist state and the Christian churches. It also restored the self-confidence of the smaller Protestant groups such as the Methodists and Baptists, who found new opportunities. It built a bridge between the Hungarian and American peoples, not least when the film made by the Billy Graham Evangelistic Association was shown across America on television. As the first of his films about Eastern Europe, it had its weaknesses, yet taught Americans much about the life and religion of the land.

The Hungarian visit was a personal triumph for Billy, and made certain the opening of other socialist countries. And it gave him a new ministry in speaking to atheist high officials and Party members about the living Christ.

One year later came the ten day "Evangelization of Billy Graham" in Poland, a country predominantly and vigorously Roman Catholic, yet then ruled by atheists. The invitation came from the Polish Baptist Union and the Polish Ecumenical Council, the latter which represents the non-Catholic minority. The Catholics opened their churches to Billy Graham in an unprecedented gesture. Cardinal Wojtyla of Kracow gave his warmest support to the invitation. When Billy reached Kracow, Wojtyla had gone to Rome to be elected Pope John Paul II on the very day that Billy left Poland.

Every meeting place was full for hours before the service. In Warsaw the main Lutheran, Reformed, and Baptist churches were used, and along with the great Catholic church of All Saints, with its fine paintings and huge baroque altar below a painting of the resurrection and the glory of Christ. The Baptist choir stood in front of the altar, and the crowds stretched out of the church onto the green. This was not church property, yet the police did not disperse them.

Here, and in his whirlwind tour of five other cities, Billy preached in great simplicity. This, and his sincerity, reached priests and people, hungry for a deepening of their lives at a time of the growing economic and social crisis, which erupted less than a year later.

At Katowice, the coal mining city that would be much in the headlines in the early days of solidarity, the enormous modern cathedral of Christ the King was filled to capacity, with 13,000 people covering the red carpets in the aisles, which converge on the altar, and out onto the terrace. They listened in total silence as Billy preached on the text from Galatians: "God forbid that I should glory, save in the Cross of our Lord Jesus Christ." Unlike most of the churches, a counseling area was available; those who made commitments to Christ went down into the crypt, with its shrine of the Franciscan priest who gave his life for another man in Auschwitz. Here 2,000 persons were counseled. The bishop of Katowice, Herbert Bednorz, had asked the Baptists: "How many members do you have in Katowice?" "Three hundred," they replied. "Then how will you fill my cathedral?" He was astonished and delighted at the great attendance, "the greatest ecumenical event in the history of my diocese," he said from the pulpit. He wrote to Billy two months later that the ecumenical meeting in the cathedral had deepened and strengthened the unity of Christians in his diocese, and that when he went to a conference of the bishops from all over Poland, "your preaching was very positively estimated."

The "Evangelization of Billy Graham" greatly increased respect and understanding among the majority Catholics for the Baptists. Many Catholics joined the follow-up groups and learned to study the Bible, thus encouraging a new movement that was already gaining ground in Poland. Billy's visit induced an immediate marked increase in the sales of Bibles. Shortage of paper prevented the demand being met fully at first, but it was no passing phase: Two years later, in the three months between November 1982 and January 1983, the Bible Society in Warsaw sold nearly 47,000 Bibles and more than 36,000 New Testaments.

If Billy Graham influenced Poland, Poland also influenced Billy Graham. It gave him more assurance, encouragement, and experience in helping Christians in the difficult circumstances of Eastern Europe. It brought him more contacts and friendships to further his ministry in socialistic countries. And it brought him the profound experience of the visit to Auschwitz.

He and Ruth had been briefed back in Montreat by a senior official of the United States government about the consequences of a nuclear war between the superpowers. The grim facts, expounded in accurate detail five years before the general public were given impressions by a television company, appalled the Grahams. Billy realized as never before that the human race could destroy itself in a matter of hours. "Man's technology has leaped far ahead of his moral ability to control his technology. As I searched the Scriptures, my responsibilities dawned on me." He determined to speak out.

He chose the visit to the Auschwitz concentration camp, which is preserved as a memorial, between Kracow and Katowice to make his first public statement on the need for nuclear disarmament by all nations: "The very survival of human civilization is at stake.... The present insanity of a global arms race, if continued, will lead inevitably to a conflagration so great that Auschwitz will seem a minor rehearsal." In a widely reported speech, he called on world leaders, whatever their ideology, to put national pride and power second to the survival of the human race, and called on all Christians to rededicate themselves "to the Lord Jesus Christ, to the cause of peace, to reconciliation among all the races and nations of the world."

He delivered his speech standing before the "Wall of Death," where 20,000 prisoners were executed. He was almost in tears after being conducted around the gas chambers and the camp, with its vivid memorials of human suffering. The wall now had a cross, where visitors put flowers. Billy and Ruth placed a wreath there and knelt in prayer. Auschwitz drove deep into Billy's mind his growing concern for nuclear disarmament. He urged it publicly and privately—not unilateral disarmament but the total destruction by all nations of nuclear, biological or chemical, and laser weapons.

To preach true peace between nations and in the hearts of men would be part of his world ministry henceforth. As he said, the arms race became his "number one social concern."

In January 1981, Billy was back in Poland to receive an honorary degree in theology before proceeding to Hungary for another, shown on state television, and then to Rome for his first private meeting with Pope John Paul II. They found an immediate rapport in their mutual love for Christ and for humanity.

Meanwhile, in Poland "The Evangelization of Billy Graham" continued to exert influence. "Your ministry has exceeded all our expectations and imaginations," wrote his interpreter, Zdzislaw Pawlik, who was also secretary of the ecumenical council. "It was really a historic event in terms of uniting all Christians around the Word of God and giving new impetus to the life of individuals and congregations." It had come at a strategic moment in Poland's history: the election of Pope John Paul II immediately after; the rise of Solidarity, the new freedoms; the period of martial law.

On June 1, 1983, the film of his 1978 tour, which had profoundly impressed America, was shown on Polish television, which had been barred to religious programs at the time of his visit. Between four and five million Poles watched this film with its brilliant photography and clear message of the need for a simple faith in Christ, "It can be regarded as a very important contribution," commented Pawlik. "It was received very well by the Polish people."

Billy Graham, already evangelist to five continents, was now plainly evangelist to the world.

18

Tidal Wave

URING THE METRO MANILA CRUSADE OF DECEMBER 1977, President Marcos of the Philippines, then at the height of his power, broke precedent by giving a state dinner for the Grahams and the team after one of the crusade meetings; no religious leader, not even Pope Paul VI or Pope John Paul II, received a similar honor. Thanking Billy for bringing "the freshness of the spirit and the joy that comes from knowing God," President Marcos continued: "You come as a peacemaker, you come as one who has the same deep aspirations for the brotherhood of all humanity. And you seek, too, to lift up that miserable two-thirds of mankind who belong to the third world, our world of abject poverty, ignorance, misery, our world desperately in need of God."

The president's words were shortly to prove particularly apt. After a closing service when 150,000 people came to Ritzal Park, Billy flew from Manila to India. While the Filipino follow-up committee was handling more than 22,000 inquirers, of whom 60 percent were Roman Catholic, including a leading film star who became a renowned evangelist, Billy conducted Good News Festivals in Calcutta and three other cities. But two weeks earlier, a devastating cyclone and the worst tidal wave since 1864 had struck the coast of Andhra Pradesh in South India, causing 10,000 deaths, wiping out villages, and inflicting untold loss and misery.

The president of India, receiving Billy in New Delhi, begged his help. As soon as Billy reached Hyderabad-Secunderabad, capital of the stricken state, he announced to the great crowd that attended the Good News Festival that his World Relief Fund would give $21,000 for rebuilding churches: The sum had been raised at the recent Cincinnati crusade. At Madras, the closing festival of the tour, he left Akbar Haqq to preach at one of the five services and flew in a plane chartered by the team to the devastated area. The government provided a helicopter from the local airport.

As Billy landed, he could see funeral pyres, and as he walked in the washed-out fields and villages where relief workers helped feed orphans and put up shelter, more bodies were recovered and he prayed over them. Survivors took his hands in theirs: "Kill us or build us houses," pleaded one, in a harrowing scene that was afterward seen on film by millions.

Billy was escorted by the state minister of education, a devout Hindu who had been at his home in the immediate area on the night of the disaster. He had taken charge of relief. It was he who suggested that Billy Graham build in his own name an entire new village. The minister pointed out that Indians always pronounce the name as "Billy Gram," and that the word for *village* in Telegu, the local language, is *gram*. Billy agreed at once.

Other organizations were sending relief quickly, but Billy's coming in person, and his grief and love, touched all India. Indians called him "Angel of Mercy."

On return to America, Billy immediately raised money. The film of the festivals and of the cyclone disaster, shown on television, brought in $100,000. Meanwhile, the team set up the Andhra Pradesh Christian Relief and Rehabilitation committee, headed by the two cochairmen of the festival: the Roman Catholic archbishop of Hyderabad and a leading Baptist, Ch. Devananda Rao, who was minister of tourism in the state cabinet, and who had come with Billy to the scene of the disaster. Plans for the new model township were quickly drawn. The state government gave nearly a quarter of the cost of the houses; the Billy Graham Evangelistic Association raised more than three quarters, and the cost of the church, and the water tower. On April 21, 1978, only six months after the tidal wave, Archbishop Arulappa dedicated the foundation stone of Billy Graham Naga.

It was not, therefore, the crowds at the festivals, nor the 12,841 recorded decisions, nor, in the words of the Bishop in Madras, the "great source of blessing to the entire Indian church," that made the true significance of the Indian visit of December 1977. Rather, it was the founding of Billy Graham Naga as a spontaneous gesture of Christian compassion.

Wherever he was, Billy Graham had never passed by on the other side. In younger days, his preaching had been affected by reaction to the heresy of a "social Gospel"; biblically based Christians had tended to forget the strong social conscience that had been one of the glories of the evangelical revival. As the years passed, Billy had done much to correct the balance among his contemporaries, while avoiding identification with particular political or social solutions to world or national problems. During the 1970s, he channeled much money to famine and disaster relief, as well as to education in the Third World, and his sponsorship of Lausanne had led to theological rethinking on the relationship between evangelism and social action.

Thus his response, and the team's, to the Indian cyclone disaster was typical, and they took close interest in the progress of Billy Graham Naga. The president of India promised to come for the inauguration of the completed township if Billy came too, but this did not prove possible.

Instead Franklin Graham, now president of World Medical Missions and of Samaritan's Purse, represented his father. On a hot Sunday, June 29, 1980, two years and nine months after the night of terror and grief, Franklin, Walter Smyth, and others from the team were met by the villagers, "bubbling with joy." Two hundred and eighty-five new houses were already occupied by survivors of the disaster, forming a mixed community of Catholics, Protestants, and non-Christians. They crowded happily around with the local leaders of church and state, as Franklin dedicated Billy Graham Naga and its new church of St. John the Baptist.

By his World Emergency Fund, Billy and the team continued to do all they could to "help people on every continent, especially when disaster strikes." Billy explained to the students at Harvard in 1982, "For example, our organization has helped build hospitals in such diverse places as Zaire, Jordan, Israel, India. We've sent plane after plane load of medical supplies and food supplies to various areas of the world where there were refugees. We helped support a boat picking up the boat people in the South China Seas. And my son worked on that boat. And I could cite scores of incidents that have come about as a result of the growing responsibility we feel toward the oppressed and the needy in the world.

"In addition, I've tried to use privately what little influence I may have had with those in high places to do something on a governmental level: not just to give relief, but to work toward changes. And, on occasion, have succeeded.

"My pilgrimage has also led me to call for morality and ethics in government. During our history, we've gone through many traumatic periods, in which we almost lost confidence in all forms of government. But the problem was not necessarily the form of government, but the ambitions and moral blindness of some of those in power. The kind of government any nation has will be determined by the kind of ethics and morality that underlie the political structure. But it also will depend on the moral integrity we demand of those in leadership. Government will never be better than the men and women who have given their lives to it.

"And they will never be better than the world- and life-view they accept, and on which they operate. Either the law of love will prevail—or the law of hatred, violence, and dishonesty will prevail."

19

$\mathcal{S}$YDNEY 1979

WHEN THE ARCHBISHOP OF SYDNEY, SIR MARCUS LOANE, WAS attending a missionary conference in the mountains of West Irian in 1975, he went for a hike by himself. While walking he reflected that 1979 would be the twentieth anniversary of the crusade of 1959, and that two years later he was due to retire. On return to New South Wales, he wrote on July 29, 1975, to Billy Graham: "I long to see a fresh and mighty spiritual impact on our city and country. Under God, I believe that you are the man to head up this task."

The archbishop was certain the crusade must not be short; when Billy had returned for ten days in 1968, many had come forward and joined the churches but the obvious impact had been small. Loane, therefore, made three weeks (four Sundays) a condition. He showed the letter to Bishop Jack Dain, still closely in touch with Billy since Lausanne. Dain commented that such an invitation was hardly worth a stamp, for Billy had not taken a three-week crusade for years, nor had he given a firm date so far ahead. Walter Smyth walked in before the letter was mailed, and expressed his gratitude to Loane but could offer no assurance of acceptance.

Billy replied on August 12 that if ever he returned to Sydney, he would like to come while Marcus Loane was archbishop, and that he favored three weeks. "However, keep in mind that I will be sixty years old and will not have near the physical vigor and stamina that I had in 1959. . . . It would be difficult for me to describe

William Franklin Graham Jr. (Billy) was born in the downstairs bedroom in this frame farmhouse on November 7, 1918, three days before his father's thirtieth birthday. His parents called him Billy Frank.

"When my decision for Christ was made, I walked slowly down and knelt in prayer. I opened my heart and knew for the first time the sweetness and joy of God, of truly being born again. If some newspaperman had asked me the next day what happened, I couldn't have told him. I didn't know, but I knew in my heart that I was somehow different and changed. That night absolutely changed the direction of my life."

—Billy Graham

Billy thought Ruth was the one God had long been preparing to stand beside him. Her intelligence, practicality, wit, determination, and wholehearted love for Jesus Christ attracted him to her—not to mention that she was the campus beauty! Ruth could see Billy was a man who had a purpose, a dedication in life, and he was a man who knew God. She said, "He was a man in a hurry who wanted to please God more than any man I'd ever met!"

The 1949 Los Angeles revival meetings were Billy's first major national media exposure. Two combined tents became the "canvas cathedral."

The early team members (front, left to right: George Beverly Shea, Billy, Cliff Barrows; back: Grady Wilson, Tedd Smith) worked together almost since the beginning.

The Billy Graham Evangelistic Association team in 1987.

Billy preached in the Harringay Arena in North London for three months in 1954.

Billy was summoned on short notice to No. 10 Downing Street by Prime Minister Sir Winston Churchill. As he left his meeting, he said to the press, "I feel like I have shaken hands with history."

On July 10, 1957, a lunch-hour meeting occurred amid the concrete canyons of lower Manhattan. The team had learned in London to take the crusade to the people. Secretaries, clerks, and financiers stood shoulder-to-shoulder in New York's financial district to hear a Gospel message.

People from Maine to California watched by television as Billy preached his farewell sermon to New York from Times Square. Broadway had never seen such a sight. Times Square had held huge crowds before—on New Year's Eve—but these people were praising God.

Historic Yankee Stadium was filled to overflowing on the hottest day of the year,
105 degrees in the shade.

Billy emphasized a point from the Bible at the 1962 Chicago crusade.

The sight of Billy saying goodbye to Ruth and Bunny was a familiar, if painful, one.

The mountaintop house in Montreat, 1968.

Since its dedication on September 13, 1980, the Billy Graham Center at Wheaton College has become an international center of information, research, and strategic training on evangelism and missions.

In June 1973, a record 1.1 million people made Yoido Plaza in Seoul, South Korea, Billy's largest meeting ever held anywhere in the world.

In Poland, 1978, Billy spoke at Auschwitz's Wall of Death, where 20,000 people were shot between 1940 and 1945.

A crowd estimated at 150,000 greeted Billy in the public square outside the Orthodox cathedral in Timisoara, Romania.

Queen Elizabeth II, Prince Philip, and the Queen Mother welcomed Billy and Ruth to Sandringham, where he preached in the chapel.

In 1984, Billy preached in a chilly wind and below-freezing temperatures in Sunderland, England, near the North Sea.

On September 22, 1991, more than 250,000 people attended New York's Central Park rally, making it the largest North American crusade event ever.

The Russian Red Army chorus sang a favorite American hymn, "Battle Hymn of the Republic," at the 1992 Moscow crusade: "Christ was born across the sea. As he died to make men holy, let us live to make men free, while God is marching on. Glory! Glory! Hallelujah!"

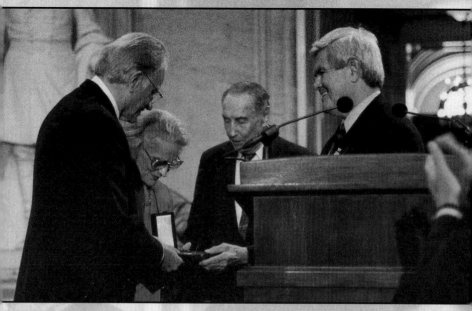

On May 2, 1996, Billy and Ruth were honored with the Congressional Gold Medal, the highest honor that Congress can bestow. Billy was the first clergyman to receive the honor for ministry, and the Grahams were the third couple to receive the award.

Franklin, former President Bush, and Billy at the opening service of the Metroplex Mission in Texas, 2002. Bush paid tribute to Billy, calling him "a genuine American hero and a man the entire Bush family is proud to call a very dear friend."

At the 2002 groundbreaking ceremony in Charlotte for the planned new headquarters of the Billy Graham Evangelistic Association.

how much large stadium evangelistic meetings take out of me physically now. By God's grace I can still do it—but I have to limit myself to the evening meetings."

Late that year the archbishop brought together the heads and prominent ministers of the other denominations. After a small hesitation because the archbishop had approached Billy before consulting them, they gave unanimous support: "There will be an enormous volume of goodwill and prayer from the beginning," Billy was assured. He accepted, in January 1976, and preparation began.

The venue of 1959, the Royal Agricultural Showground, would not be available. The only site of sufficient size was the Randwick Racecourse, which would unexpectedly be free (except for one meeting, which the Jockey Club transferred) because of a court case two years before the crusade. Geographically, Randwick was the wrong side of the city from the new areas of expansion. Moreover, the shape of a racecourse, despite expert adaptation, would prevent the sense of crowd that a stadium or the Showground gives, but it was specially suitable for interpretation to the ethnic minorities, grown much larger.

With three years to go, preparations were perhaps deeper and more thorough than any previous crusade throughout the world; all the lessons of the past thirty years were assimilated and adapted to reach a city that had changed much in population, style, and skyline since 1959. Of the twenty-six chairmen of committees, two were converts of 1959, one as a schoolboy, the other as a young professional man who had not been a churchgoer. Many committee men and women were also converts.

The diocese of Sydney fashioned its program to prepare and follow up the crusade. According to the diocesan director of evangelism, "[We took the opportunity] to do everything we had ever dreamed of doing, under the guise of getting ready for Billy Graham." Canon John Chapman added that only Billy could have brought the Protestant denominations of Sydney (apart from a very few individual churches) to work together so closely and effectively. The Roman Catholics did not cooperate but did not oppose.

By late April 1979, when Billy and Ruth took the plane for Australia, Sydney had been saturated with prayer because prayer groups had spread like wildfire. Counselors were trained; 5,000 nurture groups were ready to receive those who came forward. There had been widespread "dialogue evangelism," and training to reach the population of high-rise blocks. The churches had set so much going that all would have been worthwhile, they felt, even if Billy had been unable to come.

Billy arrived in Sydney ten days before the crusade's opening, and at once won the ear of the city through the friendly welcome of the press. Six weeks earlier in New York, he had privately met with an Australian newspaper magnate for a most constructive discussion. At the airport press conference, Billy's sincerity and humility won the immediate support of hard pressmen, who then followed the lead of one, Alan Gill of *Sydney Morning Herald,* a strong Christian.

Billy was soon on television. In 1959 he had needed to overcome the fear of Australians that he was either a "wowser" or a hypocrite. In 1979 they already admired and accepted him as "fair dinkum," but the television talk shows gave him an opportunity to put the Gospel into living rooms in a relaxed yet decisive way. Sydney loved him for his answers to a star interviewer's problems with kangaroos in the ark, and even more effective were the final moments of David Frost's show when Frost suddenly asked him to close the program with prayer.

Spring weather in Sydney is usually mild and mainly dry. Instead it turned cold and wet. On the evening that Randwick Racecourse was handed to the crusade executive to be adapted, the architect and his assistant drove in from opposite sides of Sydney through rain, only to find Randwick strangely dry until the coffee break at midnight: The women's prayer groups had prayed.

The crusade opened in rain. Evening after evening, the rain and wind made the racecourse not a pleasant place to attend a service in the open. The weather reduced the crowds but could not dampen the enthusiasm of the thousands who came as a result of Operation Andrew. Those who were not in the covered stands sat on specially provided plastic sacks.

One evening, during a violent thunderstorm, lightning knocked out the sound system after the choir rehearsal shortly before it was due to be turned on. The Australian sound crew did all they could to salvage enough equipment to reach the crowd, smaller than usual because of the storm, but without success. Bill Fasig, the team member at the control, telephoned Cliff Barrows on the platform. Cliff replied: "I will keep the choir rehearsing, and you pray." The contractor said to Fasig: "You might as well. We have done everything else!"

The sound came on exactly as the service was due to start. The contractor was astounded. "What did you do?" he asked. "I prayed," replied Fasig.

Billy was deeply grateful for the way the committee and the hundreds of crusade volunteers "faced the overwhelming problems of rain, weather, and even the venue itself." As he said to them, "You did it with courage and faith and without complaining. You took it all as from the Lord. This was an inspiration and a blessing to all of us." He loved to hear their stories and would use some in his sermons: "Forty-five minutes after the meeting ended last Sunday afternoon, a counselor saw a mother leaving the counseling area, leading two happy children away, clutching their *Trusting Jesus* books that we gave them. And the counselor asked the children, 'What did you do today?' And each replied, 'I asked Jesus into my heart.' Then the counselor asked the mother, 'What about you?' And she replied very sadly, 'I wish I had, but the children wanted to come, and now it's too late for me.' 'No it isn't,' responded the counselor. And then and there, that mother gave herself to Christ, having been led forward by her children."

Billy also related a crusade story that may be unique, about a young married professional man, a passive churchgoer, who felt bored and restless and took a flight to Singapore the previous December to escape family and business for a wild weekend. "I just heard this story today. I think that man is here tonight. And when he was flying over Singapore, they flew over the stadium where we were holding a crusade. And he saw the big crowd and he saw the lights and he asked someone, 'What's going on?' and was told what it was. He came to the meeting; he found Christ. That boredom and that restlessness all left him. He came back to his family, rejoicing that he had found Christ. And he was already in the church, but he really didn't know Christ."

The lower attendance affected finance. The budget had not been met before the crusade began, as the finance committee had hoped. Therefore, an offertory appeal was made each evening, directed solely to Christians in the audience, and emphasizing that Billy and the team received no remuneration for their services, and that the money would be spent in Australia. After a week and a half, the budget was still not met. Billy volunteered to make the offertory appeal himself.

The finance committee and its chairman, Neville Malone, a senior accountant in the oil industry, declined: Only Australians should appeal to Australians for money. With the shortfall now serious, Billy renewed his offer, provided the crusade's inner executive agreed unanimously.

Malone held out alone, and Billy stayed silent. Malone and his friends and prayer partners continued to pray earnestly, and suddenly the money began to come, but the budget needed to be increased, and Bishop Dain again urged that Billy be allowed to speak. Malone again declined. Malone spoke before the offertory on the last night in a spiritual, unemotional, and rather original way that impressed Billy so much that he took notes. On the last night, Dain made a low-key request to Christians that they give sacrificially. Many nonchurchgoers gave too.

The budget was met. Money poured in after the crusade. The big surplus would have been put to making the film of the crusade, *A Time for Decision,* had not a member of the finance committee already paid for it from his pocket. The whole experience profoundly influenced Malone's own giving. Later he left industry to serve as treasurer of the diocese.

Meanwhile, despite the rain and the wind, inquirers were coming forward. Billy preached more slowly than in 1959, and older Australians found the content deeper and more expository, the delivery less melodramatic yet equally powerful and clear, especially to the young. The percentage of inquirers stayed almost constant. The archbishop, whose unbroken attendance emphasized to Sydney the crusade's importance, said in a speech six months later: "Such a crusade is a phenomenon for which one can hardly account on a human level. The best part of Billy Graham by the grace of God is Billy Graham: a man whose face and voice have those qualities of unaffected humility and total sincerity. It will never cease to amaze when one recalls the invitation and response at each meeting; almost the same words for the same appeal, and the instant, silent flood of men and women surging quietly forward from every corner and every grandstand."

On the night of the worst weather, a federal cabinet minister's wife sloshed through the mud. Her testimony was very effective team to women's groups in the months to come. Another night came an elderly and distinguished physician, whose witness in the short remaining years of his life, and his funeral, were long remembered.

Most of those who came forward were ordinary citizens, many of them young. One night an exhausted member of the crusade executive team was tempted to give up. Then a fellow member said: "My church had a hundred referrals last week." The news was like a shot in the arm: The hard work was worthwhile for the fresh life pouring into the churches.

In the last week the weather cleared and numbers rose sharply. Meanwhile, Billy, rather to his own surprise, felt fitter than when he had begun. And the crusade was reaching right across Australia through videos and landlines, to hospitals, churches, mission stations in the outback, and even to households where neighbors would be invited. Twenty-nine out of the thirty-six television stations of Australia carried some of the meetings.

Six months after the crusade, the archbishop of Sydney declared to his diocesan synod: "I would like to think that Sydney has been stirred and touched to its depths by a mighty movement of the Spirit of God and that thousands of its people will prove to have experienced a radical and permanent change in their lives."

And in 1981, a few months before his retirement, Sir Marcus reflected on the result of his walk in West Irian all those years before: "The crusade did not make the break-through or the impact on the city at large in the way that one would have hoped, but I would say without reservation that it was a source of very great blessing to the churches, among church people, and for those whom church people were personally responsible for bringing."

20

GREAT STEPS FORWARD

O N SEPTEMBER 13, 1980, MANY EVANGELICAL LEADERS AND other guests, including George Bush, soon to be elected vice president of the United States, came together for the dedication of a fine new Colonial-style building on the campus of Wheaton College: the Billy Graham Center.

For nearly thirty years Billy had considered founding an educational institution. At one time he had thoroughly investigated the possibility of creating a new university, but every project was laid aside because it might deflect him from his primary task of evangelism. At length, in the later 1970s, he found his answer. In September 1977, he turned the first sod on a site donated by Wheaton, his *alma mater.* The building rose fast. Billy appointed a team member to raise funds and gave the center the royalties of his book *Angels,* which became a runaway best-seller and topped the American nonfiction list for weeks. The center's finances had a good start.

The Billy Graham Center at Wheaton College soon established itself as an aid to Christian enterprise and thought, to the understanding of the past, and to planning for the future. Associated with the Wheaton Graduate School, it helps prepare future leaders from all over the world, intellectually and spiritually. It organizes courses and conferences to think through the problems and possibilities confronting the church. The library provides an impetus to the study of evangelism and missions through the ages and in the contemporary world. The archives not only bring together in expert hands the vast and growing mass of papers relating to the Billy Graham crusades, and Billy's life and ministry, but they are also a repository for the manuscripts of American evangelists and thus an important center of research.

And there is the museum. During the building of the center, Billy became concerned that the museum might be a glorification of himself. He wanted to scrap it. He was dissuaded, and the finished product delighted him. Designed by a sensitive expert, it provides the visitor with "a walk through the Gospel," setting American revivals and the Billy Graham crusades into the context of church history from earliest times and featuring the varied ways in which the Christian message reaches the contemporary world.

"The museum deeply moved me and filled me with silence, wonder, and tears," wrote one of the distinguished guests at the dedication. "I wanted at the end to be alone with Jesus for as long a time as he would please to grant me."

Immediately after the dedication, Billy left for Japan. A crusade in Tokyo and three other cities, with Leighton Ford preaching at two more, had been prepared in much prayer, with outstanding thoroughness.

Billy had briefed himself fully about this highly populated industrial nation with a strongly traditional culture. The stranglehold of tradition and of the ancient religions was loosening; the young were open to other influences, though not to Marxism, which had little appeal to Japanese. Christianity had been preached freely for more than a hundred years, yet only 1 percent of the people were Christians. At a dinner before Billy's Osaka crusade, the governor of the province asked why so few people in Japan believed the Christian Gospel. He answered his own question in a memorable phrase: "Perhaps, because it has not been made clear."

Billy Graham had already helped to make it clear. Thirteen years earlier in 1967, he had held a Tokyo crusade, which had proved to be a milestone in Japanese history, turning the eyes of an inward-looking church to the urgency of the need to reach the nation. The year 1967 had done much to tip the balance away from the negative liberalism, which had dominated the united church (of the larger denominations) since before World War II.

The year 1980 carried this process a great step further. In origin and preparation, the crusade was essentially Japanese. Tensions—between local committees and the national, between the older and the younger leaders, between nationals and the American advisory team under Henry Holley—had been resolved by graciousness and a shared determination that nothing should weaken the thrust of the Gospel.

Billy arrived in the first days of October 1980. After a press conference in Tokyo, where every enterprise should begin, he flew south to Okinawa. There, and in each city afterwards, the crusade surprised even those with the most faith. Japan was startled by the great numbers that gathered, and because numbers mean much to the Japanese, they awarded a new respect to Christianity, which suddenly became more visible. In the months and years that followed, this helped to make the people more open to the message that Christians preached.

Billy knew that when he gave the invitation to receive Christ, many might come forward without fully understanding what a decision would cost to their future lives. He, therefore, made the invitation tough. As in Korea seven years earlier, he emphasized that they should get out of their seats only if they would forsake all other gods. "I thought no one would respond," wrote Billy from Tokyo, "but last night we had over 2,000. In Fukuoka, which has only 1,000 Christians, it poured torrential rain and yet we had from 15,000–17,000 people at each service sitting in the open, and hundreds responding to the appeal (in water that sometimes went over their shoe tops). I am not a church historian enough to evaluate what is happening, but I believe that Japan may be on the verge of a Christian revival."

In Tokyo, after the baseball stadium had overflowed with people and many had streamed forward to be counseled, the Japanese pastors were "shouting happy" at all that had happened. Their follow-up system went smoothly into action. The next years brought many new members to the churches; hundreds of other inquirers slipped out of sight, but the pastors were not discouraged, knowing that in Japan a conversion could be a very slow process.

Japan was not likely to see a spectacular turning to Christ as in Korea, but citywide evangelism became easier because the barriers between churches had dropped for Billy. The crusade had strengthened the faith and courage of the small minority of Japanese who were Christians, and also strengthened their determination to make Christ's message clear to their friends.

Six months after the crusade, Walter Smyth was back in Japan to meet representatives from every crusade city. "It was one of the most thrilling evenings I have ever spent," he said, for they reminded him that the average Japanese Protestant church had less than fifty members and then told him of church after church that had already baptized thirty or forty people.

Yet the crusade had been only a step. Most of their countrymen remained without Christ. The Japanese longed that Billy Graham should return in the mid–1980s, for they held that he was "God's man for this age."

Several Osaka pastors once discussed why Billy could reach the Japanese so decisively. "Billy Graham is a very humble person," said one, "and he loves the heart of common people. He knows the condition of the soul and applies the Gospel to them."

Another made two points: "One, his emphasis is on prayer. He asked how many people pray: prayer moves the power of God. Another point, his Gospel is very simple. Many years ago Billy Graham came to St. Paul University in Tokyo. He pointed out that we should preach to people so that even a twelve-year-old boy could understand."

And the third pastor said that Billy Graham has "two faces. One face: his authority when on the platform. Short sentences and strong convictions. He gave us his message. He's a very authoritative person on the platform. The other face: when we speak together around the table he's just like a servant, a very humble person. He has a heart to listen to other people's opinions."

From East to West: In the spring of 1981, Billy went to Mexico and the story could not have been more different from Japan's.

The National Mexican Congress with Billy Graham (for historical reasons the word *crusade* could not be used) was planned in two halves: the first in Mexico City and the second at Villahermosa, capital of the state of Tabasco. The constitution of Mexico prohibits large public religious meetings except on church property. This rule was not broken for the pope, though most Mexicans are nominally Catholics, and the sole exception remained a Billy Graham rally in the Arena Mexico in 1958. Hopes of inviting Billy back for a longer visit had foundered because of this problem. During 1980, however, the congress committee secured a verbal promise of the Inde-Olympico Stadium; the promise was never put in writing but was given with enough assurance to justify going ahead.

In January 1981, six weeks before the congress was due, the Inde-Olympic Stadium was suddenly closed down for the next few months because of a government official's speculation and the resulting lawsuits. The congress could obtain no alternative site until the evangelicals threatened to "take to the streets"; the government held out to the last minute, then allowed the use of the much smaller Arena Mexico where Billy had preached in 1958. All the printed publicity was now worthless.

The arena proved to be much too small for the tens of thousands who turned up to hear Billy. Many from the upcountry arrived too late and hammered on doors that had been closed by the authorities when the crowd exceeded the capacity and the fire safety point was reached. Loudspeakers carried the service and sermon into the streets.

Billy found great liberty in his preaching, and the interpreter made the English words come alive to Spanish ears. The committee and team alike were amazed by the response when Billy gave the invitation. The nominally Catholic but largely secularized Mexicans hungered for the Gospel. Down at Villahermosa where an 8,000 seat baseball stadium had at least 35,000 people in it every night, the response was overwhelming. "Literally thousands," wrote Charles Ward of the team, "surrounded the platform. The counselors could not begin to cope with the numbers, so we passed out our 'Commitment to Christ' folder and a decision card for the people themselves to fill out." Fortunately, the follow-up had been well planned.

For the first time in Mexican history, the evangelical (i.e., Protestant) church became national news. The press at Mexico City was cool at first, then warm and excited. At Villahermosa, the press gave unstinted support, as did the secular authorities. The Roman Catholic hierarchy, unlike their brethren in the Philippines, opposed the congress, though not openly until after it was over, when they declared Billy Graham a "non-Christian."

Evangelicals had been barred from preaching on television, but Billy was invited to appear on several talk shows. In answer to questions, he put the Gospel across freely and plainly. He visited the president of Mexico and opened many doors in high places that had been shut against evangelicals. Meanwhile, the School of Evangelism in Mexico City, organized to coincide with the congress, brought together more than 1,400 ministers and laypersons from all over Mexico and neighboring countries and made great impact on their lives. Billy described it as "one of the best we have seen around the world."

Billy's ten nights of preaching opened a new chapter for Mexico, symbolized perhaps by the nineteen new churches that were started at Villahermosa.

21

MOSCOW 1982 AND AFTER

AT THE END OF FEBRUARY 1982, BILLY GRAHAM WENT TO Blackpool in northern England for a conference address and a two-day crusade. The friendly crowds, and the hundreds who came forward, were unaware that he was wrestling with one of the most difficult decisions of his life: whether or not to accept a specific invitation to Moscow.

Five years earlier when he was in Hungary, Baptists from Moscow had brought a general invitation. Even before the visit to Poland, high-level negotiations had begun between the Billy Graham Team and the Soviet authorities who, being Marxist-Leninists, were committed to atheism. Soviet officials knew that Billy wished to work alongside the churches registered by the state, but he made plain at a very early stage his concern about the restrictions on religious freedom and for the prisoners of conscience.

Billy was aware that before the Communists took power in 1917, the Russian Orthodox Church and the tsarist state had restricted and oppressed the Baptists and other nonconformists. Lenin, though an atheist, had allowed these a toleration for a few years in the 1920s, which had led to great growth, while the Orthodox in their turn were grievously oppressed. Following the death of Lenin and the rise of Stalin, all Christians in Russia went through the fire of persecution until a measure of freedom was restored during World War II as a tribute to their patriotism.

Billy had visited Moscow as a tourist in 1959 and had prayed that he might live to preach there freely to a capacity crowd in a stadium. Few in 1959 would have dared to believe that he would indeed thirty-three years later. He became very interested in the great movement to Christianity among Soviet peoples, and the continued discrimination and varying pressures by agents of the Soviet state, particularly during the new wave of persecution under Khrushchev from 1959 until his fall in 1964. Billy learned from a reliable count by a Western expert that the believers in one God vastly outnumbered actual members of the Communist Party who controlled their lives.

The Billy Graham Team's negotiations led to a provisional confidential understanding that Billy should make a preaching visit to churches in several cities throughout the Soviet Union in September 1979. This was postponed after Afghanistan in December 1978. Over two years later, Haraszti learned that Billy was one of the leaders of Christian and non-Christian religions whom the Orthodox patriarch of Moscow and All Russia, Pimen, contemplated inviting in May 1982 to address a World Conference: Religious Workers for Saving the Sacred Gift of Life from Nuclear Catastrophe.

At the first direct contact between the Billy Graham Team and the Russian Orthodox Church in October 1981 at Geneva, Alexander Haraszti told Father Vitaly Borovoy, the patriarchate's chief liaison officer with the World Council of Churches, that Billy, if he came, must be allowed to preach in the Moscow Baptist Church and in an Orthodox church, possibly the patriarchal cathedral. Haraszti then went back to Moscow (one of eight visits in twelve months) and was introduced to the Metropolitan Philaret of Minsk and Belorussia, chairman of the external affairs department of the Moscow patriarchate, whose sympathetic understanding proved important to the outcome.

The decision to accept or decline the patriarch's invitation could not be easy. The Orthodox Church had come into deep spirituality through the deprivations and the persecutions of the past, yet the leadership kept in step with the state; the West expected the conference to be propaganda for the Soviet peace movement. Billy emphasized to Moscow that his deep concern for nuclear disarmament did not make him a unilateralist, and that he would come as an observer, not a participant. He would, therefore, not sign the conference final statement. He also insisted that he must, as an evangelist, preach the Gospel in Moscow without any restrictions on his message: a desire endorsed by Orthodox, Baptists, and government officials.

As Haraszti, in close contact with Walter Smyth and John Akers, went back and forth from Russia, Billy conveyed his determination to speak publicly on the issue of human rights, but as a guest he would not utter denunciations, which might win approval in the West but extinguish future ministry in the Eastern bloc. Moreover, he had taken to heart some advice from Vatican sources, that in Eastern Europe you can achieve much if you do not shout it from the housetops.

Billy also insisted that he must visit the Siberian Pentecostals who had been in the American Embassy since June 1977, hoping to be allowed to emigrate. He urged that the issue be resolved before he came, but if not, he must visit them. The Soviet authorities were surprised that he cared about the "Siberian Seven" (considered to be lawbreakers), but finally agreed with reluctance to a private, pastoral visit, with no media attention.

On February 5, 1982, Patriarch Pimen issued the formal invitation, the Baptists added their invitation, and Haraszti carried them back to America. He presented the letter to Billy Graham on Sunday, February 14, at the Essex House Hotel in New York, where Billy had brought a few close associates to discuss and pray about his answer. If he went to Moscow, it would pave the way to a longer visit, because churchmen and state officials would come to know him and he would learn much; it would help the churches by enhancing their importance in the eyes of the secular rulers, who would be impressed that their churchmen could secure such a world famous figure. It would open the door to Eastern European countries who waited on Moscow before inviting Billy. It would provide opportunity to give his testimony to Christ and preach the Gospel in high places of an atheist state, and before leaders of non-Christian religions.

The pitfalls were equally plain, and one or two of the Billy Graham Team did not want him to go, fearing he would be used. He consulted with family, colleagues, experts, the State Department, and the White House. "I discussed the advisability of my going with former President Nixon and former Secretary of State Henry Kissinger, both longtime personal friends. Mr. Nixon told me: 'There is a great risk, but I believe that for the sake of the message you preach, the risk is worth it.'" To refuse Moscow would end forever the hope of public ministry in the Soviet Union. Mr. Nixon later commented to the present writer (memo of December 30, 1986): "I strongly urged him to make his trips to the Soviet Union and to Eastern Europe in spite of the fact that most State Department and White House officials were opposed to his doing so. I frankly told him that I had no illusions whatsoever that he was going to be able to convert the atheistic Communist leaders of the Soviet Union, Romania, etc. to Christianity, but that it was important to let the people in those countries see and hear an American religious leader who could give them at least a glimmer of hope that there was a better spiritual life for them than the dull, drabness of Marxist/Leninist societies."

Billy reached Blackpool still undecided, though working on a formal letter of acceptance. He continued to agonize and pray and discuss. During each of the three days there, his mind was dominated by the pros and cons of going to Moscow, yet when he mounted the podium to preach, he could shut it right out; vigor flowed in, and he preached as if he had carried no burden all day except for the people before him.

The more Billy prayed and deliberated, the more certain he became that God had opened this door. He must go through it whatever the personal cost. But the decision once made did not flood his soul with peace.

His acceptance was announced. The criticism began: He would be a pawn; he was naïve; he would throw a cloak of respectability over the Kremlin's religious policies. The Siberians called on him to announce that he would not go if they still had not received their exit visas, but Billy already knew that the Kremlin would be unmoved by the gesture. The American press wrongly reported that the president had asked him to cancel his acceptance. In fact, when Billy had lunch with the Vice President and Mrs. Bush the Sunday before he left, and the Bushes invited the President and Mrs. Reagan at short notice, it was Billy who brought up the subject. The president said, "Don't worry about it, it will come out all right. I'm going to be praying for you."

Billy Graham reached Moscow on the evening of Friday, May 7. He could not arrive physically refreshed, for he was in the middle of the long-scheduled series of university lectures and public crusades in New England. He was projected at once into five-and-a-half days of interviews, services, meetings, tours, and functions, backed by that immense hospitality, which is typically Russian. At sixty-three-and-a-half years old, it seemed to be the most demanding schedule he had ever known.

Warm friendships sprang up between Billy and Pastor Bychkov of the Baptists and Metropolitan Philaret of the Orthodox—friendships that helped closer relations and respect between the churches.

Billy also met men of importance in the Kremlin, the most senior being the chairman of the Foreign Relations Committee, Boris Ponomarev, a candidate member of the Politburo. They spoke alone for over an hour. As Billy said later, "[At every interview] I took the liberty of telling about Jesus Christ and what he means to me and how anyone can find him."

"It was graciously done," commented an aide who was present at other interviews, "but always very directly. And Billy comes across so well at private meetings."

Billy knew that the rigid hold of Marxist-Leninist doctrine kept these men ignorant of Christianity and supposing that the things of the Spirit were delusions to be explained by political or economic circumstances. Yet each, like every human soul, had a hunger for God, however suppressed. Billy also knew of the widespread disappointment at the lack of idealism in Communist societies, the desire for answers that have eluded them.

Billy always raised the question of the Siberians very frankly, and of believers who were in prison, he had a list of about 150 in his hand.

On that Saturday evening, Billy was taken to three Orthodox churches. The faithful poured into the few churches to prepare themselves for Sunday. That night came the first hitch. The team was informed that Billy's preaching at the Baptist church, scheduled for 5 P.M. on Sunday, had been switched to 8 A.M., squeezed in before the Orthodox Divine Liturgy at 10 A.M. Because the Voice of America and the BBC had broadcast the time, the State authorities had become alarmed at the prospect of half of Moscow converging on the 2,000 seat Baptist church.

Next morning the police set up barriers and allowed only ticket holders to enter the Baptist church, but they did not break up the overflow crowds in the narrow street. Nor did they stop them singing hymns, although this was forbidden by law outside church property. The next day *The Times* in London had a headline: "Graham Breaks New Ground in Moscow." He broke new ground in another way too, when the controlled Soviet media reported his activities. No previous religious visitor (apart from proponents of Soviet "peace" movements) had been noticed. Christianity was barred from newspapers or television except as a target for ridicule or atheist propaganda, and Christians were therefore most excited to find *Pravda* reporting with respect the activities of an evangelist: His words brought Christianity to the masses.

Inside the Baptist "prayer house," as Protestant churches are called in Russia, two-thirds in attendance were Moscow Baptists and their guests, some from the farthest republics of the Soviet Union. Perhaps the other third were Western and Soviet pressmen and security personnel, so that at least some atheists were present. During Billy's sermon from John 5, a girl let down a banner for a few seconds from the left balcony; its English was fully plain to the Western press: "We have 150 in prison," but Billy was involved in his preaching and was not looking in that direction at the time.

The joyful service ran overtime, as Russian services tend to, and Billy's Baptist hosts were nervous that he would be rudely late for the Divine Liturgy at the patriarchal cathedral and bundled him out a side door. As he was getting into the car, a newsman shouted, "There's a large crowd waiting several blocks away to greet you." Billy asked the driver if he would stop immediately. His escort (including a Baptist clergyman) said, "There is absolutely no time because we are now twenty minutes late where you are expected at the cathedral." Billy, not realizing the significance of the crowd behind the barriers that wanted to greet him, but realizing the importance of speaking in one of Moscow's great Orthodox cathedrals, agreed. He changed clothes in the car, and put on his robe and hood.

Waves of disappointment touched many a home in Moscow and beyond, especially among Christians who had traveled from far to greet him.

At the cathedral of the Epiphany, the matchless singing of the choirs and the intoning of the ancient liturgy by richly vested priests continued for two hours, followed by greetings. Then Billy was invited to stand before the great golden screen or *ikonostasis* beside Patriarch Pimen. Nearby stood the patriarchs of Alexandria, Romania, and Bulgaria, and many metropolitans and bishops.

Billy thanked Patriarch Pimen. On this Victory Day (May 9), he spoke of the sacrifice of the millions in the war and then of Christ's sacrifice. "You can be partakers of his resurrection," he continued. The interpreter had no amplifier. There were cries of "Louder! Louder!" The next sentences therefore rang out through the church: "This Jesus is the perfect atonement for our sins. He is standing at the right hand of glory and will return victorious."

The conference for Saving the Sacred Gift of Life from Nuclear Catastrophe opened the next day. When Billy's turn came, he delivered a long, far-ranging speech on the "Christian Faith and Peace in a Nuclear Age." Jewish, Buddhist, Hindu, and Muslim leaders and many atheists from Soviet government circles heard his reasoned but uncompromising exposition of the biblical answer to world problems and to the nuclear threat, possibly the most resounding public affirmation of the Christian Gospel to be heard in Moscow outside a church for more than sixty years. Many of his statements ran contrary to Moscow's accepted thinking, for he emphasized the value and dignity of the individual, and that God is the Lord of history. He continued, "Lasting peace will only come when the Kingdom of God prevails. The basic issue that faces us today is not merely political, social, economic, or even moral or humanitarian. The deepest problems of the human race are spiritual. They are rooted in man's refusal to seek God's way for his life. The problem is the human heart, which God alone can change."

Billy devoted one section entirely to human rights and religious freedom. He also urged the conference to call the people of the world to prayer, and to "rededicate ourselves personally to the task of being peacemakers in God's world." He sat down to a spontaneous standing ovation. Only one other speech in the conference, the patriarch's, was applauded in this way.

Billy took no further part in the conference. He had let it be known that he would leave if any delegate abused the United States, and when a Middle Eastern delegate began to do so, Billy removed his earphones. The chairman exchanged notes with other members of the platform and no more anti-American invectives were heard.

That evening Billy Graham visited the Siberians in the American Embassy. The visit had been planned for the previous day, but Billy's staff had a hunch that his desire to exclude the media would not be respected at the original time. Even when Billy reached the embassy, he nearly had to cancel because they would not agree that no photographer or television camera record their meeting. He and his aides sympathized with the Siberians: Billy had read their story through—twice. But privacy had been pledged; the Soviet officials would never trust him again if he broke his word. He could not sacrifice the good of the many for the few; and moreover, he could achieve more for the Siberians in his own way. At last all agreed, and the curtains were closed between their basement room and the street above, which was filled by newsmen. Yet when Billy entered, having waited all this time with the ambassador, Alex Haraszti's sharp eye noticed a new crack in the curtains, wide enough for a camera lens in the street above to catch a picture. He closed it.

They had a long pastoral visit, reading the Bible and praying together. The Siberians had rather expected something dramatic like Naaman who had supposed that Elisha would "strike his hand upon the place." They were much disappointed and puzzled. But their story ended as happily as Naaman's, though not so quickly. Billy persisted in his efforts, and in August sent Haraszti to Moscow. Alex was there when they finally left the embassy in April 1983 on the first stage of their longed-for emigration. They reached the West not realizing how much Billy Graham had helped them.

By the Thursday morning when Billy returned to Moscow airport, he was spiritually invigorated: The exuberant witness of Russian Christians, despite the pressures and restrictions, had deeply impressed him. He had preached to an estimated 8,000 people in Moscow and rejoiced that he had been able to affirm his own faith, among believers and unbelievers, more often than he had expected. They had been extremely receptive. Billy said, "I found the Soviet people, in their hunger for the word of God, the same as I have found people in every part of the world."

Billy was, however, physically exhausted and had not been sleeping well, which was usual when he was under strain. The Western press had followed him everywhere, almost aggressively, throughout the visit. They had been looking for the quick scoop or sensation, but he had been thinking throughout in terms of the centuries: the almost thousand years of Christianity in Russia, the mere sixty-five years of atheist rule, the long-term future. At the airport he was asked by a journalist why he "did not speak against religious repression in the Soviet Union where the government espouses atheism."

Billy replied that he was a guest: "This is not the time nor the place to discuss it." He added that he had found more religious freedom in the Soviet Union than was commonly supposed by Americans and that thousands of churches were open. He then touched on the structure of the relations between church and state. Had he been less exhausted, he might not have used the expression "free church," by which he meant one that is not a state church "like the Church of England with the Queen at its head."[11] He was referring to historical changes since 1917, but the pressmen missed the allusion and seized upon the word "free."

Unknown to Billy, the press had already twisted an answer he gave at the earlier formal press conference on the Wednesday, before going out of Moscow to visit the monastery at Zagorsk. This was a significant occasion since it gave Billy an opportunity to speak plainly on Soviet television about Christ and spiritual revival in answer to the question, What will help bring peace to the world?

Another of the questions put to him by a Western pressman was: Had he personally seen religious persecution since he had been in Moscow? Billy, who had only been there four-and-a-half days, asked, "Do you mean, have I personally witnessed any?"

The newsman said, "Yes."

Billy answered truthfully: "No, I have not personally seen persecution." He could not possibly discuss the Siberians in this context without jeopardizing his confidential diplomacy on their behalf. And he had no idea what a storm his truthful answer would raise.

He flew back to Paris and London. Three days later he took part in a transatlantic television link up for the David Brinkley show and found himself assailed and denounced. He discovered that he had become the center of violent reproach and abuse and sorrow. He was alleged to have cared nothing for the sufferings of Soviet Christians; to have been so blind or naïve that he could go to Moscow and see no evidence of religious persecution in the Soviet Union; and had favorably compared the freedom of religion with that in Britain. The American press came out in a rash of bitter cartoons against him. Even many of his friends with no information except press reports were puzzled and dismayed.

Billy came to London to receive, at the hand of Prince Philip, the 1982 Templeton Prize for Progress in Religion: $200,000. He had already announced that he would give it away: part to relieve world hunger, and part for education in the Third World and for evangelism in Britain.

Faced by a rather hostile press conference, and again in New York, Billy could have won instant approval by revealing his confidential discussions in Moscow or by following the practice of guests who denounced the host country as soon as they have left. He kept quiet and merely set the record straight in its context. In answer to questions, he contrasted the "tremendous" religious freedom of the West with the "measure of freedom" in the Soviet Union, and spoke of religious persecution in the same way as he had in Moscow. His late hosts saw that he spoke with the same voice outside their borders as he did within and trusted him.

The Soviet press, however, misapplied his words at the airport to build him up as the man who gave America the truth about the churches being free, and claimed (as on Radio Moscow's English service) that "Graham said he had found more religious freedom in the Soviet Union than in Britain." Inevitably some individual Russian believers, misled by their press, or hearing by word of mouth or letter that he had sped past the crowds outside the Baptist church, were grieved. Billy regretted any pain caused to some of those whom he had pledged to help.

He had done what he could. Billy said privately and publicly that he knew he was in the will of God before he went. He was even more sure while he was there. In the early hours of Sunday morning, May 9, after his first full day in Moscow, he confided to Haraszti: "I feel I am in the will of God and that this visit will have an effect on the fate of our two nations and possibly on the fate of mankind," as indeed it did.

When he returned to America, Billy was yet more certain, despite the criticism. In the months that followed, he received enough evidence that his work bore fruit. In March 1983, Alex Haraszti and Walter Smyth's associate, Blair Carlson, began an extended exploratory trip through the Soviet Union, visiting many cities in Russia, Siberia, Central Asia, Georgia, and the Baltic states. They were received with open arms by Orthodox, Baptists, Armenians, and Lutherans, and state officials in every city. Two nights before they arrived in Novosibirsk, Western Siberia, Billy had been seen on television in a program about the conference. This gave joy to Christians. The two team members were left in no doubt: Billy Graham's visit to Moscow in May 1982 had been in the will of God.

Years later it could be recognized as having contributed to the collapse of atheistic communism and the restoration of freedom of religion, and thus to Billy's Moscow Mission of 1992. And it opened doors to East Germany and Czechoslovakia.

On the morning of Sunday, October 17, 1982, Billy Graham preached from Luther's pulpit in the City Church of Wittenberg in the German Democratic Republic; East Germany was ruled by Communist government, which then seemed permanent.

All the Protestant churches of Wittenberg had been invited to take part in the Lutheran worship. As Billy mounted the ornate pulpit, which makes a splash of color in an austere church, he murmured to his interpreter: "Is this a *youth* service? Just look at all the young people." A high proportion of the congregation were indeed young, with eager expectant faces. Nearly forty years of atheist teaching in the schools had not taken away the hunger for God.

Billy spoke on the faith of Martin Luther and made a great impression on the congregation and had a direct effect on young people. Afterward, many crowded around him and talked with him and received his autograph. In the church courtyard and in the walk around the Luther sites, escorted by the clergy and by the mayor (a government official and therefore a Marxist), Billy talked with ordinary people. This especially pleased him because usually in East Germany, his tight schedule and the hours spent in car travel limited his personal contacts to leaders.

That afternoon Billy and his team went to Dresden. The great baroque Church of the Cross, restored after wartime bombing, was filled to the limit: The five galleries, the aisles, the wide sanctuary were packed with over 7,000 people. Once again the young predominated; an estimated 85 percent were under twenty-two. At the end of the address, over a third raised their hands to accept Christ.

The tour in East Germany had come after four years of diplomacy by Walter Smyth, Alexander Haraszti, and John Akers in Berlin and Washington. The invitation had come from the Baptists. They were joined, after early hesitations, by the former state churches, the Federation of Evangelical Churches. They all prepared on a national basis so all of East Germany became aware that Billy Graham was coming.

When the difficulties had been smoothed away, the visit nearly had to be cancelled because in late August 1982, while in the state of Washington for the Spokane crusade, Billy had gone for a walk in the nearby mountains with his youngest son, Ned, and had fallen several feet off a wet rock and injured his back. The physicians, supported by the Board of the Graham Association, wanted him to take three months' sick leave. So much was at stake in East Europe that Billy declined the advice, but throughout the tour he was not in good health. Haraszti, as his personal physician when they were traveling together, insisted that he use a large car so he could lie full length on the journeys. Large cars in the lands of the Eastern bloc are generally limited to state or party officials. The use of one by Billy Graham caused a little heart burning among Christians, but it was necessary. In addition, the team usually had to stay at hotels reserved for foreigners, though at Görlitz they had the pleasure of staying at the church house at the invitation of Bishop Wollstadt.

The twelve-day tour was grueling, despite the support of Cliff Barrows, whose preaching was another highlight for the Germans. Myrtle Hall, the black singer whose glorious voice delighted audiences at Graham crusades throughout the world, greatly added to the joy. Apart from the burden of the preaching, the group meetings over meals, and the private interviews with leaders of church and state, Billy had an additional stress. In a Communist country, his every statement would be scrutinized, especially by Westerners, for its political meaning, even when his intention was purely religious. In East Germany whatever he said, or did not say, would be criticized by someone. He could only follow his own goal: to preach the Gospel in season and out of season, and depend on Christ's promise: "It is not you that speak but the Spirit of your Father who speaks in you."

Sometimes Billy longed to relax when the schedule demanded that he give his next address. Yet whenever he mounted a pulpit, he would be conscious of an extraordinary access of strength; weariness was forgotten and the power flowed. His faithful interpreter, Reinhold Kerstan, felt the same. Kerstan, born in Berlin, had emigrated to America when he was a young Baptist pastor. He made a most notable contribution to Billy Graham's ministry. The Germans felt that they were not listening to a foreign preacher because the rapport was so close between the two.

Many pastors had been afraid that Billy would not be able to understand the problems of the ordinary believer in an atheist society. The churches in East Germany had privileges denied those in other Communist lands, such as retaining ownership of hospitals and social institutions, and having their own schools for training, yet no one from outside could comprehend fully the spiritual background, trials, and complexities of daily living.

Billy's reading, personal contacts, and preparatory work and experiences of his staff had briefed him thoroughly, and he came with a strong desire to learn. In his preaching and conversations, Billy sought to encourage. In his interviews with high officials of the state, he pressed on them the civic loyalty and high moral standards of the believers, as well as speaking of his own personal faith. He brought a message of purity and peace through the Cross. Because he preached truth, his words went to the heart, especially of the young. And his hearers knew instinctively that Billy's words came from the heart. "He lived his convictions," said Chief Departmental Head Heinrich, officially an atheist, who traveled everywhere with the team. "His conduct was the witness."

Christians had a deeper explanation. Pastor Hans-Günther Sachse, as one of the organizers of the tour, saw much of Billy, whom he had not known personally before. "I could not help having the impression that here is a man who shows a unity of life and word. The people see that the man is behind the word. I think that this really is a radiating out power, given by the Holy Spirit."

It reached out not only to Christians but to Marxists in their atheism. In one city, a senior member of the clergy noticed how the district and civic leaders, having officially greeted Billy with flowers on his arrival at the church door, went to the seats they had reserved for themselves, though normally they would never attend a church. "They listened to Billy Graham intently. It was obvious they were under the influence of his preaching. And when the word of God is being preached, it cannot go away void and empty. One of the officials could quote Billy Graham six months later."

Billy's eleven-day visit to East Germany helped Christians endure the seven more years of atheist oppression before the fall of the Berlin Wall.

At Stendal, a small city north of Magdeburg, Billy was to preach in the evening in the twelfth century Lutheran cathedral of St. Nikolaus, which is really two churches divided by a great screen, an architectural curiosity that could be used as a pulpit on great occasions. It is reached by a very narrow twisting stairway.

Early in the afternoon, a large number of young people from Stendal and surrounding cities gathered in the forecourt of the cathedral. The sight attracted others who came out of curiosity. The doors opened and the church filled up with 2,500 people, who were mostly young. About an hour before Billy Graham was scheduled, they started singing. The quiet Christian songs and the sight of so many worshipers were unforgettable to young and old. "Our state officials," recalls one of the clergy, "were deeply impressed to see that many people, causing no disturbance, behaving decently, and come together for the sole purpose of hearing the Word of God."

A Czechoslovakian Baptist pastor, Jan Kriska, had been an atheist in his youth. Several of his companions rose to high positions in the Communist Party and the state. He had long nourished a hope of bringing in Billy Graham for a preaching tour, but his government friends laughed at the very idea. Early in 1982, however, one of them told him that after Billy's visit to Moscow, they would consider him for Czechoslovakia.

In due time Kriska sent a letter, which was handed to Billy in Moscow, inviting him to stop in the Czechoslovak Socialist Republic on his way home in May. He was unable to accept. After negotiations by Smyth, Haraszti, and Akers with Czechoslovak officials in Washington and Prague, a five-day visit was arranged to follow East Germany.

Billy flew from East Berlin after a delay from bad weather and rested three days in Vienna. Here he was brought the final schedule for Czechoslovakia. He winced when he saw it. From his arrival and press conference at Prague airport on Friday, October 29, which was shown on state television, until his departure on the following Thursday morning, his days were full to the limit of his strength.

In the beautiful city of Prague with its historic buildings, Billy preached on Sunday morning in the Baptist church to 1,200 people. He then preached in the evening at St. Salvator, a seventeenth century church of the Evangelical Czech Brethren, which is the largest Protestant building in Prague. Wherever he preached, tickets were issued through the churches, to prevent overcrowding. The demand exceeded the supply, and St. Salvator could have absorbed considerably more than the 3,000 who listened to Billy that night. Scores who could not show a ticket were courteously turned away by the police, who would not permit them to linger outside during the service.

The Czechoslovaks loved Billy's simplicity, directness, and little touches of humor. In Prague, in Brno, chief city of Moravia, and at Bratislava, the city on the Danube, which is capital of the Slovak republic, there were memorable incidents. A hundred strong youth choir in Prague, with the men in blue suits and white shirts and the women in blue skirts and rose-colored blouses, sang contemporary Czech Christian music and then joined Myrtle Hall, who had sung spirituals, in a rousing "Amen." In Bratislava, a forty-member children's choir sang in front of the pulpit and then presented Billy and each member of the team with a red rose.

At Brno in the Hussite church, seventy people came forward for counseling—so many that they had to be directed into side rooms after the service. But at Bratislava, in the modern church building of the Brethren, the twenty-five were able to kneel at the pulpit. This was the first time in Billy's ministry in a Communist country that inquirers had come forward publicly during the service. Among them was a farmworker whose mother was a Christian. He had rejected faith, got into bad company, and become an alcoholic. He went forward in repentance and faith. Late that night on the twelve-and-a-half-mile (twenty-kilometer) journey home by train and bus, he was singing the songs he had learned at the meeting to the surprise of neighbors who knew him as a drunk. At home he told his wife. She began to cry, threw herself on her knees, and prayed aloud to be freed from chain-smoking. She gave her life to Christ. Both of their children became Christians, and the whole family was baptized together.

Though only about ten thousand people in Czechoslovakia heard Billy Graham in person, many millions heard him on television. The state television and radio were opened to the Christian Gospel during Billy's visit, the first time in a while. Christians wept with joy when they found that his testimony to Christ was not cut from television news. At Lidice, in the memorial gardens on the site of the village that the Nazis had wiped out with virtually all its inhabitants, Billy laid a wreath and made a strong declaration against nuclear war. Television viewers also heard him say: "There is no excuse for terrorism, whatever goals it may claim. There is no excuse for the oppressive domination of one nation by another. Terror breeds terror, and cruelty breeds cruelty. How can this cycle be broken? As a Christian, I believe the basic need in our world is for a radical conversion of the human heart, a conversion which God can bring, and which will replace hate with love, greed with compassion, and the lust for power with sacrificial service."

Billy also laid a wreath at the Slavin monument near Bratislava. Some Czech and American Christians had been upset when this engagement was announced, because Slavin is a memorial to the Russians who died in war. Then churchmen, atheist state officials, and the television viewers saw the text on Billy's wreath: "Greater love has no man than this, that a man lay down his life for his friends [John 15:13]." He spoke not only of Americans and Russians who had died for the liberation of Czechoslovakia from the Nazis; he turned the occasion to the glory of God. "Those of us who are Christians are reminded of the greatest sacrifice of all, the sacrifice of Jesus Christ who gave his life on the cross so that we might be freed from slavery of sin and death. He died not just for one individual or one nation, but that people from all nations might put their faith in him and acknowledge him as Lord of all. Today he commands us to turn from our selfish way of living and follow him in loving service and witness."

Such words had never been heard on Czech state television. Marxists might complain that "he is putting this Jesus Christ into everything," but many among the young, who in Czechoslovakia were taught indifference rather than open hostility to Christ and were left ignorant of Christianity, were listening. Requests for Bibles showed a marked increase. Christians found neighbors more willing to ask about Christ.

Billy Graham made a deep impression on the whole nation. State officials, to whom he spoke frankly about his own faith and about the problems and sufferings caused by the Marxist attitude to religion, were almost as warm as his Baptist hosts in pressing him to return for a longer visit. And the encouragement to ordinary Czechs and Slovaks to be true to their convictions was surely a step toward their recovery of freedom only seven years later.

22

NEW ENGLAND

"I HAVE HAD THE PRIVILEGE OF PREACHING THIS GOSPEL ON EVERY continent and most countries of the world" Billy once said. "And I have found that when I present the simple message of the Gospel of Jesus Christ with authority and simplicity and quoting the very Word of God, he takes that message and drives it supernaturally into the human heart—whether it's at a university or whatever group it may be in. It is a supernatural message, a supernatural authority, a supernatural power, the power of the Holy Spirit.

"So when I stand up to preach the Gospel today, I no longer worry about whether anybody is going to respond or anybody is going to find Christ. I know that in every audience I talk to there are some people whose hearts God has prepared if I am faithful in presenting the message of Christ. I may not see any visible results. We are not to preach for results. We are not to count. We are to be faithful and vindicate the righteousness of God by presenting his Word."

Billy is always keenly aware that he is on a battlefield: "Especially at the invitation there is a great spiritual conflict. This is part of the evangelistic service that wears me out physically and psychologically and spiritually more than any other. I sense that Satan is battling for the souls of men." Yet giving the invitation can bring him personal blessing. "Many a time under my own preaching I've recommitted my life to the Lord, standing there—because we all have moments when we feel that God is speaking in a very special way to us ... and many times I come forward with the people, in my heart, to make a recommitment of my own life."

The conflict and the blessing were real wherever he preached, and the opportunities seemed limitless. Billy was receiving such a stream of requests from every continent that he could have spent all his strength, and his team's resources, holding crusades overseas, ignoring the equally full stream of requests from home. Love for his own country, his desire to help the churches, and to call yet more Americans and Canadians to Christ's service throughout the world made him reserve a part of every year for North America. Moreover, without these crusades, which usually were shown nationwide on television later, he would have lacked the prayer support and finance that enabled him to hold missions in lands where the church might be small and money short.

Therefore, Billy and the team had crisscrossed the North American continent, holding three to five carefully prepared crusades every year, at cities chosen for their strategic importance to a whole region.

The New England crusade of March to June 1982 stands out historically for the width of its range and the boldness of the strategy, and for its impact that exceeded even the expectation. Billy's director of North American crusades, Sterling Huston, had outlined a boldly imaginative plan to reach all New England, the only part of the United States that thinks in regional rather than state terms. It is also the greatest center of learning and higher education. The plan had emerged after Allan Emery, then president of the Billy Graham Evangelistic Association and a prominent New Englander himself, had taken soundings throughout the region. It called for a four-pronged approach: Billy would give evangelistic lectures in the universities; his associates would conduct seven crusades in cities of the six states from Maine to Rhode Island, with Billy preaching at the concluding rallies. Then an eight-day Billy Graham crusade would follow in Boston. Finally, a few weeks later, a television crusade could reach into almost every home in New England.

Sterling Huston, with his team directors, found at once "an overwhelming sense that we were about to experience God at work. The people were hungry for renewal, ready to devour any training and preparation that we could offer. At Providence, Rhode Island, for example, our team counselor training instructors were teaching every night of the week. We were unable to have more than four class locations, but at every location there was standing room only, and we had to move to larger facilities. Over and over again, our committees requested more instruction, more assistance, more guidance. They wanted to make sure that they did absolutely nothing that would hinder the work of the Holy Spirit through the Crusade ministry in their city."

No less than twenty-five institutions of higher education requested an evangelistic lecture by Billy Graham. The plan allowed only for five. The selection committee had a most difficult task. And such was the sorrow and complaint of universities that were declined, that Billy agreed to speak at another seven.

At Harvard he spoke twice. By common consent, these lectures were the high point of his university tour. On April 20, he spoke at Harvard's John F. Kennedy School of Government and the following day at Memorial Church.

Some people had been worried that an official invitation to a famous evangelist would create dissension in the secularized, sophisticated world of Harvard. His lecture at Kennedy was given at their regular *Forum,* which distinguished statesmen had addressed. Professor Peter Gomes, the Harvard University chaplain, described the lecture as "an elegant and deeply moving *apologia pro vita sua,* which won many heads and hearts." Billy held his cautious and critical audience spellbound as he spoke frankly and humbly of the lessons learned in his pilgrimage and of his conviction that true peace lies only in knowing Jesus Christ.

The address at Memorial Church on the following evening was the first by an evangelist since George Whitefield, more than two hundred years before. Billy was somewhat conscious that he stood before a university. Some of those present wished he had preached with his old, free fervor, for which the modern student was more ready than his predecessors. As it was, Billy could sense that his listeners were open to the Gospel, and he tried to adjust his sermon accordingly. The program, in the form of a Sunday service, did not allow him to give the invitation to come forward. Chaplain Gomes, however, told Billy to give the invitation if he wished. Billy decided to keep to the original plan. More than a hundred response cards were handed in.

"Your mission was a great time for Christians here at Harvard," wrote the assistant minister, "and has had a real effect upon the whole university." Yet it was only one episode in the grueling schedule in New England, made more strenuous because Moscow and London for the Templeton prize, had to fit in the middle.

"While you have been in Russia," wrote Jim Roberts, one of the chairmen, and himself a convert of an earlier crusade, "more than 3,000 New Hampshirites have been rejoicing over the results of the Dr. John Wesley White/Billy Graham Rally and Crusade held in Manchester. We had that many people working together to make the effort a success and all of us are praising God for the results.

"There were more than 10,000 present at your May 1 afternoon Rally and 1,000 came forward. More than 1,000 also came forward during the six nights with Dr. White. How thankful we are for all of this and how grateful we are to you for including New Hampshire in your ministry. With the state population of only 800,000, you can quickly see how profound an effect all of this will have."

The climax came in Boston, and with it the rain. The worst storm since 1906 hit Boston on the closing Sunday afternoon of the crusade, June 6, 1982, yet 19,000 went to Nickerson Field on the Boston University campus to hear Billy Graham. "With their faces almost hidden by rainhats, raincoats, and umbrellas," recalls Sterling Huston, "the crowds of people sat on chairs, bleachers, and even on the wet artificial turf, which in some places was covered by several inches of water that had accumulated over the weekend."

All of Boston was amazed that so many should go to an open stadium when the weather forecast offered no hope of a letup in the rain. When Billy gave the invitation, nearly a thousand splashed through the mud to make a decision for Christ and were joined by another thousand to counsel them. Rain cascaded on counselors and inquirers during the vital first moments of follow-up.

"The presence of the Holy Spirit could not have been more real in any of the previous evangelistic thrusts or awakenings in the history of New England," wrote the crusade chairman, Lawson L. Swearingen, to Billy. "Although I had faith to believe that New England would respond when I agreed to devote two years to this project, I could never have sensed the magnitude of the response; and now that we have experienced it, I am more convinced that the awakening is real, and that some of us should devote the next few years to make the most of the possibilities."

Prayers could not cease, nor the great reservoir of counselors melt away, for a few weeks after the Boston crusade came the fourth stage of the New England campaign. The Houston crusade was being shown across the nation. In New England it was delayed one week and shown with shots of the Boston crusade hurriedly edited in. In September the Boston telecast itself was shown. By this means, a high proportion of New England's 13,000,000 inhabitants had heard Billy Graham in 1982, either in person or on the screen.

The television ministry was made all the more effective by the development of telephone counseling. The team had tried this experimentally for years, adapting the idea from the call-ins used by politicians. Finding an effective way became a particular ambition of Sterling Huston, who wanted to see a narrowing of the gap between the high numbers of viewers who were moved toward commitment to Christ by a telecast, and the comparatively few who afterward became strong Christians. He recognized that many viewers could never be adequately counseled by mail.

In May 1980, three weeks after the Indianapolis crusade, the team set up a number in the city with forty lines and showed telecasts of three of the meetings. They received an encouraging 800 calls. That November, when the Reno crusade was to be carried live on three Christian networks, the team opened 150 lines at Minneapolis. Despite the limited viewing, 15,000 people called, many of whom made the same commitment as at a crusade. After a telecast in March 1981, counselors dealt with 7,000 telephone inquirers but were astounded to learn that 73,000 attempts were registered by the telephone company's computer.

By the time of the telecasts of the Boston crusade, the team was using 557 lines in six centers in the United States, with 4,000 trained counselors on the phones. (An early experiment of having less lines and a "callback" offer, as at Melbourne in 1959, was dropped because few callers would give their number until trust was established.) Every time Billy Graham goes on television for three nights, some 20,000 people are counseled by telephone, yet careful survey has shown that a further 40,000 may have tried and given up.

According to the team, "People struggling with alcoholism, suicide, illness, adultery, abuse, marital problems, and the occult all seek spiritual help. Some receive Christ, others only talk about their problems and then hang up. Atheists, agnostics, Satan worshippers, and others call to challenge the counselors." The bulk of those who call are in earnest. A telephone inquirer has chosen to watch the telecast, write down the number given, then call at his own expense (one American Indian youth walked a mile to a pay phone to seek counsel). "We find," says Huston, "that they are much more ready to receive Christ and receive spiritual help than many who come forward at crusades. They have a real responsiveness: they want help and they trust the people at the other end." By September 1983 nearly 200,000 people had been counseled by telephone, extending Billy Graham's ministry, through modern technology, without adding a mite to his physical burden.

At the end of 1983, the telephone ministry was taken a further step, after the crusade in Oklahoma City that October. Charlie Riggs, head of counseling and follow-up, and his assistants held training sessions in twenty-five cities of the state of Oklahoma. In December, when Billy Graham telecasts were shown on three nights, and the telephones began to ring, the answering counselor would ask the caller at the end of their conversation if he or she would like someone in their city to visit the next morning. In this way, the contact was quicker, local, and more personal.

Sterling Huston sums it all up. "We have been astounded by the demand and the spiritual hunger."

23

AMSTERDAM 1983

IN THE EARLY 1980S, BILLY GRAHAM FOUND ANOTHER BURDEN weighing on his heart. Six years after the Lausanne Congress, he had no doubt that it had been epoch making with profound consequences to the strategies and growth of the Christian church throughout the world. Yet neither Lausanne, nor Berlin eight years earlier, nor the regional congresses, nor the conference at Pattaya in Thailand four years after Lausanne, had been quite what Billy had intended when he had first thought of the idea in the late 1950s.

The congresses had done much to define and strengthen evangelism, but they had been meeting points for leaders, staff officers, and generals of the Christian churches rather than for the foot soldiers on whom all depended. Billy thought continually of men and women, mostly unknown, who, like the apostle Paul and Timothy, did "the work of an evangelist," often enduring hardship and poverty and sometimes persecution. Those who pushed bicycles through jungle trails to proclaim Christ from place to place, or held missions in dense urban areas at the invitation of churches, or used other means.

Billy had no idea how many there were, but he determined to hold an international conference to help them. It would be specifically for *itinerant* evangelists, otherwise any local pastor who counted himself an evangelist might expect to be asked. Never in church history had there been an international conference of evangelists.

It would be sponsored and organized by the Billy Graham Evangelistic Association, who would also raise funds. Every participant would pay at least part of his expenses, and some would pay all, but no one would be kept away by the cost of travel. Billy asked Walter Smyth to be executive chairman. They chose Amsterdam for its excellent communications and facilities, and because hardly a country in the world would withhold visas from citizens whose destination was Holland.

They set the date for ten days in July 1983. Billy appointed Werner Burklin as director, a West German who had worked for Youth for Christ and for the team on both sides of the Atlantic. Werner built up an international staff of men and women with different skills and backgrounds. As he said, "[They were all] competent and above all spiritually motivated. To everyone I hired I said, 'As the staff goes, so will the conference.' And I was convinced that everyone had to live a holy life, not only in the office but off working hours."

Werner Burklin, on his own initiative, traveled all over the world to explain to church leaders the kind of men and women who were intended to be participants. He knew that in some countries, the leadership would expect to nominate themselves or their relations or the usual conference hoppers. In other countries, no younger person would dare apply if older men wished to go or even if they had declined. But Werner's explanations opened the eyes of local leadership to Billy's vision, and news of the coming conference spread quickly into the remoter areas of lands far distant from Amsterdam. Billy had laid down that 70 percent of the participants should come from the Third World and that a good proportion be under forty.

Unlike Lausanne, where the participants were nominated by committees in their own countries, the Amsterdam secretariat made the final decision on every invitation after sifting through the advice from handpicked screening committees. This ensured that each participant came as an individual rather than to balance a delegation or represent a viewpoint. Originally, Billy had planned for 2,500, but applications poured in and continued to arrive even after the conference began, totaling 11,000. The secretariat found it heartbreaking to refuse suitable applicants when the conference was already full. Even the smoothest arrangements could not handle too big of a number if the purposes were to be fulfilled. The final figure was almost 4,000. Yet, to the last moment, the staff did not know if every air ticket had reached its destination, or whether participants from more distant corners would negotiate the hazards of travel or local regulations to arrive on time.

On the hot evening of Saturday, July 12, 1983, the International Conference of Itinerant Evangelists, "Amsterdam 83," opened in the great hall of the RAI center. As the organ played, a citizen of every country that was represented brought his national flag to the platform in a colorful procession. Flag after flag came by, an impressive witness of the spread of the Christian church, until 132 flags were on parade. That evening, after the ceremonies of welcome, Billy Graham gave the keynote address: "The Evangelist in a Torn World," the first of five addresses, including a question and answer session, he gave in the ten days. Well-known names from the East and West also spoke at the plenary sessions, which were interpreted into nine languages, and at the workshops in the middle of the day, when the participants separated into smaller groups according to language and interests.

From the start, Amsterdam 83 proved to be a most happy conference. Lausanne, struggling with mighty issues, inevitably had its tensions, which were absent from Amsterdam where the atmosphere immediately became relaxed and joyous. Most of the participants had never traveled outside their own countries. They delighted to share and pray with kindred spirits from other lands, and to discover that their problems and pressures were not peculiar to themselves. Many had never seen more than a few hundred Christians together; now they could sing, pray, and listen with thousands. Many had suffered from lack of spiritual counsel. Amsterdam provided trained counselors to whom they could unburden in confidence. And all along, in the broiling heat wave, they were learning fresh methods and finding better ways, or contributing their own hard-won experience. Nor were practical needs forgotten. Evangelists from the Third World were given cassette-players and clothing for themselves and their families provided by Dutch Christians and administered by Samaritan's Purse, the relief organization headed by Franklin Graham, Billy's elder son.

Billy himself was in effect the conference's host for the ten days. At Lausanne he had deliberately kept in the background. At Amsterdam he was on the platform, with Cliff Barrows and Bev Shea, and introduced the speakers and shared his knowledge and memories. The affection of five continents flowed toward him from the massed participants, not least those from Eastern Europe, who included two Orthodox Metropolitans from the Soviet Union. The East Germans were delighted to see him relaxed and in good health. "Graham in Amsterdam was more mobile, active, joyful, free than he was in our country."

The conference ended after ten days with a great service of Holy Communion conducted by the Bishop of Norwich from England, when the 4,000 participants and the stewards and staff took the elements together. Previously, they had read aloud in unison the fifteen Amsterdam Affirmations: A small committee had worked long hours to draw up affirmations that would express the heart of the conference and provide a nonbinding code of belief and conduct. Thus the thousands who were present had words in which to rededicate themselves to the proclamation of the Gospel by life in the power of the Holy Spirit and to the building up of the church. "We share Christ's deep concern," was the fourteenth affirmation, "for the personal and social sufferings of humanity, and we accept our responsibility as Christians and as evangelists to do our utmost to alleviate human need." The final called on the whole body of Christ to join in prayer and work for peace, for revival and evangelism, and for "the oneness of believers in Christ for the fulfillment of the Great Commission, until Christ returns."

Amsterdam had reaffirmed, as Billy put it in his final address, "that while the social needs of man call for our urgent attention, we believe that ultimately these needs can be met only in and through the Gospel. Man's basic need is to be born from above—to be converted to Christ. Man must be changed. Man's biggest problem is man himself."

Amsterdam 83 did not end when the participants scattered to the four corners of the earth to put into practice what they had learned. Billy appointed John Corts from his team to head a follow-up office based on Amsterdam. During the conference, as John wrote, "We saw so many opportunities, so many needs of evangelists that would break your heart." The Association wanted to be a catalyst to make the needs known and to help supply them. A worldwide Fellowship of Itinerant Evangelists would form a loose link. Membership would probably grow to some 40,000. Plans were already forming for a second conference, since Amsterdam 83 had been unable to take all who applied and should have been there. The follow-up office would promote the high standards of personal and vocational life, which the conference had emphasized, and would act as a clearing house for fresh ideas.

The possibilities were as limitless as the need. Billy Graham had sent a surge of encouragement across the world. He had strengthened the rising generation. Helped by hundreds, from famous speaker to humblest youthful steward, he had been the human agent in a spiritual renewal that only the future can measure.

Part Four

1984–present

24

THE QUEEN'S GUESTS

IN JANUARY 1984, THE QUEEN AND THE DUKE OF EDINBURGH invited Billy and Ruth Graham for a weekend at Sandringham, with Billy to preach the Sunday morning service in the parish church. On Sundays during her winter holiday in Norfolk, the Queen usually had the Bishop of Norwich first and then other bishops to preach and stay. For a non-Anglican, non-British preacher, a Sandringham weekend was therefore an exceptional honor.

Billy had attended private luncheons with the Queen on several occasions since his sermon at Windsor in 1955, but this invitation was special. As soon as the rector of Sandringham had brought the Grahams up to the house on the Saturday afternoon, the Queen began to ask about his Mission England, the forthcoming series of stadium meetings across the country being prepared for that summer of 1984. He thought that perhaps the Queen hoped her invitation would focus the attention of the nation.

The next morning was bitterly cold and snow was falling fourteen miles away, yet over 2,000 people stood outside the little village church in the park, listening to the entire service by loudspeakers. In the church, the royal family sat in the chancel. The nave holds only 115, with the robed choir, and all were either members of the royal household or parishioners or their houseguests. The rector, Gerry Murphy, had visited every family in his group of parishes the previous week, and some came who seldom went to church. The congregation was the nation in miniature: the sovereign and her subjects.

The hymns and lessons focused on the Good Shepherd. Then Billy mounted the ornate pulpit of oak and silver, a gift of an American millionaire in memory of King Edward VII. Behind Billy stood a silver processional cross, which was 400 years old. Above him was the bas-relief portrait memorial to King George V.

As usual, Billy planned to begin with a little humor. "That day at Sandringham in my notes I had scribbled out in my own handwriting a number of possible stories—about four or five. I didn't know, until I stood up, which one I was going to tell." Wanting to put at ease a fellow guest who was a Roman Catholic and a keen horseman, and knowing the enthusiasm of the Queen and the Queen Mother for bloodstock breeding and racing and that most of the congregation were used to cattle and horses, he told the story of the Baptist from Texas who went to the New York races.

The Baptist noticed a Catholic priest bless a horse before each of the first four races. The horses that he blessed all won. So when the priest blessed a fifth horse, the Texan backed it with everything he had. Halfway through the race the horse dropped dead. The Texan ran up to the priest to complain. The priest said to him, "You must not be a Catholic, my son."

"No, I'm a Baptist."

"Ah, well," the priest replied, "If you'd been a Catholic you'd have known the difference between a blessing and the last rites!"

When the burst of laughter subsided, Billy had the entire congregation in his hand. He preached on the Twenty-third Psalm, which had been sung earlier to Crimond. Speaking quite fast, he gave a simple, strong message of hope, for he showed how the Good Shepherd meets the human problems of sin, suffering, death, and the future. Everyone is searching for purpose and meaning in their lives. Their souls needed to be restored to God. "God is saying from the cross, 'I love you. Turn to me.'"

After the service the Queen, the Queen Mother, and the Duke stood with the Grahams and the rector in the churchyard for a photo, another exceptional gesture ordered by the Queen. After the Royals had left (the Grahams were going to a reception at the rectory before returning to the house for luncheon), Billy Graham spoke to the millions who would watch the news that evening. "My job is to be faithful, to proclaim the Gospel wherever I am.... It is always a time of tremendous soul searching for me, and a great privilege, with a sense of humility and unworthiness, to preach the Gospel at anytime."

Back in London, Billy had numerous official and media interviews. At Lambeth Place, the Archbishop of Canterbury (Robert Runcie) hosted a reception for fifty church leaders, drawn from every denomination, and gave them three reasons why he warmly welcomed Billy Graham and supported Mission England. Billy went to 10 Downing Street for a private talk with the Prime Minister, Margaret Thatcher. Afterward, she personally escorted him to the front door, a favor usually reserved for heads of State. That evening, although very busy, she attended the reception in his honor in the State Apartments of the Speaker's House, which the Houses of Parliament Christian Fellowship had put on. The Fellowship had been founded nearly thirty years earlier as a direct result of Harringay. Mrs. Thatcher not only stayed for the buffet supper and Billy's talk, but also for the question period. In the words of one of her close aides, "A great mark of her admiration and appreciation of Billy Graham and all he stood for—and had done for the British!"

Billy was returning to England as the result of many years of persistence by British evangelicals that he should again hold a nationwide crusade or mission. In the years since the 1967 All-England crusade by television from Earls Court, Billy had been back for several more limited occasions. In 1973 he held a youth training week in London's famous Olympia Stadium. In 1980 he returned to both Oxford and Cambridge Universities and felt that the response in Cambridge was deeper than in 1955. But despite formal invitations to return for a national crusade, Billy was convinced that the time was not ripe. He would have sectional but not fully national support.

Finally, in July 1981, a small high-powered group representing both older and younger generations, led by Gavin Reid, later Bishop of Maidstone, presented a plan to Billy in person while he was staying in the South of France. They were sure more than ever that England was a mission field needing a clear, resounding proclamation of Christ and his Cross, and that Billy Graham was the only man on earth who could bring the English churches together for a mission that would command the nation's attention.

Their plan was for a three-year "Mission to England with Billy Graham." The first year, 1983, would be for prayer, local evangelism, and thorough preparation by the churches. During 1984, Billy would preach at missions, eight days long, in different regions of England except London, using the football stadiums of strategically placed cities. The effect would be cumulative, right across the nation. (A mission to London with Luis Palau was already being planned by him independently.) The third year, 1985, would not merely follow up converts: The Billy Graham missions would be the launching pads of an even wider evangelism, in market towns, cities, and the countryside, as each diocese and district made the most, under God, of the interest and spiritual hunger and the flood of new converts eager to pass on their faith.

The group begged that they might return to England and say that Billy was willing to come, and that it would be the summer of 1984, if—. The "if" was that the churches understood that he was not coming to do a crusade in itself like Harringay or Earls Court, but to share a three-year, open-ended endeavor by them all.

Billy replied: "You are asking me to come and do something *for* you, and I am not sure whether that would be right. If you are asking me to come in and do something *with* you, I find that very exciting." He agreed, exceptionally, to hold open an entire three months until they could test the response.

During the autumn of 1981, the plan was put to each region in a genuine sounding of opinion. All five responded favorably. A little incident at Norwich was a token of what might happen. When the speakers were eating lunch after the meeting, they were interrupted by their waitress. "Do you mind if I say something?" They looked up surprised. "I do hope Dr. Graham comes back. Because twenty years ago it was he who ... well ... brought me to God!"

Despite the favorable response, Billy did not give an immediate acceptance. Then he went to Blackpool in the last days of February 1982—the time when he was deciding finally about Moscow—to address the Christian booksellers conference.

He had accepted the invitation because of the affection of the whole team for the conference secretary, Jean Wilson, formerly of his London office. Once it was announced that he would be coming, West Lancashire Christians had begged that he stay on for a mini-crusade. The thorough preparations, size, warmth, and affection of his audience at the two rallies, and the high response to his closing invitations to decide for Christ, moved Billy Graham profoundly. The local press gave generous coverage, commenting that he had drawn the largest audiences in the town's history. Although, said one paper, there were other famous evangelists in America, "none is more welcome on this side of the Atlantic than Dr. Graham himself. His message to mankind does not change and is so simple that a child can understand it."

After Blackpool, Billy went to Manchester for a private meeting of clergy and laity drawn from the five proposed regions. The title "Mission England" was proposed and adopted to cover the entire three-year concept. A formal invitation was drafted, typed out, signed by all who were present, and given to Billy Graham. He had no further hesitation. Within a few weeks, he sent his acceptance for the summer of 1984.

The concept caught on at once. In one region, which was not originally included in Billy's schedules, the three diocesan bishops had approached the Mission England office and secured a change of plan. Another bishop whose diocese was not well placed geographically for the stadium chosen for that region, tried to get his city included, but the schedule was now as full as Billy's strength would allow.

The time seemed ripe, a new spirit stirring in the nation, a new hope and sense of purpose. The courage and sacrifices of the war in the South Atlantic had crystallized a widespread desire to return to Christian values. All over the country, men and women were recognizing the emptiness of the materialism, permissiveness, and self-seeking that had sapped the national character. They looked for deeper answers to the fearsome problems and anxieties of the age. Ears and hearts were open again to the message of Christ.

During 1983, the preliminary rallies and preparations for Mission England were already bearing fruit. Local leaders, a small central office, and members of the Billy Graham Team all worked closely together and many imaginative plans were in progress. "What we long to see," said Walter Smyth, "is that this mission—six centers but one mission—should be the beginning of spiritual renewal throughout Great Britain."[12]

Billy's preliminary visit in January 1984 ended with a great rally in Birmingham where he addressed 11,800 ministers and lay leaders who had converged on the National Exhibition Center from all six regions, despite snow.

"As I look upon the vast masses of this country and think of Mission England," he told them, "my own attitude is this. I say, 'Who is sufficient for all of these things?'

"I come in May with my team in fear and trembling. I come rededicating my life afresh and anew to the Lord Jesus Christ and the ministry of the Gospel. I come with a sense of expectancy that God is going to do great and mighty things beyond which we could even dream today. . . . All the elements of successful evangelism seem to me to be present in the preparation of Mission England. The harvest is white; the instruments provided by modern technology are sharper; and because of spiritual hunger, the urgency is greater.

"You are beginning to see for yourselves that this is not a Billy Graham affair. It's all of us working together, a team of people working for three years—a year of preparation, the year of public meetings, and then the year of follow-up in the churches. . . . I believe we can see England touched for Christ this summer. I believe we can see a new sense of moral values. We can see a turn-around in the country.

"And this could affect the world. Because, whether you like it or not, England is still looked upon by the rest of the world for moral leadership. . . .

"I want you to know that I will come here on my knees as your servant—not as a great preacher or great evangelist, but as a servant in Christ's name to serve you, to join hands with you, and to give our very best for the sake of the Gospel."

25

MISSION ENGLAND

B ILLY ARRIVED IN LONDON ON FRIDAY, MAY 4, 1984, WITHOUT
a voice. During the recent Alaska crusade, it had given out
entirely during a sermon, due to laryngitis. He had recovered and
finished the crusade, but the trouble had resurfaced.

He was taken at once to a Harley Street doctor he knew and
trusted, who decided to find a specialist. After fruitless calls because
of the holiday weekend, he approached a leading ear, nose, and
throat surgeon a few doors down the street, who saw Billy at once
and arranged to operate with laser techniques in his usual hospital
at 8:00 next morning.

Waking from the anaesthetic, Billy murmured to T. W. and
Maurice Rowlandson that they had better cancel his engagements.
They told him to rest. The surgeon had promised that Billy would
be well enough to preach that Sunday evening. He went from hospital bed to Westminster Chapel, the famous and large Free
church. He preached in little more than a whisper (well-amplified)
with a box of tissues at hand, for a possible nose bleed, and the
plastic tag on his wrist. Gavin Reid noted that he was obviously
weak, but when Billy "made his famous call for people to leave
their seats and 'accept' Christ, the first fruits of what was to be a
record harvest were there for all to see as some 200 people came
forward." He returned to the hospital and the next day, still not
discharged, attended a lunch given in his honor by Rupert
Murdoch, the owner of *The Times,* for the editors of the national
papers. They appreciated his personality and mission. Thus

Mission England had a most understanding national press from the start, in contrast to 1954.

By the opening of the first mission ten days later at the Ashton Gate football stadium outside Bristol, Billy was not only recovered but had fulfilled a grueling schedule of media interviews and the making of a four-part program for the BBC. And England was ready. Across the nation, over 100,000 had been involved in preparations. Of these, nearly 50,000 had attended Christian Life and Witness classes and 14,000 had attended the follow-up training course. Of particular value was the new concept, which would become a feature of crusades all over the world: Prayer Triplets— three people, each selecting three friends they wished to pray for, would meet to pray that all nine would come with them to the meetings and go forward. An estimated 30,000 groups were praying for 270,000 people.

At Bristol, thousands converged on Ashton Gate from throughout the southwest and south Wales in happy anticipation and an almost picniclike atmosphere. Ruth Graham had hoped to fly over to join them, but was taken to the hospital for surgery. As Billy began, he could reflect that thirty-eight years before, in bomb-damaged Bristol, he had preached the first sermon of his first little-known mission to England with Cliff Barrows, in a small backstreet Gospel chapel, long since demolished. And both George Whitefield and John Wesley had first preached in the open air at Bristol.

The Bristol mission exceeded the organizers' rather cautious expectations, not merely in the figures (nearly a quarter of a million attending over the eight days and 20,000 of them coming forward) but in the momentum it generated, not least by videos of the meetings shown in churches and halls. "A new emphasis of outward looking and mission has begun," wrote the area director, Anthony Bush, six months later, "and is still underway in hundreds of churches. A vicar wrote recently from Calne in Wiltshire saying, 'I am thrilled with the number of parish missions that have sprung up throughout the area since Ashton Gate.' Ashton Gate was a marvelous focal point that fixed the attention of over a thousand churches in the southwest on evangelism. The fact that God moved more than 20,000 people to respond to Billy's appeal has given people confidence that conversions are possible and lives are changeable in the power of the Holy Spirit. A mission took place in four little villages near Glastonbury recently at which a hundred people came to the Lord in one week. A church in Corsham is fuller now than it has ever been since it was built in 1900 or so. Many churches report larger congregations than they have had for many years."

Anthony Bush was a farmer. One morning during the mission, he took Billy with T. W. out to the dairy farm. "He seemed very relaxed and most interested, and reminisced about his early days helping on his father's dairy farm. . . . A humble and 'ordinary' man when visiting my farm became a giant of communication and spiritual conviction on the platform." Looking back seventeen years later, Anthony Bush highlighted the "wonderful cooperation between a broad band of churches, which resulted in the most exciting series of giant meetings ever seen in the West. Thousands of Christians giving their time and talents over eight days, and for some, much longer, to see a wonderful harvest. A real sense of excitement and happiness."

Billy was not satisfied with his Bristol sermons. On the train to the next mission at Sunderland for northeastern England, he asked Gavin Reid to help him assess and improve them. When an aide demurred that he had not done at all badly (with that response of 20,000), Gavin "saw the only touch of iron in the man that emerged all summer. 'No!' he almost snapped. 'You *know* it wasn't good. I've got to do better.'" In England, background knowledge of the Bible and Christian belief and terms was more faded among the mass of the people than at the time of Harringay in 1954 or even of Earls Court in 1966. The secularization of Britain had gathered pace despite the zeal of the Christian minority. Billy must make sure that his every sentence could be understood by all ages and cultures, every illustration appropriate, that the issues of sin and salvation be so clear so that every hearer be brought face-to-face with Christ.

At Sunderland, the catchment area for the mission at Roker Park Stadium was heavily industrialized, with much unemployment, and affected at that time by the miners' strike. Billy made a point of meeting a group of unemployed men. They so impressed him that he often referred in his preaching to all he learned about their frustrations and difficulties. The northeast had been called the graveyard of evangelists, but the people flocked to hear Billy Graham, many out of curiosity.

The greatest contrast with Bristol came with the cold and the rain and the biting wind blowing in from the North Sea. "I had on long underwear," Billy recalled years later. "I had on my heavy wool suit, I had on the heaviest wool coat I could get, I had a scarf around my neck while I was singing, and I had a hat on for the first time in my life preaching. I was so cold I could hardly get my mouth opened!" The hat was a cap that Billy had with him, unaware that in the northeast the cap is a trade mark of "Geordie" working-class men, immortalized in the comic strip *Andy Capp*. It endeared Billy to the people.

Yet on the coldest, wettest night when numbers were down to 10,766, almost the lowest of the summer, more than 1,500 people came forward to stand in the bitter cold and rain after Billy had given the invitation—the highest percentage of the whole mission.

From Sunderland, Billy went south again to Norwich in East Anglia, as predominantly rural as the northeast had been industrial. The bishop of Norwich, Maurice Wood, when vicar of Islington thirty years earlier had been one of Billy's chief supporters at Harringay. Wood's suffragan (assistant) bishop of Thetford, Timothy Dudley-Smith, the distinguished hymn writer, had been the founding editor of *Crusade,* the British magazine launched as a consequence of the Wembley crusade of 1955. He was now chairman of the local Mission England committee. The scattered population and comparatively poor communications of Norfolk, with the cautious attitude of many churches despite the Episcopal leadership, had made preparations slow. And the Norwich mission had a particular handicap because the Carrow Road football ground had been reseeded. The directors were adamant that no one should walk on the turf. Even the platform had to be cantilevered above it. Inquirers therefore could come no further than the dusty red perimeter track, with the counselors facing them as they came down from the stands instead of joining them as they walked toward the platform. These factors helped to lower the statistics. But the four days at Norwich saw happy crowds who listened to Billy Graham in silent concentration. One Norfolk landowner had given tickets to tenants and agricultural workers on his estate. The next morning one of them jumped off the tractor to shake his hand, exclaiming, "If everyone listened to Billy Graham there wouldn't be no wars!"

Geography and history dictated that the East Anglian region must have two venues, north and south. Billy therefore agreed to return to Ipswich in Suffolk, as rural an area as Norfolk, for the final four days of the whole series, following a short rest and then a week each in two metropolitan areas.

The Ipswich mission director, Victor Jack, wrote many years later, "All the memories I have of Billy and Cliff Barrows and team are totally positive. Billy was a joy to work with and I found him a very humble man who was totally open to what we felt was best for the area." Billy was particularly keen to be accessible to local people. When he received dignitaries, he took close interest in their activities and families, "after which he always shared with them a potted version of his message for that night. The natural and spontaneous way in which he shared the good news of Jesus was very impressive."

Numbers could not be so high as in the big cities, but the effect was considerable. Churches that had worked in isolation or rivalry came together in the preparations and in the projects that followed.

The training in prayer and in the disciplined nurture of converts bore fruit, not only in the follow-up of the mission, but as an integral part of many church programs in the following years. Thus a Christian night school was started in the cathedral city, Bury St. Edmunds, to build on the interest and interchurch cooperation.

Before Ipswich, Billy had preached at stadiums in Birmingham and Liverpool, centers of huge populations. These missions could be counted among his great crusades. Birmingham, with its big Asian and African minorities, brought all colors and races to crowd the stands. And the huge television screen imported from Japan was in full use for the overflow in the park beyond the stadium. The mission chairman, David MacInnes, was fascinated to find "a younger generation who was thrilled to hear a man in person who was something of a legend from the past. It was intriguing too how many came with the intention of being converted! It was as if the mission freed them from the pressure of peer group and media agnosticism. It was all right to be converted by Billy!" Some of Billy's talks were "quite rambling, and yet when the challenge came at the end, the air was electric, and I remember a large burly police inspector with a huge moustache coming down from the top of one of the stands with tears running down his cheeks."

Then came Liverpool, a city where poverty and crime had recently sparked riots. Historically, it was deeply divided by a great barrier of mistrust between the mainly Irish Roman Catholics and the Protestants. The coming of David Sheppard, famous as a cricketer, to be Anglican bishop of Liverpool and of Derek Warlock to be Roman Catholic archbishop had opened a new era as they worked together in a way never seen before in Liverpool. Bishop Sheppard had been Billy's supporter when serving among London's poor. He and Worlock brought their people right behind the Mission England preparations. They had to overcome local prejudices. Thus, at the opening service at Liverpool's famous Anfield football ground, it was realized that a Roman Catholic archbishop on the platform might anger extreme Protestants. The two prelates therefore sat together with other church leaders in the press box, from where the bishop of Liverpool came to the platform to welcome Billy on behalf of all the churches.

Huge crowds came, mostly from the immediate neighborhood of the city and suburbs. Their good humor was very impressive in a region of tensions, although they were noisy, talking during testimonies and singing along with soloists. One night the widow of the legendary Bill Shankley, the manager who had made Liverpool Football Club world famous, was present. Cliff Barrows led the crowd in the club's anthem, "You'll never walk alone." He made the slight change of "Walk on ... walk on ... with *Christ* in your heart...." They sang it movingly with great power.

Billy's addresses were heard in profound silence and led to the highest response of the six regions (27,412 inquirers in eight days), especially among the young.

Between May and July, from Bristol and Sunderland to Liverpool and Ipswich, more than a million people had attended. As in previous crusades throughout the world, Billy heard many stories of lives turned around and families reconciled, like the man and wife at Bristol who were engaged in divorce proceedings. Each came separately; each went forward. Meeting to mutual surprise at the bus stop, they soon tore up the divorce papers.

Surveys a year later found that a high proportion of those who had gone forward were keeping true to their commitments and many others were being brought into the churches, for the third follow-up year of the three-year mission had already begun as Billy, after a rest of less than three weeks, went to preach in Korea and then in cities of the Soviet Union. In England, the momentum quickened when in July 1985 he returned for an eight-day mission in Sheffield, which had pleaded to be part of the 1984 series, but could not be included. Billy had been doubtful whether to return, but was convinced of the need by the suffering caused in that area by the failed miners' strike. During the mission he talked with the miners' leader, Arthur Scargill, and visited a mine. Sheffield was a specially happy mission for Billy because Ruth was with him, and leaders noticed how close they were and her positive influence on his ministry.

The response at Sheffield went beyond all expectations, with a total of 26,000 coming forward, two-thirds of them being under twenty-five. On the final night, the stadium was crammed with 49,500 people. Several older evangelical ministers wept as they exclaimed that they had never dared expect to see such a sight in their beloved city.

Nor was the mission confined to Sheffield. About four months earlier, David Rennie of London, founder of an electronic business and organizer of relays from earlier crusades, pointed out that it would now be possible to transmit the Sheffield mission by satellite. Fifty-one locations across the British Isles were chosen for Livelink missions, small or large, prepared as if Billy would be present in person. And because the satellite was positioned over Nigeria, the meetings were watched in Zambia and carried by national television in Zimbabwe. The effectiveness of these satellite missions determined Billy and his advisers to explore the possibility of reaching the whole world, although, as Billy said, "Modern technology is no substitute for old-fashioned praying."

As for Sheffield itself, the mission chairman, Philip Hacking, wrote sixteen years later that "this event brought us together in a way that has never been destroyed. There have been slips along the way, but the church was given new confidence." This was true across all the regions. One bishop wrote that the impact had been much wider and deeper than was generally realized. "As I traveled around the Diocese a year after the mission, I find parishes that have been greatly influenced by the experience, but not in ways one can analyze statistically. I mean that for parishes of all ecclesiastical traditions, outreach has become much more central to their life as well as the nurture of Christians new and old."

Four years later Billy came again for the three weeks Mission 89, which covered Greater London. He preached in Earls Court once more, and in two other centers, and one morning in the Guards Chapel next to Buckingham Palace, to the First Battalion, Coldstream Guards, at the invitation of the Commanding Officer.

These missions from 1984–89 formed an important foundation for the Archbishops' Decade of Evangelism before the millennium year. And, as in the crusades of 1954–55, they increased the numbers of men and women offering for Christian ministry. The effect on the national culture was less than in 1954–55 because of secularization, aided by the lure of humanism and Eastern religions and the pace of life, but they had reemphasized for England the power of straightforward preaching based on a clear proclamation of the life, death, and resurrection of Christ and his power to redeem.

26

ROMANIA AWAKES

WHEN A HUGE FRIENDLY CROWD NEARLY CRUSHED BILLY Graham in the square outside the Orthodox cathedral in the Romanian city of Timisoara in September 1985, no one realized that this was a foreshadow of the revolution that began four years later by another huge crowd in that same square, who overthrew the ruthless atheist dictatorship of Ceausescu. Nor did anyone realize that Billy's preaching tour of the country was unwittingly an important step toward Romania's recovery of freedom.

Romania, like Poland, is mostly a religious country, predominantly Orthodox, but including a strong Reformed minority and a growing Baptist and Pentecostal presence. It was now in the grip of Nicholas Ceausescu, his family, and the secret police. The people seemed powerless against Ceausescu's personality cult and almost absurd building schemes, his growing personal fortune while their standard of life declined, his discrimination against believers.

In 1977 Bucharest suffered a severe earthquake. When Walter Smyth brought a contribution from the Billy Graham Evangelistic Association's World Emergency Fund, he made tentative inquiries about an invitation to Billy, but the government and Orthodox leadership were against a visit.

Two years later, Alexander Haraszti began prolonged negotiations. He knew that the government wanted the United States to renew Romania's so-called Most Favored Nation status in trade, and by July 1983, he had convinced Ceausescu's ministers that if they were to persuade Congress, against all the evidence, that there was religious toleration in Romania, they must invite Billy Graham. The Orthodox patriarch was, therefore, apparently informed that he must come, but the government wanted to ensure that few people would hear him. It did not allow advance media interest or posters or public notices outside churches. However, the leaders of all the denominations, including the Orthodox, worked together to make the visit a national occasion.

Billy Graham and his team, including Franklin Graham, arrived at Bucharest to an official welcome on Friday, September 7, 1985, and flew some two hundred miles the next day to Suceava in northern Moldavia. The Romanians had provided two Russian-built planes. One was for Billy and his party, and the other was for his radio, television, and film crews and equipment. This support had been agreed to grudgingly, and only because the government expected that relays would be little needed and that their own technicians, under the eye of secret policemen disguised as tourist aides, could censor the Americans' shots for the film to be shown on television.

On arrival at Suceava, Billy was taken by Metropolitan Teoctist into the glorious scenery of the mountains to visit several ancient monasteries with their remarkable wall paintings, inside and outside, by which the church, in earlier centuries, had taught Bible stories and the great Christian truths when the country people were illiterate. Billy was struck by these paintings and referred to them in his sermons. And his Orthodox hosts were immediately drawn to Billy, "by his warmth as a personality," recalled Father (later Bishop) Nifon, "his spiritual warmth, by his calmness."

While Billy was in the mountains, people were already converging on the monastery of Verona in the plain, a fair distance from the city. The Metropolitan had graciously arranged that Billy's visit should be on the Sunday of a festival in honor of the Virgin Mary, which always attracted many thousands of pilgrims, together with a traditional market. The monastery had a large walled courtyard with a wide-open space beyond. The team's technicians, under

David Rennie from London, had spent the day mounting loud-speakers on the wall so everyone could hear. In the evening, as men, women, and children were already camping on the open space, a state official hurried back to the city and demanded that Haraszti order the technicians to redirect all loudspeakers inward to the courtyard, for as in all Communist countries, legal religious activity was restricted to church property. Rennie had to round up his men from their hotels.

The next day as Billy was driven out to Verona, he overtook a stream of people walking or riding in carts toward the monastery, where he was astonished to find a crowd, estimated at 30,000, jammed together in the courtyard and in the church, with a further 10,000 beyond the wall. The festival liturgy continued for nearly two hours. A group of Pentecostals who were standing in the church grew restless and began quietly singing evangelical hymns, which was somewhat embarrassing for Billy because it showed a lack of courtesy to his Orthodox hosts.

At length the liturgy ended and the Metropolitan brought Billy to a pulpit arranged overlooking the courtyard and introduced him with warmth and graciousness. Billy's sermon was translated phrase by phrase as he spoke of the beautiful scenery and historic associations he had seen and of his own farming background. He then wove his message around the words of the Virgin Mary about her Son, "Whatever he says to you, do it," leading to a plain unfolding of the need to be not only devout but to receive Christ into the heart. The Virgin they honored in the festival wanted us to trust in Jesus alone for salvation, for that is what he says we should do.

The next morning Billy was flown to the industrial city of Cluj-Napoca in Transylvania, which had been part of Hungary before 1918 and had a largely Hungarian population, a cause of political tensions. As Billy recalled in his memoirs, "Both the Romanian government and the local ethnic Hungarian leaders attempted to pull us into the controversy—something I was determined to resist." Nothing, however, could dampen the zeal with which both civic and church leaders made him welcome with banquets and sightseeing. He was scheduled to preach in the Reformed cathedral. At the luncheon, the Roman Catholic bishop begged him to preach also in St. Michael's Cathedral, an invitation gladly accepted.

That evening as he was driven toward the first service, people were standing six or seven deep in the streets to greet him. Both cathedrals were packed to the limit even though the Catholic bishop's last-minute invitation had never been publicly announced. Permission to put relay television screens in other churches had been revoked. Rennie's men had erected loudspeakers outside, as agreed by the authorities, but they stayed silent, officially because of a short circuit. However, it was later learned that the secret police cut the wires.

The Director of the State Office for Church Affairs, Ion Popescu, always outwardly friendly, was becoming alarmed at the great crowds determined to hear Billy. Each evening as Smyth, Haraszti, and Akers hammered out the next day's arrangements with him, he twisted and turned. On one evening, Akers had to report to Billy a danger that the tour would be stopped and Billy expelled, but the international furor would have been too great. Popescu tried another tactic. Before they approached the city of Oradea, he told Billy that the Baptist church (where Billy particularly wanted to preach) desired only a short greeting, not a sermon. And the Baptists were told that Dr. Graham was now very tired and wished to be brief. The tour was indeed exhausting, especially as in Transylvania his every sentence must be interpreted twice, into Hungarian and Romanian.

The Second Baptist Church at Oradea had been a center of controversy for many years. Its rapid growth in membership caused the Communists to persecute pastors and members, then to announce that the old building must be demolished to make way for housing, a threat not carried out owing to international concern and the intervention of the American ambassador.

Early in the morning of Tuesday, September 10, people wanting to hear Billy were already arriving from all over the region, drawn by word of mouth and announcements on foreign radio. "By 5 A.M. they filled the streets around the church and the traffic was stopped," recalls the younger of the two pastors, Paul Negrut, then aged thirty-two, who had given up his profession as clinical psychologist four years earlier and had already been confined six months in a military concentration camp for his faith. The police and city authorities demanded that he and the senior pastor, Nic Gheorghita, dismiss the crowd. "We didn't dismiss the crowd. We spoke to the deacons of the church and took all the pews out from the building so we could get in as many people as we can. Then when we saw that the crowd was still growing, we discussed with the deacons and took the loudspeakers of the church and put them in the trees and on the rooftop of the buildings surrounding the church so the crowd could hear. We were arrested for that and threatened with prison if we do not bring the loudspeakers in. We refused." One deacon, stringing a loudspeaker to a tree with the eager crowd milling around, retorted to a policeman who ordered him to take it down: "I can't. You do it if you want to be killed!"

The pastors were not allowed to meet Billy earlier to discuss the meeting. They waited in the church where every inch was filled. "At five minutes to 7 P.M.," continues Negrut, "when Dr. Graham came with the team, the official interpreters, and a number of secret police officials dressed as tourist agents with tourist agent badges, one of them got so confused that he missed the chair where he was assigned to sit on the left-hand side of Dr. Graham. But he left that chair empty. I immediately took it and whispered: 'Dr. Graham, I don't know what they told you, but they told us that you do not want to preach. Probably they told you that we asked that you do not preach. Are you willing to preach for an hour tonight?' And he said, 'Yes, my brother.' Then I jumped and grabbed the microphone and I welcomed Dr. Graham not as a political leader or as a politician but as an ambassador of Christ. And I asked the crowd,

'Are you willing to stand for an hour and hear Dr. Graham preach?' And the roar came from the crowd, 'Yes.' So that was it. Dr. Graham accepted the challenge and he preached for one hour, an extraordinary message on the healing of the blind man Bartimaeus. He spoke about the blindness, the darkness of sin, what it means for people to live without God. He gave an invitation and so many people on the streets, in the building, in the corridors of the building, people raised their hands. Nobody could see them but just those around them, and God."

Billy was deeply impressed by the spiritual hunger of Romanians of all ages, not only in Oradea, but in each of the six provincial cities and Bucharest where he preached. The most astonishing scene of all came in Timisoara, the very city where the revolution broke out four years later. And although without the slightest political intention, it seemed in hindsight like a dress rehearsal.

Timisoara had a large population of both Hungarian and Romanian. Billy was scheduled to preach in the magnificent Orthodox cathedral, which stood in a square at the head of a broad street. During the day he was taken on a walk around the historical sites, in the center of the city, stopping to talk to passersby by interpretation. Meanwhile, hundreds upon hundreds of men, women, and children, with a very high proportion of young people, were converging from all over the region to see and hear him. By the time his motorcade attempted to approach the cathedral, the wide street was blocked by a sea of humanity, a vast friendly crowd estimated at 150,000, who cheered and sang as Billy walked, smiling and waving, along a corridor cleared by police and helpers. This was an astounding sight as the crowd parted, then reformed behind his party up the long street to the cathedral steps.

Once again, every inch in a cathedral was packed, with 6,000 standing shoulder to shoulder as Metropolitan Corneanu led Billy to the front of the icon screen while a choir in the balcony sang hymns. He preached from Paul's address on Mars' hill in Athens very simply with illustrations. Outside, the huge crowd could see loudspeakers, but again they were silent, the wires cut or disconnected by the Communist authorities. Many people, unable to hear the preacher they had come to hear, became so restless that the police sent for reinforcements, fearing a riot.

Billy reached his final words: "I say to you tonight: Come with Christ, stay with Christ, go with Christ.

"Let us bow our heads and pray silently. You pray for yourself. Ask God to search your heart. Are you prepared to meet God? Does he have first place in your life? Is he the Lord of your life?

"Can you say in your heart, 'I *do* want him to be first in my life. I want to have the assurance that I really know Christ. I want to work for him. I want to be the kind of man or woman that God wants me to be'? Then I ask you to raise your hand, and I will remember you in this closing prayer.

"O God, we thank thee for the people here tonight who are holding up their hands. May this be a life-changing experience for many people. In Jesus' name. Amen." Hundreds of tape recorders clicked off; thousands of hands shot up.

When the service ended, the Metropolitan escorted Billy through the congregation, into the foyer where they were singing "How Great Thou Art," and onto the floodlit outer steps. As soon as Billy and the Metropolitan emerged, the crowd surged forward with a great chant: "Billy, preach to us. Billy preach to us."

"But without amplification, I could not do so," records Billy, "nor would the police have allowed it.

"As we came down the steps, the crush of the crowd was so great that I didn't know if we could make it. The people were very warm and friendly, though; even if I couldn't preach to them, they wanted to see or touch us."

In Haraszti's words: "Billy Graham was knocked sideways, nearly to the ground. The police were terrified, scrambling to get us out of there. I truly thought we would die in the crush. There was no fear. I just thought, *What a way to go, to die beside Billy Graham here in Romania.*"

The Communist government had wished and expected very few to hear Billy, but 150,000 had come, drawn by a word-of-mouth network. No one dreamed that three years later, on December 16, 1989, an equally big crowd would throng that street and square to stop the arrest of a Protestant pastor, the event that sparked the revolution.

In Bucharest, President Ceausescu was so alarmed and surprised by the multitudes in city after city that wanted to hear Billy that he cancelled his scheduled meeting with him, lest it seem an endorsement of what had happened. "He may also," as Billy commented in his memoirs, "have interpreted the huge crowds as a cloaked demonstration against his regime. In some ways I was sorry; I had been looking forward to sharing my faith in Christ with him."

Four years later, the dictator was executed. Freedom returned. Perhaps Paul Negrut of Oradea was justified in his conviction, uttered in September 1985 while Billy Graham was still in Bucharest, that his visit was "one of the most important miracles at the end of the twentieth century here in Romania." It proved beyond doubt, as Negrut said later, "that faith in God is stronger than atheism, Communism, and Marxism." Hundreds of thousands of people across the country came to hear the Gospel preached, "coming freely—nobody pushed them—when Communist leaders could not gather a crowd unless they forced people through company leaders, secret police, and Communist activists." The people's response to the preacher of the Gospel showed that faith in God was having the upper hand in the country of Romania.

Negrut was charged with politically slandering his country and placed under penal investigation for six months. To Negrut, the Graham tour was an encounter between the kingdom of darkness and the kingdom of light. "And what was special about Dr. Graham was that his message was not simply a sermon; it was the real presence of God. And the Word of God came alive so powerfully that even in 2000 we baptize people in our churches who accepted Christ in September of 1985 when Dr. Graham preached in Oradea and other cities of Romania."

In the years following the revolution of 1989, Billy Graham's daughter Anne Graham Lotz visited Romania twice in her Bible teaching ministry. She was astounded to learn that Christian leaders were convinced that her father's visit was a vital factor in the dictator's overthrow: "For years and years Communism had told them that God was dead, that the church was defunct. And then Daddy came, and when people turned out by the thousands, they suddenly knew that they had been lied to, that there were people of faith all over the country. This insight revealed that there were not only spiritually oppressed people who yearned for a Savior, but politically oppressed people who yearned for freedom. They had been so isolated in their thinking—they didn't even know that there were other people who thought like they did. Daddy came in and suddenly they not only knew there were thousands of people who desperately wanted to be set free spiritually, but also politically. All of a sudden the light came on."

27

$\mathcal{R}$EACHING $\mathcal{O}$UT TO $\mathcal{W}$ASHINGTON

B ILLY GRAHAM HAD DECLINED SEVERAL INVITATIONS TO HOLD a third crusade in Washington, D.C. The year 1952 had confirmed him as a national figure. He had held a second crusade in 1960 in the closing months of the Eisenhower presidency. "Washington," covering a far wider area than the District of Columbia, was an uneasy mixture of groups and professions, divided politically and socially, with extremes of wealth and poverty. In the District itself, by 1986, the resident population was predominantly black (they were not yet known as African Americans), and Billy was determined not to come for a crusade except with the full participation of black religious and civic leaders. In 1960 the black churches had mostly kept aloof. Crime, homelessness, hunger, drugs, and prostitution were rampant in the shadow of the Capitol. Billy longed to minister to all who actually lived in the District as well as to the politicians, lawyers, service people, and diplomats of Washington who lived in the suburbs.

By 1986 Billy was able to accept, for the invitation had the full endorsement of the most prominent blacks, including Dr. Ernest R. Gibson, senior pastor of the First Rising Mount Zion Baptist Church and director of the National Capitol Council of Churches. In 1960 Gibson had opposed; in 1986 his enthusiasm for a crusade was the key to black participation. The controversial mayor, Marion Barry, and his predecessor, the greatly loved Walter Washington, were also endorsing the crusade.

Ernest Gibson became cochair of the executive committee with Colleen Townsend Evans. The former actress who had known the Grahams since the Los Angeles crusade of 1949, Mrs. Evans had moved to Washington when her husband, Louis Evans Jr., had been appointed senior minister of the National Presbyterian Church. She was the first woman to chair a Billy Graham crusade. Black and white together, each with wide contacts and experience, the Evans-Gibson team became a powerful force for good. Each subcommittee also had black and white cochairs, so that "unity was built into the process," as Colleen Evans put it, "but also unity happened as we met together for a year planning the crusade. We fell in love with each other. It was wonderful and then when Billy came, that wonderful, disarming, loving personality, he was so willing to meet with black leaders, to meet in quiet, unpublicized back rooms. He, I believe, convinced the black community of the love of the white community."

Washington 1986 broke new ground, beyond the normal preliminary rallies and training, in being much more than the eight days (April 27 through May 4) of services in the usual pattern. It covered a longer period in which Billy came five times for a few days. He made unpublicized visits to soup kitchens, old peoples' homes, missions working among the homeless, drug addicts, and alcoholics.

Billy also met privately with high-level groups. On March 4, he went to the Pentagon to a luncheon attended by the Joint Chiefs of Staff and their civilian equivalents. Billy did not give an address but answered questions and discussed points, "a very good and lively dialogue around the table," in the opinion of Mark Petersburgh of the Christian Embassy, one of several small private organizations dedicated to the spiritual welfare of government officials at all levels. Two days later Billy spoke on the Twenty-third Psalm at a luncheon for eighty of major general's rank or above. Some of them had met him in the battlefields of Korea or Vietnam when they were younger. Some would be senior commanders in the Gulf

War five years later. The impact of his words could be symbolized by the major general who was crying as he came up to Billy and silently shook his hand before leaving without a word. Every guest was later given a copy of *Peace with God*. On other visits, Billy spoke at luncheons for the judiciary and for editors.

President Reagan, an old friend, would be out of Washington during the crusade, but Billy dined with the Reagans at the White House on March 21, as often before. He had talks with Cabinet ministers including Vice President Bush together with Secretary of State Schultz. George Bush, a longtime personal friend, looked to Billy Graham as "pastor to the nation." These "wonderful one-on-one quiet meetings," as Colleen Evans termed them, kept strictly private, were an important aspect of his pastoral ministry. Doug Coe, organizer of the National Prayer Breakfasts, who over the years had often been present as Billy's confidential aide, commented in 1986 that "it is not really as much what Billy says as his presence. The Gospel can be preached powerfully by presence. And I have watched it many times when he sits down personally with people whether there is one person, two people, five or ten people, he just can talk about the weather and about what is going on that day around the world, or whatever, but the people are irresistibly drawn, and are never really satisfied until he begins talking about the Lord."

Thus, in Washington, many people who had spoken with Billy in private were present when he spoke or prayed in public. On March 19, as guest chaplain, he opened the sitting of the House of Representatives with prayer and was the guest of honor and speaker at a House-Senate luncheon, and then, in an unscheduled stop, sat in on the weekly Bible study attended by members from both the House and the Senate.

On April 23, four days before the crusade began, Billy opened the proceedings of the Senate with a long prayer, thanking God for his grace to the nation and for "the firm moral and spiritual values of our forefathers." He continued, "But, our Father, we confess we are in danger of slipping away from the moral and spiritual values which have made us great. We are in danger of losing our way in the midst of other voices that would urge us to put our trust in man rather than in you." He prayed for spiritual awakening; he prayed for blessing on their families, for wisdom for "each elected Senator," and for the president. He ended with, "Give us a new passion for justice, a new zeal for peace, a new commitment to compassion and integrity, and a new vision of what you desire us and this Nation to be."

The assistant secretary of the Senate determined that the prayer should be inscribed on vellum. She gave it to the chaplain, Richard Halverson, a strong supporter of the crusade, to hang in his office. Halverson suggested that every senator should have a similar, finely inscribed copy for his office and received many expressions of appreciation when this was done.

The crusade, so long prepared, opened at the Washington Convention Center on the afternoon of Sunday, April 27, 1986. George Bush, with Barbara beside him on the platform, welcomed the 21,000 people jammed together in a remarkable display of ethnic unity—blacks, whites, and Hispanics together, with a vast choir directed by a black with Cliff Barrows. The Convention Center was not an easy venue, but Billy wished to hold the crusade in the District itself, not in a more convenient building in the suburbs. The final service on Sunday, May 4, took place at the Robert F. Kennedy Stadium, with 36,000 attending and 2,215 coming forward.

The crusade had followed the usual pattern, including a Love-In-Action program to give food to the homeless and deprived. The thousands who came forward were from all classes and colors, including many regular church people from the suburbs who had never made a personal commitment. One leading pastor nearly jumped off the platform when he saw one of his most wealthy and respected members, whom he knew had never taken the step of faith, waiting humbly to be counseled.

Beyond the hundreds of individual stories was the wider impact that gave a new unity to a deeply divided city and a new strength to the churches. Cities and suburbs, black and white, were doing things together that they had never done in the past. The national capital's population is inevitably always changing, so that, in one sense, the crusade's local effect cannot easily be assessed years later. But as one leader said with conviction later that year, "There is no voice for Christ more influential in the nation's capital than Billy Graham's." And Billy had no other interest than to promote Christ. Many Congressmen were influenced for good. Ten years later Congress would mark its respect and gratitude in a special way.

28

$\mathscr{S}$IDELIGHT ON $\mathscr{A}$MSTERDAM II

A YEAR AFTER BILLY GRAHAM'S SECOND WORLD CONFERENCE for evangelists, Amsterdam 86, a member of his team who had a leading role in the preparation of both conferences, put down his thoughts. Bob Williams later became Director of International Ministries on the retirement of Walter Smyth, but died of lung disease at the age of fifty. He had done much to prepare the third millennium conference of evangelists at Amsterdam in August 2000 and died on the day after it ended.

His comments throw light on the importance of Amsterdam 86. He writes: "Following Amsterdam 83, my personal feeling was one of having left a task unfinished. While Amsterdam 83 was very successful, I was concerned with the number of qualified, committed, but very needy, young, unknown, uneducated evangelists who had applied but were turned away due to the lack of space and finances. During the preparations for Amsterdam 83, I personally reviewed every single application. I knew the kind of people that were being turned away. I knew their quality, their commitment, their need. I knew that their ministries were struggling due to the lack of training and guidance in the field of evangelism. Therefore, when the decision was made in the summer of 1984 to conduct Amsterdam 86, I was excited and relieved that we were given an opportunity to complete the unfinished task.

"In the fall of 1984, eight of us spent five months in the suburbs of Atlanta reviewing all that we had done in 1983, and being constructively critical; all of our work was directed toward perfecting the processes and procedures, but all of our prayers were directed towards the Lord giving us real sensitivity to the persons to whom we would be ministering through Amsterdam 86.

"We reviewed the 8,000 applicants who were turned away in 1983. We decided to develop a more detailed application process and ask everyone to apply again. We also wrote to over 750 denominational leaders, leaders of parachurch organizations, religious schools, theological colleges and seminaries, sharing with them the kinds of individuals who would benefit the most from Amsterdam 86. We strove to communicate that Amsterdam 83 and hopefully Amsterdam 86 were not really conferences. They were in essence 'Training Schools' for the young, uneducated, unknown itinerant evangelist who may have some form of Bible training but very little training concerning the practical 'how to's' of evangelism. We weren't certain these leaders would understand our goals. We were also fearful that they might simply recommend themselves and some of their more highly educated colleagues rather than the 'little' men and the 'unknown' men who did not have such a high profile and were not considered to be leaders.

"To our amazement, over 50,000 recommendations were made by these leaders and almost 30,000 applications received. We put more attention on trying to get not only many countries that were not represented in Amsterdam 83, but many regions within countries. In 1983 we had 40 or 50 participants from Brazil, but most of them were from the coastline cities such as Sao Paulo and Rio. For Amsterdam 86, we strove to find the evangelists who were working in the jungle, in the northern part of Brazil along the Amazon River—evangelists with less support and with a greater task ahead in some of those unreached areas of the country. We were very effective in getting a more broad cross-section of each country and also a cross-section of the denominations within the countries. We also worked to move past the typically evangelical aligned denominations and into more mainstream denominations that were not necessarily evangelical but had evangelical and evangelistically minded individuals, hoping in essence to infiltrate those organizations and create a greater commitment and desire for evangelism. This same process happened in other countries such as Ghana, Nigeria, Sri Lanka, Mexico, etc. We were much more successful in getting a more representative group of evangelists.

"We also recognized that there were part-time evangelists who were also part-time pastors or school teachers or government workers, etc. In a lot of countries where finances were low and the economy difficult, very few evangelists were capable of supporting their ministries unless they had a pastorate or job. We felt that we were by-passing some of the most effective if we were not giving the appropriate attention to those who were part-time. Amazingly, most of the part-time evangelists were doing more evangelism than most Western full-time evangelists.

"We also discovered that in some cultures evangelists are not recognized unless also attached to a church in some form of a pastor or assistant-pastor position.

"We had many difficult moments as we were reviewing the applications. With India, we had received over 3,500 but were capable of accepting only 500. We filled 465 of the available positions with very qualified applicants. We realized at that point there were only 35 places still available but over 350 additional competent, qualified, committed applicants. We could not believe that we had to eliminate nine out of ten. At that point, Mark Abraham and I, who were working on that particular country, were overwhelmed with emotion. We went through the 350 applications two or three times, trying to narrow the 350 to 35. But, every time we read the applications to determine which were better qualified and more in need of the conference, we were overwhelmed with emotion, realizing that these people had a passion and a desire to preach the Gospel but were crippled by the need to learn from others, to be trained, encouraged, inspired, equipped. We felt almost as if we were potentially making or breaking ministries because we knew that Amsterdam 86 was that important, and their ministries were vital to the people of the world to whom they'd been called. Many of them would become discouraged and disgruntled and would leave evangelism unless they had the encouragement and training of Amsterdam 86. Only a Sovereign God could bring the right people and keep the wrong people away and allow those who were to come to Amsterdam to go back and reproduce in the lives of those who were unable to come.

"The preparations for Amsterdam 86 were much more difficult than 83 even though we were trying to learn from our trial and errors and lessons of Amsterdam 83. To double the number of participants from the 5,000 of 83 to the 10,000 of 86 did not simply double the work but in many cases quadrupled it. In 83 we dealt with 35 hotels but in 86 we surveyed over 350 hotels and finally contracted with 85 and in addition built a dormitory about 25 miles from Amsterdam to house about 4,000 participants. We dealt with one airline in Amsterdam 83 but because of the great number of seats needed to bring people into the conference from 174 countries around the world, we dealt with initially 62 different airlines and finally contracted with about 25.

"Simply writing people and telling them that 'no, they couldn't come,' required more personnel, translators, language ability, equipment, more office space, since there was much more knowledge of our task and our goal, much more enthusiasm around the world, much more desire to attend as a result of the perceived success of Amsterdam 83.

"The Lord brought us a tremendous staff, committed to the principle of remembering that we were dealing with not only process, procedures, and papers but with people. We were committed to being most effective and efficient, especially with the big money items such as the millions of dollars spent on airlines and hotels and meals. Every time we lowered the cost by 1 percent or 2 percent, we were capable of bringing more people. Our airline, hotel, and meal costs were averaging 43 percent cheaper than in

1983 due to our gained expertise in dealing with the airlines and hotels. The logistics were absolutely phenomenal and the statistics were staggering. Bringing 10,000 staff, stewards, participants, program personnel, media people from 174 countries; housing them for 10 and sometimes running up to as many as 20 nights, providing meals and the various diets that were required due to health problems or cultural concerns. But our staff was committed and for that we are very grateful.

"The work was long and seemingly never ending. The more we reached into the jungle and out to the outer islands to find the deserving evangelist, the more difficult our task of even communicating to him since many countries simply do not have mail systems outside the major cities.

"I don't believe we will ever be able to know the true results of the Amsterdam conferences. How many evangelists have continued in the fight for precious souls who would have become disheartened or discouraged without the encouragement, inspiration, and fellowship of Amsterdam? How many more people are reached by the evangelist who is even a little more effective? How much more reproductive are the converts who experience better follow-up, growth and integration into the body of Christ due to evangelists placing more priority on and being more effective in follow-up due to training regarding follow-up and discipleship at Amsterdam? How many people really heard the Gospel for the first time due to the evangelist learning how to make the Gospel message clear, simple, and authoritative?

"How many evangelists are leading more committed, pure, holy, and powerful lives due to the emphasis on the evangelist's personal life? How many returned to their patch of the world to preach Jesus Christ with power, purity, and success? How many returned 'to teach others also' the things which they learned at Amsterdam? Only the Lord knows."

The hard work of Bob Williams and his team, of the conference director, Werner Burklin, and all others involved bore abundant fruit.

As Billy Graham wrote in his autobiography, "From the opening ceremony—with its torchbearers, parade of flags, and lighting of an Olympics-style 'flame of salvation'—the multinational, multiracial, multilingual, multidenominational throng sang, prayed, studied, and witnessed as one in Christ." On the last night, following the service of Holy Communion with more than 10,000 communicants, the same torchbearers rekindled their torches from the central flame they had ignited on opening night. "Lifting the torches high, they carried them from the meeting to symbolize carrying the light of Christ to all the continents of the world.

"As convener and honorary chairman of the conference, I hoped the participants would return home with my words ringing in their ears. 'Our primary motive,' I told them, 'is the command of our Commander in Chief, the Lord Jesus Christ.... We are under orders. Our Lord has commanded us to go, to preach, to make disciples—and that should be enough for us.'"

A personal experience of Billy and Ruth beautifully sums up the spirit of Amsterdam 86. With several thousand other participants, they had entered the huge dining hall and happened to sit down next to an African and shook his hand. Billy recounts the experience: "From his clothes, we suspected that he came from a poor country and had very little. But his face had a gentleness and joy about it that was immediately apparent; it also revealed the sense of purpose and commitment I had seen often during the opening days of the conference.

"'Where are you from?' I inquired.

"'I am from Botswana.'

"In response to my gentle prodding, he told us something about his ministry. He said he traveled, often on foot, from village to village, preaching the Gospel of Christ to anyone who would listen. It was, he admitted, discouraging at times, with frequent opposition and very little response.

"'Are there many Christians in Botswana?' I asked.

"'A few,' he replied. 'Only a very few.'

" 'What is your background? Did you go to a Bible school or get any education to help you?'

" 'Well, actually,' he said, 'I got my master's degree from Cambridge University.'

"I was immediately ashamed that I had stereotyped him as an uneducated man. I was also humbled, not only because he was far better educated than I was, but because of something else: Any man returning to his underdeveloped homeland of Botswana with a coveted Cambridge degree would have virtually unlimited opportunities for political power, social position, and economic advancement. And yet this man was completely content to follow Christ's calling for him as an evangelist. He could truly say, in the apostle Paul's words, that 'whatever was to my profit I now consider loss for the sake of Christ' [Phil. 3:7].

"Who could say what impact for Christ a man like this would have in the Africa of the future? I said a silent prayer of gratitude for his dedication, and for the opportunity God had given us to bring together such a unique group from across the world, about 8,000 itinerant evangelists from 174 countries, for training and encouragement."

29

CHINA 1988

BILLY HAD PREACHED IN EVERY CONTINENT, BUT NOT IN CHINA with its huge population ruled by atheist Marxists. Because Ruth had been born and brought up there, the Grahams had a great love for China. They knew that despite intense persecution during the Cultural Revolution, Christianity had spread very vigorously and that most Christians worshiped in house churches not registered with the government-sanctioned China Christian Council (the Three Self Patriotic Movement[13]) and were therefore illegal. Yet any invitation to preach could come only from the Council, regarded with suspicion by many house churches as compromisers.

In 1980 Ruth and her sisters and brother had been allowed to visit their hometown of Tsingkiangpu, which was not open to tourists, and the welcome they received made Billy all the more eager to preach in China. An invitation came from the Christian Council, and at length, after a last-minute postponement seven months earlier when he broke a few ribs in an accident, he and Ruth, with Franklin and their team of experts and a film crew, arrived in Beijing to an official welcome on April 12, 1988, as the blossoms were opening on the trees.

At the welcome banquet in the Great Hall of the People (a vast modern building), Billy and Ruth were surprised and pleased when their cohost, who had been Chinese ambassador in Washington, announced a moment of silence so that Christians could pray a blessing. "Never in all my previous travels in the Communist world," commented Billy, "had this happened." Ambassador

Zhang, chairman of the Chinese People's Association for Friend-ship with Foreign Countries, had already made "a most gracious, generous" speech of welcome, followed by Bishop Ting of the Christian Council, whose words "rang clear and true as a Chris-tian speaking of the risen Christ," recorded Ruth in her diary.

The most memorable event in Beijing, beyond the sight-seeing to the Great Wall, or Billy's preaching to 1,500 in a church that seated 700, or his addresses and discussion groups in academic set-tings, was his interview with the new premier, Li Peng, who had been elected by the People's Congress only a few days earlier. Against precedent, the interview had been publicly announced and took place in the Pavilion of Lavender Light within the ancient walled Forbidden City of the former emperors. Li Peng, a bespec-tacled, pleasant-faced man of medium size came out to greet the Grahams and their advisers.

The interview was not exactly private. Billy and the premier sat on two chairs with their interpreters behind. Ruth was seated near Billy; facing them were Franklin, Bishop Ting, and Ambas-sador Zhang, the American ambassador, and others to listen in on the conversation. Li began: "Although we have different faiths [don't have the same God] that doesn't prevent us from having a good talk." When Billy responded to Li's remarks, he forgot the Chinese custom that the guest must speak no longer than the host: "I got carried away and took off on the Gospel" until Ruth was silently praying that he stop. The Premier exclaimed, "You really do believe what you preach!"

Billy was particularly struck by Li's emphasis that China could never be prosperous with only material development: "We need moral power too," and his candor in admitting they had not always preserved the freedom of religious belief, which the Constitution guaranteed. "But I must say," he added, "that there are not too many believers in China," a fact which the Grahams never forgot, despite the great increase of recent years. Li's remarks and attitude gave hope of a more relaxed approach to religious believers.

The conversation lasted fifty minutes. The Premier went public about it on television and radio, and in the press and thus it, in Billy's words, "created visibility and credibility for us that we could never have gotten otherwise and opened many doors for us. In addition, it gave an unusual degree of visibility to the Christians and churches of China I was visiting."

The seventeen-day tour covered two thousand miles and five major cities and, according to Billy, "packed in more speaking and preaching engagements, interviews, social events, and even sight-seeing than I remembered from any other trip I'd taken (though not as much sight-seeing as I would have liked).... In no place we visited was there any restriction on what I could say, and I took advantage of that to expound the Gospel to respectful and attentive audiences." In Nanjing he also visited the Amity Press, an operation of the Three Self Movement with government permission, which printed Bibles. But they printed them in the old characters, which younger Chinese were not taught and therefore could not read; and large numbers of copies remained in warehouses. Billy urged the directors to print Bibles in modern characters and to distribute them: "People are starved for them." He was informed that preparations were already being made. Soon after his visit, the first Bibles in the new characters came off the press.

The Grahams met Zhu Rongji, the newly installed mayor, in Shanghai. Mr. Zhu was later Premier of China, and they would meet again in Beijing when Billy was en route to his pioneering visits to North Korea, a story in itself to be told some future day.

In Shanghai, as Ruth recorded in her diary, one of the registered churches where Billy preached was the Pure Heart Church in a distant and rather shabby part of the city. After they had tea with the pastor according to custom, Ruth was led to her place while the choir was singing. "There were a lot of young people (the most this far). It was a happy service and as Bill began preaching on the Seven I Am's, a bat flew in (Chinese symbol for happiness and the character is the same). All during the sermon he swooped and flew up and down and around the church. The Chinese paid no attention (a few of the foreigners flinched.)" The sermon was "a powerful message. So simple yet profound."

While in Shanghai, the Grahams paid a call on the legendary church leader Wang Ming Dao, who had spent long years in prison and was still officially a nonperson. He refused to join the Three Self Movement. To the house churches he was a hero, now old and frail and nearly blind. The Grahams and their party climbed three flights of dirty concrete steps to reach his room, where they found him with his head bent over his little table, praying or asleep. His young male helper roused him and explained who his visitors were. He grasped each by the hand as Mrs. Wang came in, also blind but not so deaf.

After conversation but before the Grahams produced their gifts, as Ruth recorded, "Bill asked if he had a word from the Lord for us. He was silent for long seconds, then said: 'Be thou faithful unto death and I will give thee a crown of life.' 'Be faithful unto death. . . .' 'Be faithful. . .' Then he began to reminisce, haunting memories of an old man from which he cannot escape."

The Grahams's visit was not surreptitious in the least. All that they did, wherever they went, was cleared with the official hosts, who had been nervous at first as to what Billy might say or do, but his openness, graciousness, and kindness disarmed them. In Guangzhou (Canton), the Grahams and their party visited a cele-brated house church in the backstreet home of Brother Lin Xiangao, who had spent sixteen years of hard labor in a coal mine for his faith during the Cultural Revolution. The official hosts would not accompany them, except for a security man, who was useful in pushing a way through the crowded rooms. "There were three floors and the board steps were narrow and steep with one or more people on each step," recorded Ruth. Each room was filled with people on narrow benches or up against the walls. The lower floors had a homemade closed-circuit TV and on the third floor Brother Lin stood on a slightly raised platform. In front stood a narrow table where young men and women sat, each with an open Bible. The ceiling had been removed to allow electric fans, but the atmosphere was stifling and Billy had a momentary faintness as the people sang and prayed, but recovered to bring a short message, interpreted into Cantonese by Pastor Lin, with his strong face and strong voice.

The evening was continuing with Bible teaching as the Grahams squeezed themselves again down the stairs. "Back out in the steaming, crowded alley with the smell of people, vegetables, and something good cooking," Ruth felt she had been in the catacombs of the early church.

Billy was exhausted, but trusted he might be a bridge between the registered and unregistered churches. As an indication of the tensions, he had word that day of an independent pastor who had been arrested in a Beijing park, reportedly on his way to hear him preach. Billy contacted "the highest authorities," but the pastor was not immediately released. Billy had frequently raised the subjects of religious freedom and human rights in private conversation with state officials, who admitted that discrimination was still practiced against Christians. And in August of that very year, Brother Lin's house church in Guangzhou was closed down for some months as an illegal meeting. A well-placed Chinese observer in Hong Kong, with extensive contacts both in Three Self churches and the house churches, wrote in the immediate aftermath of the tour that it might possibly turn out to have been a turning point toward the relaxation of state controls on religion. But the totalitarian clampdown after the Tiananmen Square massacre the following year meant that the Christians' road would continue to be hard and stony.

House-church leaders themselves were grateful that Billy did what they could never do: He shared Christ and his Gospel with Li Peng and other top Communists who wielded enormous power. He made a vigorous case for Christianity to play a role in China's development, just as a new law on religion was being drafted, and he was able to discuss the message of Christ with atheistic scholars and students.

For Billy and Ruth, the high spot of the China trip was their visit to Ruth's birthplace and early home at Tsingkiangpu, now part of the city of Huaiyin, across the Grand Canal. Indeed Ruth seemed reinvigorated by this return to her roots.

They were flown in an old Russian propeller plane to the port of Lianyungang, with its sad memory for Ruth of the Bell family's evacuation in 1937 from Japanese-held territory and their sorrow at being forced to leave Chinese friends and the patients of the missionary hospital where her father, Nelson Bell, had been such a happy, brilliant surgeon and evangelist.

They drove almost due south, as Ruth described in her diary: "We passed through miles of 'old China'—little villages, mud farmhouses with thatched roofs, each with their own little pond of green water, a few ducks, chickens, sometimes a water buffalo, an occasional dog. It was growing dark as we finally entered Huaiyin."

The Grahams were overwhelmed by the way their hosts made them feel comfortable and welcomed. At the banquet that night, the charming and attractive young mayor (who "made it quite clear that she was an atheist") presented Ruth "with an exquisite framed relief picture of the old compound in mother-of-pearl."

The stone in the picture, she said, "reflects the strength of the relationship between you and the Huaiyin people. The pine represents the everlasting nature of our friendship. The maple tree (feng tree) symbolizes the warmth of the feelings of the Huaiyin people for you when the leaves turn red in autumn."

The next day, when they drove to the old missionary hospital compound, thousands lined the streets. They were probably curious about the invasion of foreigners, some having never seen one before. It had been forty-seven years since Nelson Bell left China.

At the old compound, the Bell house had been emptied and swept clean. As they went around together, Ruth poured out her happy memories to Billy and Franklin, who had heard so much of this place. Chinese friends had also located the Chinese house where Ruth was born. In one of the two small upstairs rooms, they had placed benches around the walls and flowers on a table. Ruth told them how in later life someone had asked her father how many of his old patients were still living. He thought a moment, then replied, "I would guess 90 percent are now dead, which only shows that what we did for them spiritually is the most important." A face in the crowd listening lit up with a big understanding smile, and Ruth recognized there was one who remembered and believed what the missionaries had taught.

They went to other buildings in the compound. Ruth wrote, "We met an old lady—a Christian who had known the missionaries. 'I am a Christian,' she said in Chinese, her strong old face calm, unsmiling for the pictures. She gave me an old faded picture of the hospital staff. They took pictures of us together and when I said in Chinese, 'God bless you,' she replied with a smile, 'Thank you and God bless _you_.'"

A few minutes later in the office, the civic leaders proudly showed the Grahams a large stone slab that had been unearthed during the excavation for the new hospital. It was the stone that had been above the main gate of the hospital compound, with the characters for "Love and Mercy Hospital" carved on it in old Chinese letters.

Then they presented Ruth with a handsome brocade box. Opening it she found the old, rusty swing hooks from their front porch—Ruth's sister Rosa had spotted them back in 1980. Nothing could have touched Ruth more.

From the hospital, they drove to the school building where Ruth and the other children of the station had been tutored by a missionary teacher. At the entrance a double row of Chinese children, with brightly rouged cheeks and bows in their hair, chanted loudly, "Welcome! Welcome!" And as they left, the children shouted, "Come back! Come back!" (or "So long! So long!") Ruth shook hands with every old granny in the narrow street who watched them walk by in case there might be one who remembered the missionaries. And then, with Billy, they walked the few steps to the house next door. They were standing in front of the former home of "Uncle" Jimmy and "Aunt" Sophie Graham, the much-loved senior missionaries who opened the station in 1889 and had only one convert in the first three years. When the Bell children had come back in 1980, the house was a wholesale grocery store.

And now, in 1988, ninety-nine years after Uncle Jimmy and Aunt Sophie had arrived, and seventy-two after Ruth's parents had joined them, Ruth, Billy, and Franklin mounted the thirteen steps to the porch of the square and ugly house—no longer a missionary's home—and no longer a wholesale grocery outlet: It was the local church.

Beside them walked the elderly pastor, Pastor Fei. In the house "the walls to the living room and dining room have been removed," noted Ruth, "and a partition built at the foot of what used to be the divided staircase. Here the pulpit stands. The old living room fireplace mantel is still in place but Chairman Mao's picture has been removed." The room "soon filled with people crowding the wooden benches. The pastor explained that every Sunday the place is filled to overflowing, the porch and also the courtyard—over 800 people." He said that there were 130,000 Christians in the greater Huaiyin area—population nine million. *What are these among so many?* thought Ruth, and at once another thought came: *They are salt and they are light.*

30

MISSION NEW YORK STATE

B ACK IN MAY 1982, SHORTLY AFTER THE CONTROVERSIAL VISIT
to Moscow, which would later bear such fruit, Billy Graham
was looking out of a hotel window in Hartford, Connecticut, with
Sterling Huston beside him. Billy was in, according to Sterling,
"one of those visionary and pensive moments that he has." They
had finished another rally in the series of one-night stands across
New England, where interest and response had built up as the
meetings followed each other. Billy's thoughts had turned to
another region: upstate New York. A hundred and fifty years earlier Charles Grandison Finney had so fanned the flames of revival
that it had been called the "burned-over" area. By the late twentieth century, however, the cities had 70 percent Roman Catholic
populations and the Protestant denominations tended to be theologically liberal, making an "evangelist's graveyard."

Billy turned from the window. "Sterling," he said, "I believe in
God's time we could go all the way around New York State and
touch all of that area that's called the burned-over area. We could
go from Buffalo and Rochester and Syracuse and Albany and down
into Long Island and northern New Jersey and the City."

For a year or two, Billy and Sterling took no action except to
pray. Billy was fully engaged with Eastern Europe, Mission England, and his preaching in the Soviet Union, and domestic crusades.
Then he began to receive invitations, unprompted, from several of
the cities of his vision in Hartford. When Sterling followed up with

them, he found a most encouraging attitude among both Protestant and Catholic leaders: "We need to reaffirm the preaching of the Gospel."

A plan was drawn up. Mission New York State, thoroughly prepared, would cover the entire Empire State with seven crusades spread over four years. They would be the only domestic crusades, except for Little Rock, which Billy would undertake in that period.

And so, on August 1, 1988, following his tours of China and the Soviet Union, Billy Graham opened the Greater Buffalo-Niagara crusade at Buffalo's new stadium, Pilot Field. The people of this maritime and industrial center on the shores of Lake Erie, the second largest city of New York state, responded warmly. The local newspaper reported each sermon in full, and radio and television carried extensive coverage. "Graham has brought an unprecedented spirit of unity, growth, and sensitivity, which has cut across racial, denominational, and cultural lines," said Justice Norman E. Joslin of the State Supreme Court, who was the crusade chairman.

The weather was somewhat extreme, for after a steamy four days that Friday brought torrential rain. "We're very fortunate to have any amplification at all," said Billy in his preliminary remarks before preaching. "I guess we've held a hundred meetings in the rain like this, and the first thing that usually happens is the amplification goes. Then the next thing, the lights begin to pop out. And the next thing—well, I won't tell you the next thing. The next thing, the people begin to disappear! But you people here have a strength and a stamina that we will never forget. I thought certainly a while ago in that downpour—and all the wind that was coming, and I thought it was hailing: it sounded that way, but it wasn't. But you stayed! And then when it let up a little bit, you came from somewhere. I don't know where you went in between time. It's amazing."

That night, after the sermon and the invitation, inquirers poured onto a soggy field. Two days after, at the closing service, the contrast in weather could not be greater. In broiling heat, 20,000 people were present. "The Buffalo campaign resulted in energizing the Christian community in this area," wrote Justice Joslin twenty months later, affirming that all the churches that took part had gained in membership and vision and that the community at large was more sensitive to spiritual matters.

Buffalo had also given Billy, always eager to understand opponents of the Gospel, an unusual opportunity. A humanist convention was meeting on the campus near his hotel. He read in the newspaper that they had referred to him. "So I put on old clothes and looked like somebody that was working in the garden, or on the lawns there. And I walked in, and I sat down several times and listened to what they had to say. And it was very interesting. They didn't know I was there. And I would walk back to the hotel with them; they didn't know it was me. It was interesting to listen to their conversations."

A month after Buffalo, Billy and the team returned to the "burned-over area," to Rochester, eighty miles eastward, the city on the plateau divided by the gorge of the Genesee River near its mouth on Lake Ontario. Rochester had been the scene of Finney's revival of 1831 when the young city's 10,000 inhabitants had reportedly all turned to Christ. It was now renowned for technology.

Billy flew in from North Carolina, but on the plane a swelling on his left foot got worse. "It was a cold, windy day. They were building something to the airport, so we had to walk a long way into the main terminal. And I could hardly walk, and my shoe felt like it was going to tear off my foot." A doctor sent him at once to the hospital where they found that he had been bitten at the top of the foot by a small but poisonous spider—a brown recluse *(loxosceles rucousa)* that must have crept under the sheets at Montreat. As Billy said, "It didn't bite Ruth. He was after me. And we found two others in our room. After I left, Ruth had it all fumigated and everything, and paid a lot of money to get it done. And we've found two more since then. And Cliff told me he'd found two or three at his house, so he's watching out for them."

Billy had to stay in the hospital during the preliminary events of the crusade and was given antibiotics day and night. He was discharged two hours before the opening service at Silver Stadium. He felt weak and spent much of each day in bed, yet his preaching reached so widely that a total of more than 11,000 came forward for commitment and counseling, nearly double the then usual percentage of attendance at his North American crusades.

Radio and television reported the crusade even more fully than at Buffalo. The local newspaper granted forty-two full pages of coverage over a two-week period. The publisher reported that they had not done this for any other event in the history of the community. In Huston's view, "Almost every inch was positive."

The Episcopal bishop of Rochester, William G. Burrell, crusade chairman, wrote afterward: "Having overheard a few discussions of those who came forward with their counselors, I was moved by the sincerity and profound nature of these discussions. I have no doubt that many lives were changed for the good." He saw the crusade also as a great instrument of unity, since fifty-one denominations were involved. He added, recalling the Love-In-Action program, when Billy urged those who came to bring food for the poor and homeless, "that all too often the proclaiming of the good news of God in Christ is separated from the crucial tasks of serving those in need and striving for justice and peace. It is rare in any of our churches to see combined in one person these two crucial gifts of proclamation."

The crusades of Mission New York State were woven in with Billy's international schedule of 1988 through 1991, but marked also by continuing physical problems. When he returned to the Niagara region for the Hamilton, Ontario, crusade five weeks after Rochester, his foot was still swelling up in the evenings. Shortly before the Syracuse crusade for Central New York in April 1989, he was diagnosed during a routine checkup with the early stages of Parkinson's (or a Parkinson's related) disease. This was not publicly announced. Syracuse had a special poignancy because 38 students of Syracuse University were killed when Pan Am Flight 103 had been blown up over Scotland in December 1988. They were much in mind and memory when the crusade opened in the Carrier Dome on the campus.

The Capital District crusade at Albany, scheduled for April 1990, had to be postponed because Billy had fallen accidentally, leading to persistent pain in his chest. A portion of rib was removed for examination at the Mayo Clinic on April 11. Even when the postponed crusade opened on July 8, he was unable to preach on the first five days: One of his associate evangelists, Ralph Bell, took his place. Billy preached at the last three services.

Nevertheless, Mission New York continued strongly. Albany was followed by Long Island, where the crusade at Nassau had been prepared by churches throughout Long Island and eastern New York City. Nearly one year later, with the Hong Kong crusade and Mission Scotland behind him, and also the Moscow School of Evangelism, which would have been impossible a year earlier, Billy and the team went to the sports complex at East Rutherford in northern New Jersey. This was a few miles across the Hudson River from Manhattan and a convenient focal point for New York City, Newark, and the vast urban and suburban area.

The climax came one week later on Sunday, September 22, 1991, with Mission Metro New York, the rally in Central Park, which astonished America. Sterling Huston's contemporary report catches the wonder of that day: "The Central Park Rally can best be described in the words of the psalmist, 'This is the Lord's doing, and it is marvelous in our eyes.' It was, indeed, a great day of witness for the Lord in Central Park, with an absolutely cloudless day and a perfect temperature to provide the celebration-like setting across the Great Lawn. Two hundred and fifty thousand people gathered, crowding the entire lawn area and extending out into the trees in what was the largest crowd for any religious event in the history of the city, and the largest audience that Billy Graham has spoken to in the Western Hemisphere. The program included marvelous music, such as the Salvation Army Band, the Brooklyn Tabernacle Choir, the Korean Choir, Sandi Patti, Marty Goetz, Buddy Greene, Johnny and June Cash, the a capella group Take 6, and, of course, Bev Shea. The standing-room-only crowd seemed to love every minute of the three-hour service.

"Mr. Graham spoke twice. Early in the service, he addressed the city and its residents ... speaking about the problems and possibilities of New York City and emphasizing the need to turn to God to solve the difficulties of that city. Later in the service, he preached clearly, simply and, powerfully, the Gospel of Jesus Christ, using John 3:16 as his text. At the end, with the crowd pressing shoulder-to-shoulder, and standing across the Great Lawn, it was not possible to ask people to come forward, so Mr. Graham invited them to wave their packet to indicate they wanted to respond. (Everyone was offered a packet containing counseling material, a gospel of John, a response card, and a pencil.) Thousands of hands were raised. After Mr. Graham counseled the people, he invited them to pray and an estimated one-third of the audience offered that prayer of confession and commitment. Counseling is still going on as people are mailing in those cards, and the final count will only be revealed in eternity.

"The media coverage was extraordinary, with over 200 media registered for the rally. There was front-page coverage in the *New York Times,* as well as coverage in several other newspapers and all the TV local and network stations. This positive treatment by the media greatly extended the witness of that day, which was unprecedented in New York.

"More than 50 percent of the audience was ethnic, as the diversity of the city came together in the most harmonious, peaceful, loving, and positive setting of any event that has happened there in recent memory. Indeed, it was a great day of witness for the Lord, and a great day for his church. Church leaders are highly encouraged, and already are planning ways to conserve this new witness and spiritual momentum for their city.

"We are rejoicing in the results and now look forward to the television special to be shown across the nation, when we believe tens of millions will also share in this moment of victory for the Gospel."

31

MOSCOW 1992: A DREAM COME TRUE

ON AUGUST 20, 1992, THE PRESIDENT OF THE UNITED STATES, George Bush, was addressing an ecumenical service in his home city of Houston, Texas. Giving thanks for the end of the Cold War he said, "I remember when ten years ago one of God's great soldiers went to Eastern Europe and the Soviet Union. Returning to America, Billy Graham predicted that freedom would outlast tyranny. He felt that religion was alive way back then, and the doubters said he'd been tricked. But Dr. Graham knew something they didn't. He knew the chains of oppression forged by men were no match for the keys to salvation forged by God." Two months later in October 1992, Billy saw the most moving evidence of this in the Olympic Stadium in Moscow when he held an amazing mission that would have been illegal in the Soviet Union. But the Soviet Union had been dissolved. Freedom of religion had returned after seventy-four years. And history will confirm that Billy Graham had been one of those responsible.

In Communist times, Billy had increasingly felt a moral responsibility to build bridges of understanding between the Westerners and the Easterners to lessen the risk of nuclear war. Communist governments, which appreciated his attitude, opened doors for his evangelism. Thus, following his attendance at the controversial Moscow Peace Conference in 1982, he had preached in four Soviet cities in 1984, although restricted to Orthodox cathedrals or Protestant churches. In 1985 Hungary allowed the huge television screen used in Mission England to be erected on the steps of the Roman Catholic cathedral at Pecs for the overflow crowd.

In 1988 in the Soviet Union, Billy took part in the celebration of a thousand years of Christianity in Russia where Gorbachev's policies were bringing more freedom of religion. Many Orthodox churches were reopening, including the Kazan Cathedral in Leningrad from which the atheist museum had been expelled. When Billy preached in St. Vladimir's Cathedral in Kiev, the Red Army brought generators to carry his sermon to some 10,000 persons packed inside and outside. Later, the head of the Council of Religious Affairs for the USSR, Konstantin Karchev, officially an atheist, thanked Billy warmly for his help in liberalizing Soviet religious policy. Kharchev claimed that Communism and Christianity had a common desire for higher moral principles, but, he said, "We have never found ultimate truth. I would like to believe it exists somewhere." Billy replied that ultimate truth does exist, in the Person who said, "I am the way, the truth, and the life." Billy had entertained Karchev earlier in Washington, and now gave him a Bible and said he would pray for him.

In 1989 the law was changed, the Soviet government admitted that the antireligious policy had been wrong, and church bells rang across the land again. That same year Hungary allowed Billy to preach in the People's Stadium at Budapest. Ninety thousand people came. The vast rally was broadcast live and much of it shown on television. More than 27,000 people streamed forward at the invitation. Billy thought they had misunderstood, but they would not go back to their seats. The 800 counselors had to toss follow-up packets over the heads of the shoulder-to-shoulder crowd around the platform, to reach outstretched hands behind. According to Billy, "It was one of the most wonderful sights I've ever seen. Every church in Hungary cooperated, and they all came together and made it a great and glorious day. And that was before things began to change as rapidly as they did. They were already changing; you could sense it."

That winter the Berlin Wall fell. In March 1990, the German churches organized a rally outside the Reichstag for Billy to preach to a united Berlin, a story in itself.

In the summer Billy convened a School of Evangelism in Moscow. Patriarch Pimen of the Russian Orthodox Church encouraged him warmly but died before it began. Billy's hosts were the evangelical churches, their leaders somewhat dazed by the suddenness of the change from government regulation to freedom. Five thousand clergy and laymen were on their way from all over the Soviet Union to the Lenin Sports Complex "Druzhba" when Soviet bureaucracy suspended the project until the last minute. After three days of emergency discussion at Zurich, Billy said, "It just looked as though we wouldn't have a conference. And I got on the plane in Zurich to go to Moscow and I said, 'Lord, we've done all we can. I just leave it in your hands.' And all of a sudden things just opened up and the Lord did it." The School of Evangelism was electric with hope and deep devotion, enhanced by the incomparable singing and a vision for their land.

Accompanied by the school's chairman, Grigori Komendant of Kiev, head of the Evangelical Christians-Baptists, Billy was invited to the Kremlin for private talks both by Gorbachev and by Boris Yeltsin, the newly elected president of the Russian Federation. Three weeks after the school dispersed came the attempted coup by hard-line Communists, defeated by the courage of Yeltsin and the people of Moscow. The Communist Party was dissolved. Complete religious freedom arrived with the newly won democracy. The church leaders invited Billy to hold a nationwide crusade in October 1992. Billy appointed Blair Carlson, Director of European Ministries, with his experience of Eastern Europe, to direct it. He was free after handing the preparations for Mission Scotland to Rick Marshall.

The Soviet Union was falling apart. By the time it ceased to exist on December 26, 1991, and became the Commonwealth of Independent States (the Baltic States regained their sovereignty outside it), Blair and his five associate directors had started work in close accord with an indigenous interdenominational team. The outdoor Lenin Stadium, where Billy had prayed in 1959, was unsuitable for late October weather. They chose the indoor Olympic Stadium. They named the crusade "Vozrozhdeniye 92," the word meaning both renewal and awakening.

Despite the political upheaval and economic uncertainties, they met encouragement and goodwill on every side, with full access to the media. "We had primetime monthly slots on TV for Billy Graham to preach all across the former Soviet Union, and also the first ever live radio talk show—an hour and forty-five minutes long—where people from anywhere could call in with their questions about faith. The follow-up to the mail responses to these programs was monumental."

The team found spiritual hunger with excitement at living at last in a free country, puzzlement at the chaos, hope for the future, and a resurgent pride in Russia's historic past.

Mail and phone systems could not be relied on. Thus, the bimonthly meetings of the Inter-republic Preparation Committee (600 church leaders present in January, over 800 in March, and 1,000 in May) were essential means of communicating details to every part of the CIS and the Baltic States. "One representative," Blair reported to Billy early in April, "even came from Vladivostok. All denominations were represented. During the daylong meetings, participants broke down into small groups to discuss evangelism and training in their own areas and then specific involvement in the Moscow project. In Moscow, individual task-oriented committees to advise and prepare for music-choir, counseling, and follow-up, etc., have been formed." Difficulties came from the representatives' lack of experience in organizing large-scale Christian outreach, and from their having been trained under the Soviet system not to make decisions but to accept them from a higher authority.

The Russian Orthodox Church, now regaining its position as the national church, did not publicly endorse Vozrozhdeniye 92, but the new patriarch, Alexei II, supported it practically, like the mayor of Moscow, the president of the Duma (Russian Parliament), and Boris Yeltsin himself. The patriarch's public caution arose from fear that Orthodoxy might be undermined by the "huge number" of foreign Christian workers (and some from pseudo-Christian cults) who were pouring in since the opening of the borders. Billy was sensitive to the Orthodox fears. He had met with Patriarch Alexei II before the meeting at the Olympic Stadium. Having been their guest for his earlier visits, he appreciated their glory in the resurrection and triumph of the living Christ, and that many thousands of secret or lapsed believers had returned openly to the church. But Communism had kept millions from Christian background or Bible knowledge. They could be confused by elaborate rituals and priestly robes, so that the evangelical churches were already reaping a harvest. As always, Billy would not proselytize, but preached Christ.

During the spring and summer, the public's awareness of the coming crusade or mission was enhanced by the visits of General Charles Duke, the astronaut, who opened doors to the military and astronauts in the Russian "Star City," and of the famous disabled Christian, Joni Eareckson Tada, and the showing of her film. Tada gave lectures to social workers on care for the disabled and conducted evangelistic meetings for the disabled. Meanwhile, the worlds of sports, music, and business were each imaginatively penetrated.

On July 30, Blair reported, "Vozrozhdeniye 92 is becoming an evangelistic movement with historical significance and dimensions. Christians from the entire CIS are looking to Vozrozhdeniye 92 as the one organization who will be able to make an impact on the entire country and, furthermore, be a resource place and revive and educate the churches.... Close to 200 evangelistic teams are working throughout the former Soviet Union under the umbrella of Vozrozhdeniye 92. They are conducting mini-missions and youth festivals, they are ministering in schools and prisons, they are teaching Christian Life and Witness classes. The reports from those evangelistic teams are coming into our office constantly telling us of the great things that the Lord does through their ministry."

An enterprising company erected great billboards at strategic points in Moscow, empty except for an invitation: "Your advertising will beautify our city." (Billboards had been restricted to Communist slogans.) The mission snapped up fifty-two and placed huge posters, printed in Finland, showing Billy Graham with one word, *pochemo,* meaning "Why?" which is the question Muscovites were asking about their difficult life and times. The posters, the first advertising in post-Soviet Moscow, included various questions, and ended: "Millions have listened and many have found answers for themselves.... Billy Graham, a man talking with people." The theme was repeated in smaller form in Metro trains and stations, on buses and television, and in leaflets to every household.

"Mr. Graham, these are amazing days," wrote Blair. "We feel almost like coaches standing on the sidelines seeing the team take their places and prepare for action. The air here in Moscow is filled with expectation. We sense in a very real way the hand of our 'senior manager,' our loving Heavenly Father."

On the evening of October 23, 1992, more than 40,000 people crowded into the Olympic Stadium. In chairman Grigori Komendant's words, it was "a historical event. Truly, God has done a miracle having gathered us in this place." A religious meeting in a public area had been unlawful for so long, until some eighteen months earlier, that the English-language *Moscow Times* assumed that the idea would be too strange for the general public, and published a cartoon caricaturing the posters: A puzzled Billy looks at an almost empty stadium, above that is the word, *Why?* The newspaper could not have been more wrong.

Special trains had been run from St. Petersburg (as it now was again) and Kiev and ten other cities, and hundreds of buses from nearer places, but the bulk of the audience were Muscovites. Many would attend from curiosity and some, untouched by the sermon, might go forward from wrong motives, especially if that meant receiving a gift of Christian literature. To prevent this, every person received the follow-up packet on entering the stadium. It included a decision card, a copy of Luke's gospel, and, most strategically, a list of the follow-up centers. The packets were handed out by stewards. Many of these were among the 5,000 young men and women studying in the nationwide Youth School of Evangelism, held in a suburban hall each day, which had been organized by young people under the direction of an experienced American. The students attended lectures in the mornings, did street evangelism in the afternoons, and served in the choir and as counselors and follow-up team in the evenings.

The covered stadium was oval-shaped with the platform at the south end. Behind it sat the 7,000 member choir, dressed in black and white, which included men and women from more than eighty cities of the CIS. In front was the open space ready for those who came forward. Because the stadium filled up fast, latecomers were allowed to stand at the back of the open area, behind a line of Salvation Army officers. During the first night, there was some distracting movement of people coming and going as in a typical Orthodox church, but a way was found to stop it.

Each service followed the traditional pattern of a Billy Graham crusade: the choir numbers, the congregational singing led by Cliff Barrows, the Russian and American soloists, the testimonies, and the guest choral groups. But it all had a dreamlike quality, especially when the famous Alexandrov's Red Army Choir sang Russian religious songs and choruses of the faith that were for so long disallowed to them. And when they sang "The Battle Hymn of the Republic" in carefully learned English, it was realized that the Cold War had certainly ended.

Billy Graham had come to the platform slowly, on the arm of an aide. But age and infirmity fell away when he preached Christ with great simplicity from John 3:16: "God so loved the world...." His sermon was interpreted by Viktor Hamm, who had interpreted the *Hour of Decision* into Russian for many years, while living in

Canada. Viktor's father had been converted in a labor camp of the Gulag in Stalin's time. On release he had become a fervent evangelist with the unregistered Baptists until expelled from Russia by the Soviet authorities. Now aged, he was so overcome by the wonder of being in a great congregation in a state-owned building, listening to the Christian Gospel proclaimed by Billy through Viktor in the heart of Moscow, that he spent the whole service in tears.

Billy ended his sermon: "Do you want Christ to come into your heart today? Repent and begin to trust Jesus Christ. Trust him, and him alone. Remember: now is the day of salvation. Come to Christ!" The very moment that Viktor had translated the last phrase, people surged forward. It looked, wrongly, as if the line of Salvation Army officers were marching briskly ahead according to some plan, but they were being pushed and could not stop. Over ten thousand inquirers were counseled that night. The next night, a much larger space was left and the Salvation Army officers did not form a line but moved quietly during the prayer, to stand below the platform facing the people.

Billy preached on the Prodigal Son (and a show of hands had suggested that at least half the audience was under twenty-five). He ended by saying, "God is waiting for your repentance and your trust. Today you must decide: I will follow him, and I will live for him. The Spirit of God is ready to enter your life and to transform it.

"Therefore I am asking you now, wherever you are, come forward to pray. Remember that you have come to the Loving God. I don't have any supernatural power to do something for you. I am just a man, like you are. I am just a preacher. And my message is that God loves you, he accepts you and forgives you. He is ready to enter your hearts today. Bow your heads in reverence to him and pray."

Even before Viktor had completed his translation, people not merely surged but ran toward the pulpit. Billy looked surprised. "You must not run," he said. As they pressed and pressed and pressed, a Western friend who had traveled widely among Soviet Christians at the height of the Khrushchev persecution recalled,

"[I] could see Billy was near to tears at the scene and certainly so was I, as I heard the murmur of this vast crowd praying the prayer after Billy. And I looked down at their serious faces, and I felt that seventy years of atheism had blown away like an evil mist and that the deep Christianity of the Russian people a thousand years old had stood the test."

On the third and final afternoon, about 50,000 people squeezed into the stadium and another estimated 20,000 stood outside in the bitter cold, following the service and sermon on the giant television screens. It looked to Billy as if half the audience came forward at the invitation—at least 20,000. And 12,000 decision cards were handed in. That evening, as Billy watched the first snow fall on the cupolas and crosses of the Kremlin and Red Square, he thought back to the day in 1959 when he and Grady Wilson had stood in the empty Lenin Stadium and prayed for the miracle that had come.

A total of 155,000 attended the meetings and 42,000 had gone forward. With so few churches yet open in Moscow, thirty follow-up centers had been arranged (and forty in other cities) for a six-week course of basic Christian teaching, using dubbed British videos. The thirty centers eventually became thriving permanent Moscow churches.

Vozrozhdeniye 92 soon proved to be a launching pad for a widespread evangelization by the evangelical Christians, which Billy Graham encouraged by inviting Viktor Hamm (who had been working for the Family Life Network) to become one of his full-time evangelists. As Viktor traveled throughout the CIS conducting missions and schools of evangelism, he would often ask younger or middle-aged leaders where they had come to faith or how their group started. Again and again he would be told the Moscow crusade, Vozrozhdeniye 92. The preparatory seminars, the two schools of evangelism, and the stadium meetings had helped to raise up a new generation who had endured the fires of the past.

At the dedication service, Billy had warned that harvest time might be short. "We don't know for how long it will continue. I was raised in the country, and I know how precious harvest time is." And indeed the law that had granted unrestricted freedom was later replaced under pressure from the Orthodox Church, seeking the unrivalled position it had held under the tsars. But freedom was still real, despite constraints, especially for long-established evangelical churches who were able to found theological seminaries and plant new centers of worship and organize two or more schools of evangelism a year. And whereas the Amsterdam conferences of 1983 and 1986 had each seen a mere handful of participants from the USSR, Amsterdam 2000 had over seven hundred from the CIS and the Baltic States.

32

MILLENNIUM HARVEST

THE RUSSIANS IN 1992 HAD INVITED BILLY TO RETURN FOR CRU-
sades in four cities, but he was unable to accept. Instead, he
gave them a full part in the missions by satellite—a great feature of
his ministry in the mid-1990s.

The use of satellites to extend the reach of the Sheffield (1985)
and Paris missions (1986) had encouraged Billy to appoint a team
to study the possibility of taking a crusade live to hundreds of cities
around the world. After studying the technological and administrative factors, the team responded with enthusiasm. But it would be
the biggest project Billy had ever undertaken. He hesitated. "I do
not recall in my ministry when I've had such an inward struggle
over any opportunity or vision such as I have personally had over
Mission World," he told his board in November 1987. "I have had
more conversations, sought more counsel and advice, and prayed
more about this decision than possibly any decision we ever made
except possibly the Lausanne Congress of 1974." Finally, he and
the board decided to go ahead step-by-step. Three nights of Mission 89 from London would be beamed by satellite to Africa.

More than 16,000 churches in Africa prepared as if Billy Graham
would be coming to their land in person, while the Graham Team
prepared African programs to wrap around Billy's sermons from
Earls Court in London. The organizer commented, "We needed to
have Africans singing about Jesus Christ. We needed to have
Africans giving their testimonies," as well as the choir and soloists
and others from Earls Court.

And thus in those summer nights of 1989, while 250 Livelink centers in Britain and Ireland were receiving the mission by satellite television, twelve African countries showed Billy's sermons live at prime time. Another twenty-two countries recorded them for their prime time, and the programs were transferred to film for showing in remote forest clearings or mountain communities without television.

In South Africa, six telephone counseling centers of 170 lines needed to stay open around the clock for six days and the network that aired the programs was swamped by telephone calls from inquirers. As he heard the reports from Britain and Africa, Billy told the people in Earls Court that it was surely "a spirit of revival, because we are seeing so many people rededicate their lives to Christ, so many people come to Christ, and so many churches feeling the impact of what God has been doing." He continued, "Many people ask me how I feel about it. I feel that I'm only a spectator. I'm watching something that God is doing."

On the same pattern, Mission World Asia went out from the Hong Kong crusade of November 1990; South America from Buenos Aires in 1991; and Europe, including the former Soviet Union, from Essen in 1993. Each was a massive operation of organizers, technicians, and interpreters, backed by prayer, to reach the people of a continent by scores of languages.

By 1995, the time had come for the Global Mission—the whole world to be reached from one crusade. The Koreans begged that this should be from their new Olympic Stadium in Seoul; Los Angeles begged that Billy return to their Coliseum, scene of his celebrated crusade thirty-two years earlier. Billy had a strong feeling that the Global Mission should be beamed from Puerto Rico, the self-governing territory under the American flag but not "America." San Juan, the capital, had a good stadium and superb facilities, ease of access for the great force of technicians and interpreters, and a thriving church life with strong emphasis on mission.

By March 1995, everything was ready. The satellite company had set up their equipment in a building beside the stadium and said the operation was bigger than their transmission from the recent winter Olympics in Norway.

First came a worldwide school of evangelism—the lectures reaching about 500,000 participants. The evangelistic mission followed. As the Spanish interpreter, who was beside Billy on the platform, translated him phrase by phrase, seventy-eight interpreters sitting with earphones in the backup building sent his sermon across the world. Some transmissions had silent spaces for local linguists to insert their minority language.

Billy was seen on huge screens in stadiums in Korea and in countries of South America; in sports palaces and prisons in Russia, in theaters, cinemas, and warehouses. On the Rwanda-Zaire (Congo) border, the BGEA had set up screens on the hillside for 2,000 civil war refugees in the valley. In one country recovering from years of Marxist rule, the people watched in the capital's main square. The total audience was probably around a billion people: American newsmen suggested that no man in history had addressed so large an audience directly, and that it was the widest single outreach of the Christian church in history. Many thousands of praying Christians had brought their friends and neighbors to meetings of whatever size and were ready to follow up with them.

"Every night," Billy had told the staff on the eve of the Mission, "I want to bring just a simple ordinary message of the Gospel. I want it to be just as simple as can be. We are not going to get involved in any politics, no church differences, we're just going to proclaim the Gospel of Christ and what Christ did on the cross by his resurrection, what he can do for us through the Holy Spirit now."

By the year of the Global Mission, Billy Graham and his team had taken a leap forward in their outreach to the youth of America.

In 1992 Rick Marshall, later the Director of North American Crusades under Sterling Huston, had returned from directing Mission Scotland to prepare Philadelphia. The crusade was about to begin. Rick and Becki's four children ("crusade kids") were now all teenagers. When Rick asked them which night they planned to bring their friends, he met a stony silence. Then the fifteen-year-old blurted out: "Dad, we don't want to go to the crusade. It's so old, and there is nothing in it for us." Rick was stunned. After the crusade, he looked at statistics and found a slow erosion of attendance among young people despite three evenings being designated as Youth Nights. He realized that a cultural block was affecting the Billy Graham ministry. "We could have a thousand churches working together, but something was missing."

For a whole year Rick thought and prayed and was very discouraged at first. Then the Youth Committee chair at Cleveland, Ohio, in 1993 said, "Our vision for this crusade is to go outside the safe boundaries of the church to reach the next generation," and gave exciting examples. Rick began to study the contemporary youth culture outside the church. He learned they worshiped technology; violence and illicit sex seemed normal; drugs and divorce and the suicides of friends were facts of life. They were angry with parents who were so often absent while pursuing careers. The environment, the homeless, and the disadvantaged mattered. They had dropped church yet were passionately spiritual, searching, yet supposing that Jesus, Buddha, and Muhammad were equally valid. They craved movement and excitement and variety, and above all, they loved loud music. Music was the key.

By the Columbus crusade of September 1993, Rick's ideas had been shaped enough for him to open his heart to Cliff Barrows as program director and suggest that at the next crusade, at Cleveland, Ohio, one night should be a "Concert for the NeXt Generation," featuring Christian pop bands and singers who had reached the charts, such as dc Talk, Michael W. Smith, and Kirk Franklin, along with testimonies from top athletes and music too loud for parents. When the noise subsided, Billy would give a strong message.

Cliff said that Rick must speak with Billy Graham. In a long call, Rick urged Billy that they needed variety and high energy "and music louder than their parents might like, and a large Jumbotron screen showing music videos that communicate in the vernacular of the next generation. And then a straight talk from a caring adult. That's you."

Billy replied, "That's not a youth night. Let me tell you what we used to do." He described those early days of Youth for Christ, with its motto "Geared to the Times, Anchored to the Rock," how they wore eye-stopping jackets and fancy ties, how Cliff had a battery pack in his pocket and would push a button and his tie would light up; of the Gospel horse, trained to tap a hoof in answer to a Bible question; and the hundred pianos crashing away on one stage, until Rick was laughing down the line. "But I realized that I had Billy Graham's heart in principle."

"I said, 'Billy, I don't want you to dress up crazy, and I don't want any talking horses. But I want the same vision and enthusiasm and risk-taking in the year 1994 that you took forty-five years ago.' I said, 'Will you give me permission to do it?' And there was a long silence, and he said, 'Let's do it.'"

In the run-up to the Cleveland crusade of June 1994, young people listening to their favorite pop radio or watching television or billboards were thrilled to know that there would be a "concert to benefit its own audience," instead of stars charging high prices. "Nothing, nothing," ran one radio spot, "compares to the intense rush, the total gratification, the really huge swell factor of a free concert. Get a shot of musical adrenaline. Get to the Concert for the NeXt Generation. It's totally free." After giving the time and place and the names of the stars, it ended: "There will even be a special appearance by the man himself, Billy Graham."

Rick was a little nervous that few would turn up for the 7:00 start, but at 2:00 the police reported that no less than 35,000 young people were waiting outside, who poured in when the gates opened. More than 65,000 were present when the musical program began with its movement, humor, noise, and color, the audience joining in. An athlete gave his testimony, followed by a specially made video, "A Place in This World," featuring Michael W. Smith, until the kids were so stimulated that they were ready to listen.

Billy had been waiting in a soundproof trailer. When Rick brought him out in a golf cart, the kids leaped to their feet, roaring, "Billy! Billy!" When he reached the stage, the bands hugged him and sat down behind him, as if to say, "We're going to listen. You listen too." Billy said to the crowd, "I love all these guys, and I'm thrilled that they could come and be with us. I know them all personally. They believe in God. They believe in Christ. And Christ has changed their lives and made them new people. And it's a wonderful thing that we can gather here from different ethnic groups and different backgrounds and different languages and all talk about the same person, Jesus Christ." He then explained John 3:16 in the simplest way. So many came forward that they ran out of counseling materials.

Over the next eight years, the eighteen Concerts for the NeXt Generation beat stadium records twelve times, always had a high percentage of unchurched inquirers, and marked up a million attendances by October 2002. But the concert met criticism. At the Sacramento crusade press conference, a reporter said, "Dr. Graham, I'm shocked to know that you're using rock music." Billy was visibly disturbed. Then he replied, "Some say it's rock, but I would rather say it's contemporary music. I've met these musicians, I've prayed with them, I've read their lyrics. When I went to Russia or China or Korea, I needed an interpreter to reach those audiences. These bands are my interpreters to reach this generation."

Some in the team argued against the concerts. Billy recognized that there were dangers. An accident or incident when kids were worked up could damage the ministry. But he said, "God has laid this upon my heart. Ruth and I have been praying from Psalm 71:17–18: 'Since my youth, O God, you have taught me, and to this day I declare your marvelous deeds.' Here I am in my seventies, but this is my prayer, that 'even when I am old and gray, do not forsake me, O God, till I declare your power to the next generation, your might to all who are to come.'"

Ruth added, "When we were younger, just getting started, we had a lot of criticism. We called those critics old fuddy-duddies. I prayed and so did Bill that when we got older we would not be old fuddy-duddies. I don't know what all the fuss is about. The bands stock the pond so Bill can go fishing."

Eight years later, the singer Toby McKeehan ("Toby Mac") of the dc Talk trio gave a vivid account of the "pond" and the "fishing" at that first concert: "Walked out to the stadium there in Cleveland, and it was just completely overwhelming. A full—absolutely full stadium with spillover in the parking lot with TV massive monitors running so they could see it. Didn't get asked to change anything we did. I was climbing scaffolding, jumping off of it, singing my guts out, screaming my guts out, sweat towels everywhere, water's kicked over, instruments laying on the ground. We finished our set, introduced Billy Graham, and here he comes walking up. Didn't change the set, didn't move the guitars, the broken-strings, didn't move the water bottles or the towels. We were sweaty. We hugged him. [He] went up and spoke the most simple message and saw a—more than a river—an ocean of people come down to accept Christ for the first time. It was unbelievable. Never forget it as long as I live. And it happens the same way every time.

"And the beauty is he's wise enough to not ask us to change anything. He recognizes that the young people want to hear that kind of music; and at the same time he's wise enough, even though it's not his style, to embrace it and to recognize the need to have an interpreter. And kids just respect him because of that. If it had been a choir there or some older school, maybe southern gospel music, I just think it would have been difficult to have a stadium full of kids on a youth night. But because he chose those bands and because it was Billy Graham, they pack out every time."

In October 2002, from Dallas, Cliff Barrows reminisced to listeners on the *Hour of Decision* as he sat in one of the skyboxes overlooking Texas Stadium where thousands of teenagers and mothers and dads had gathered for a Saturday night Concert for the NeXt Generation. At the first concerts, he said, "We were astonished at how many of them responded. We went up to the Minneapolis area and way up to Toronto. And I remember we had so many people responding that Bill didn't know what to do with them. And I said, 'Well, let's give the invitation again and make it harder.' So he started over again and talked about what it costs to really take a stand for Christ, a cost among their peers. They would have to say no, and they would have to be willing to change their direction and way of living. And he gave the invitation again. And when he asked them to come forward, there were over 13,000 that filled every available space. And, of course, those kind of numbers are just overwhelming.

"But we have since heard from so many who have gone on with Christ and who are entered into the regular follow-up work of a regular mission. And we have an opportunity to continue to encourage them. . . . And many of them will take some time to sort through all that it means. But we're seeing evidences of lives transformed and communities changed, whole attitudes in schools. And in the various areas of a city, particularly in areas where they've had difficulty, we've seen those areas change. And we are thankful for what God is doing through the faithful preaching of his Word."

On May 2, 1996, being the annual National Day of Prayer, the senators and representatives of the 104th Congress came together in the magnificent rotunda on Capitol Hill. Congress had resolved unanimously to confer the Congressional Gold Medal, the highest award the legislature could give, on Billy and Ruth Graham jointly. George Washington had been the first to receive the Gold Medal, which had been conferred only 113 times. Billy would be the second clergyman and the Grahams the third couple to be honored. The North Carolina representative who introduced the bill said, "Mr. Graham's character and strength have made him America's most admired man. He has used his immense popularity to confront major social problems such as racism, the homeless, and hunger." President Clinton signed the Act of Congress into law and later presented a framed copy, with the pen, to the Grahams. By Constitutional convention, the president could not be present at the award ceremony, so instead President Clinton received Billy the day before and spoke at the gold dinner, which followed. President Reagan had conferred the Executive's highest award and the Presidential Medal of Freedom.

The presentation in the rotunda was attended by 700 people, including diplomats, churchmen, medical men, and scholars. The Grahams's five children, nineteen grandchildren, and one or two of the great-grandchildren were there, along with the team. As Billy said in his acceptance speech, "Our ministry has been a team effort, and without our associates and our family, we could never have accomplished anything. I'm especially grateful to my wife, Ruth. We're both being given this honor. No one has sacrificed more than Ruth has to God's calling for the two of us." Ruth had been in the hospital, and Billy too had been unable to fulfill public engagements due to bad health.

The speaker, Newt Gingrich, said that they were gathered "to honor one of the great civic leaders of the twentieth century." The vice president, Al Gore, said in his speech: "Few individuals have left such lasting impact on our national life. In presenting this Gold Medal, the United States of America makes a powerful statement about what is really important in our national life."

Bev Shea sang "God Bless America" and then the Resolution was read before the presentation of the medal: "Ruth and Billy Graham have made outstanding and lasting contributions to morality, racial equality, family, philanthropy, and religion.

"America's most respected and admired evangelical leader for the past half century. Billy Graham's crusades have reached a hundred million people in person and over two billion people worldwide on television.

"Billy Graham, throughout his 77 years of life and his 53-year marriage to Ruth Graham, has exemplified the highest ideals of teaching, counseling, ethics, charity, faith, and family.

"Billy Graham's daily newspaper column and 14 books have provided spiritual counseling and personal enrichment to millions of people."

The final paragraph referred to the charitable cause, which was featured on the reverse of the medal: The Ruth and Billy Graham Children's Health Center at Asheville, an extension of the Memorial Mission Hospital at Asheville where Nelson Bell had worked. Its "vision is to improve the health and well-being of children and to become a new resource for ending the pain and suffering of children." The gold medal showed the Grahams's heads, and on the reverse the new buildings of the center.

In his address of thanks, after giving his personal testimony and saying that anything they had accomplished had been because of the grace and mercy of God, Billy spoke of America's crisis of the spirit and of hope in Christ: "As we face a new millennium, I believe America has gone a long way down the wrong road. We must change roads, turn around, and go back. We must repent and commit our lives to God and to the moral and spiritual principles that have made this nation great, and translate that commitment into action in our homes, neighborhoods, and our society...." Very graciously, he called his distinguished audience to yield to Christ.

Thanking them he said, "As Ruth and I receive this award, we know that someday we will lay it at the feet of the One we seek to serve.... We pledge to continue the task that God has called us to do as long as we live."

33

"LIGHT A FIRE"

WHEN BILLY CELEBRATED HIS EIGHTIETH BIRTHDAY ON November 7, 1998, he was actively preparing a third Amsterdam world conference for evangelists. Since 1986 he had been asked time and again for another, and about every two years he considered it. "We would do some research," recalls Mike Southworth, then Director of Field Operations for BGEA's International Ministries, "and he would talk about it and pray about it, and God never seemed to let the desire really build in his heart until late 1997." In March 1998, Billy authorized a letter to be sent with his signature to about 2,900 leaders in 185 countries asking their opinion, whether to hold a conference in the year 2000.

Out of some 1,000 replies, 970 were overwhelmingly positive that a new generation needed the training and encouragement that 1983 and 1986 had given, and only Billy could bring it about. The leaders trusted him and held him in high esteem. Wherever team members went, especially in Africa, Asia, South America, and Eastern Europe, they were told how the earlier conferences had greatly helped evangelism and spiritual life.

Amsterdam 2000 was the most extensive single project ever undertaken by the Billy Graham Evangelistic Association. New technology allowed much of the preparation to be done at Minneapolis, but the logistics for selection, travel, board, and lodging for more than 10,000 participants and staff, and the preparation and support of the program were immense. Nothing could be left to chance or inefficiency. And as Billy had emphasized in his letter to leaders, without the backing of prayer, the conference would be as a sounding brass or a tinkling cymbal. More than 117,000 prayer groups formed across the world. Prayer was kept to the forefront in the Minneapolis headquarters, on the website, and at the Cove, the short-term training school and conference center near Asheville, which the Grahams had founded in 1993 on land quietly bought some years earlier. The weekly *Hour of Decision* alerted listeners to pray and a new daily radio program, *Decision Today,* included the latest requests.

The conference was scheduled to begin on July 29. Billy held a successful but exhausting crusade at Nashville, Tennessee, in the first four days of June. Shortly afterward he entered the Mayo Clinic at Rochester, Minnesota, for tests and therapy to combat his progressive Parkinson's condition. He had recently been troubled by increased pressure within the cerebrospinal fluid (Normal Pressure Hydrocephalus). The doctors decided on surgery to insert a shunt in his head. They expected that he would be discharged in time for Amsterdam, but his recovery was slow and he could not be present. A satellite link was installed so he could watch. As the 10,000 participants arrived from 200 countries, their disappointment was transformed by their certainty that "whether Billy Graham is here in person or absent, God is here, and God is going to do his work."

The opening ceremony included a colorful procession and the singing of the African Children's Choir. Billy had hoped to deliver his prepared keynote address on video but had been too unwell, so Franklin read it for him. That night, and throughout the conference, Franklin substituted for his father, with great acceptance, which seemed to symbolize that the torch was passing to the next generation.

Day after day unfolded in an atmosphere of eagerness, excitement, and desire to learn. The plenary speakers, including the Archbishop of Canterbury (George Carey) on "Preaching Christ in a Broken World," Anne Graham Lotz and Franklin, Billy Kim from Korea, Paul Negrut from Romania, and Viktor Hamm; the seminars, the workshops, and the task-groups of theologians preparing the Amsterdam Covenant; Sir Cliff Richard singing the Lord's Prayer; the choirs, the hymns sung by the whole ten thousand, each in their own language; the friendships made across national, racial, and religious divides—all contributed to an unforgettable ten days, especially for those who had never seen so many Christians together. The vibrancy of the faith across the world could not be mistaken: "Believers of many races and many languages united in worship and praise of our almighty King! Participants have been refreshed, encouraged, and challenged. We have seen and heard stories of forgiveness and reconciliation, of repentance and obedience, of surrender."

The conference ended on the Sunday evening with Billy expressing his love and hopes for them all, as he spoke by video from the Mayo Clinic, before the deeply reverent service of Communion. In the course of his address he said: "I want to be among those who represent a generation of evangelists that hands the torch to a new generation of God's servants. I believe that the fire of God the Holy Spirit has fallen on this conference and that we have rededicated our lives in a new way to reflect the light of the glory of God.

"We will go out from Amsterdam with a new fire burning in our hearts to touch a lost world.

"The story is told of two Christian martyrs in the sixteenth century who were burned at the stake. As the fire was being lit, one of them said to the other, 'Be of good cheer. We shall this day light a fire that by God's grace shall never be put out.' Their bodies were consumed, but their message of Christ's saving grace lives on to this day.

"I do not believe that we should spend our time cursing the darkness. I do not believe we should spend our time in useless controversy, trying to root the tares out while harming the wheat. I do not believe that we should give in to the forces of evil and violence and indifference.

"Instead, let us light a fire."

Billy urged them to light a fire that would banish moral and spiritual blight, guide men and women into tomorrow and eternity, roll back the poisons of racism, poverty, and injustice. "Let us light a fire of renewed faith in the Scriptures as the Word of God and in worship and evangelism as the priority of the church.

"Let us light a fire of commitment to proclaim the Gospel of Jesus Christ in the power of the Holy Spirit to the ends of the earth, using every resource at our command and with every ounce of our strength.

"Let's light a fire in this generation that by God's grace will never be put out...."

Amsterdam 2000 continued long after all had said their farewells. By August 2002, more than 45,000 evangelists and leaders had attended one or more of 60 regional Beyond Amsterdam conferences worldwide.

Billy Graham himself was able to leave the hospital and to preach at the Jacksonville crusade. Franklin took over as Chief Operating Officer in November 2000 and had a heavy schedule with his evangelistic festivals in America and overseas, and with his work as president of Samaritan's Purse. Billy remained as chairman. The opportunities for evangelism and discipleship training throughout the world had increased and diversified to such an extent that the BGEA offices were no longer adequate; yet further expansion at Minneapolis, where they had been located very happily for fifty years, was not possible. The board therefore bought sixty-three acres of open land on the Billy Graham Parkway on the edge of Charlotte, North Carolina, where all departments could be together in custom-built offices in a landscaped compound. This momentous change (announced in November 2001) would be phased in over three to five years.

Due to his extended recuperation, Billy was unable to accept the invitation of the new president, George W. Bush, to pray the invocation at his Inauguration in January 2001. Franklin took his place. It would have been Billy's ninth Inaugural prayer. George W. Bush in his autobiography had written of a stroll and talk with Billy some years earlier, which was "the beginning of a new walk where I would recommit my heart to Jesus Christ," becoming a man of prayer and faith and spiritual strength, which would mean much to the nation in the unprecedented crisis to come.

Billy spent much of the first half of 2001 as an outpatient or inpatient, mostly at the Mayo Clinic. Ruth also was not well, "but she has a determination and more energy than anyone I have ever known," Billy told an English friend. "She is almost totally confined to her room, but her smile lights it up." One time when she was in the hospital, Gigi was with her when Billy came to visit. As Gigi said, "I stood back and observed these two very dear lovers as he entered the room. Her eyes once again lit up. As he made his way to her bedside, he tottered and almost lost his balance. Leaning over, he bent down and gently, tenderly kissed her. It was obvious that her desire and prayer as a young bride to 'never let it end, God, never' had been answered."

It was a time of sorrow too, for on May 24, Billy's lifelong friend and longtime associate, T. W. Wilson, died after a heart attack at age eighty-two. Until his stroke in 1999, T. W. had for many years traveled with Billy. His humor and graciousness and gift for friendship guarded Billy's privacy, and as a deep Bible student and evangelist, he was his personal pastor when on tour.

In June came the first of the two crusades scheduled for 2001. "By faith," wrote Billy, "I ventured out and held a four-day crusade in Louisville, Kentucky, where we had large crowds in their stadium (from 40,000 to 57,000 each night). Hundreds of people responded to the invitation each night, and I was grateful to the Lord for the strength he gave me and the older members of our team, who also are not too strong." Bev Shea was now ninety-one and Cliff Barrows was seventy-seven. Billy preached in a strong voice, and over ten thousand people had come forward. Once again the Concert for the NeXt Generation saw 46,000 people, mostly in their teens, listen quietly and attentively after the noise and excitement of the contemporary music.

The Billy Graham Evangelistic Association was renewing its strength and outreach by reorganization and recruitment under Franklin's direction. Films, books, website, the weekly *Hour of Decision,* the daily *Decision Today* radio program, the schools of evangelism, and the televising of crusades gave an ever widening ministry.

Then came September 11, 2001.

34

"A Day of Victory"

Like all America, Billy Graham watched in horror, shock, and revulsion as the hijacked planes with their innocent captives slammed into the World Trade Center and the Pentagon. He issued a statement at once: "These unspeakable acts of brutality strike at the very heart of our free society.

"Our heartfelt prayers and sympathy go out to all who have been directly touched by this tragedy, and their families. I call upon all Americans to pray especially for our President and for all who advise him, that they may have divine wisdom as they respond to this insane and horrific act.

"In times like this we realize how weak and inadequate we are, and our greatest need is to turn in repentance and faith to the God of all mercy and the Father of all comfort. If ever there was a time for us to turn to God and to pray as a nation, it is now, that this evil will spread no further. It is also a time for us to remember the words of the psalmist: 'God is our refuge and strength, a very present help in trouble.'"

The president proclaimed a National Day of Prayer and Remembrance and asked Billy Graham to give the address at the interfaith, interdenominational service in the National Cathedral in Washington on Friday, September 14, three days after the terrorist attack.

Billy had thirty-six hours' notice to prepare an address that reached the highest number of people in his entire ministry, for it was seen and heard on almost all American television channels and radio stations, and carried across the world.

He had great difficulty in reaching Washington from Montreat because all scheduled flights had stopped and all airports were closed. A private plane was hired but even with the White House working on the problem, he was delayed nearly eight hours before takeoff, and the plane had to land at Dulles International Airport. He stayed overnight at a hotel and was still making last minute changes to his text while driving on Friday morning to the cathedral.

After the congregational, choral, and solo singing, and prayers and readings from Muslim, Jewish, and Christian leaders, Billy was helped slowly to mount the pulpit. "The presence of this great man of faith, so old and frail, yet always strong and reassuring," moved some to tears.

After thanking the president for calling the day, he began speaking in a strong voice: "We come together today to affirm our conviction that God cares for us, whatever our ethnic, religious, or political background may be.

"The Bible says that he is 'the God of all comfort, who comforts us in all our troubles. . . .'

"Today we say to those who masterminded this cruel plot, and to those who carried it out, that the spirit of this nation will not be defeated by their twisted and diabolical schemes. . . .

"But today, we especially come together in this service to confess our need of God. We've always needed God from the very beginning of this nation, but today we need him especially. We're facing a new kind of enemy. We're involved in a new kind of warfare, and we need the help of the Spirit of God. The Bible's words are our hope: 'God is our refuge and strength, a very present help in trouble. Therefore we will not fear, though the earth give way and the mountains fall into the heart of the sea.'

"But how do we understand something like this? Why does God allow evil like this to take place? Perhaps that is what you are asking now. You may even be angry at God. I want to assure you that God understands these feelings that you may have. . . . God can be trusted, even when life seems at its darkest.

"But what are some of the lessons we can learn?

"First, we are reminded of the mystery and reality of evil.

"I have been asked hundreds of times in my life why God allows tragedy and suffering. I have to confess that I really don't know the answer totally, even to my own satisfaction. I have to accept by faith that God is sovereign, and he's a God of love and mercy and compassion in the midst of suffering....

"The lesson of this event is not only about the mystery of iniquity and evil, but secondly, it's a lesson about our need for each other.

"What an example New York and Washington have been to the world these past few days! None of us will ever forget the pictures of our courageous firefighters and police, many of whom have lost friends and colleagues, or the hundreds of people attending or standing patiently in line to donate blood. A tragedy like this could have torn our country apart, but instead it has united us and we've become a family.... We are more united than ever before.

"Finally, difficult as it may be for us to see right now—this event can give a message of hope—hope for the present, and hope for the future.

"Yes, there is hope. There is hope for the present because I believe the stage has already been set for a new spirit in our nation.

"One of the things we desperately need is a spiritual renewal in this country.... And God has told us in his Word, time after time, that we are to repent of our sins and we're to turn to him and he will bless us in a new way.

"But, there is also hope for the future because of God's promises. As a Christian, I have hope, not just for this life, but for heaven and the life to come. And many of those people who died this past week are in heaven right now, and they wouldn't want to come back. It's so glorious and so wonderful. And that's the hope for all of us who put our faith in God. I pray that you will have this hope in your heart.

"This event reminds us of the brevity and the uncertainty of life. We never know when we too will be called into eternity. I doubt if even one of those people who got on those planes, or walked into the World Trade Center or the Pentagon last Tuesday morning thought it would be the last day of their lives. It didn't occur to them. And that's why each of us needs to face our own spiritual need and commit ourselves to God and his will now.

"Here in this majestic National Cathedral we see all around us symbols of the Cross. For the Christian, I'm speaking for the Christian now, the Cross tells us that God understands our sin and our suffering, for he took upon himself in the person of Jesus Christ our sins and our suffering. And from the Cross, God declares, 'I love you. I know the heartaches and the sorrows and the pains that you feel. But I love you.'

"The story does not end with the Cross, for Easter points us beyond the tragedy of the Cross to the empty tomb. It tells us that there is hope for eternal life, for Christ has conquered evil and death, and hell. Yes, there is hope.

"I've become an old man now and I've preached all over the world, and the older I get the more I cling to that hope that I started with many years ago and proclaimed it in many languages to many parts of the world....

"We all watched in horror as planes crashed into the steel and glass of the World Trade Center. Those majestic towers, built on solid foundations, were examples of the prosperity and creativity of America. When damaged, those buildings eventually plummeted to the ground, imploding in upon themselves. Yet underneath the debris, is a foundation that was not destroyed....

"But now we have a choice: whether to implode and disintegrate emotionally and spiritually as a people and a nation—or, whether we choose to become stronger through all of this struggle—to rebuild on a solid foundation. And I believe that we are in the process of starting to rebuild on that foundation. That foundation is our trust in God. That's what this service is all about and in that faith we have the strength to endure something as difficult and horrendous as what we have experienced this week.

"This has been a terrible week with many tears but also has been a week of great faith."

After quoting from the eighteenth century hymn, "How Firm a Foundation," Billy ended: "My prayer today is that we will feel the loving arms of God wrapped around us, and will know in our hearts that he will never forsake us as we trust in him.

"We also know that God is going to give wisdom and courage and strength to the President and those around him. And this is going to be a day that we will remember as a day of victory.

"May God bless you all."

The entire congregation burst into spontaneous applause. As Billy moved from the pulpit, Cardinal McCarrick, an old friend, stepped forward and embraced him.

In the days and weeks that followed, the Billy Graham Evangelistic Association and Samaritan's Purse played a full part in helping the nation. They set up a Billy Graham Prayer Center a few blocks from Ground Zero, with a team of trained volunteers and ministers, including pastors of famous city churches, to give spiritual help to the firefighters, police, and rescue workers. Local people provided facilities so that by telephone and personal ministry, many hundreds of those devastated by the disaster could be given scriptural comfort. In the weeks that followed, the Prayer Center handled more than 1,500 calls and distributed more than 15,000 Bibles and 200,000 tracts, pamphlets, and books. Billy's book *Facing Death and the Life After* was especially welcomed. At Minneapolis, the counseling department had a huge number of calls. As Billy said, "Our nation is undergoing an unprecedented search for purpose and meaning, which God can use for good to turn individuals back to him in repentance and faith."

This was shown vividly by the response, despite intense security, when Billy preached at the long-prepared Central Valley crusade in Fresno, California, early in October. Despite breaking three bones in his right foot when he slipped in his hotel room and having to wear a fixed-sole splint, he was able to preach standing and seemed to get stronger each of the four evenings. At the opening meeting he preached on "September 11 and the Love of God." "Much of the world is feeling the effects of terrorism and war right now, but there are other things that are bothering us: disease, poverty, racism, hate, loneliness, AIDS, unemployment, divorce, psychological problems, boredom, murder statistics—the world didn't stop sinning or getting bored after September 11 ... we know that something is wrong with human nature. Sin is what's wrong with the world and only Jesus Christ can solve it."

The 42,000-seat stadium averaged 46,000 over the four nights, with the Saturday youth concert bringing no less than 62,000. A total of 14,731 came forward in the racially and culturally diverse area of California, to be followed up by the 500 churches representing over 50 denominations in the agriculturally rich Central Valley. In the prisons, 23,000 inmates attended the events arranged by the crusade, with 4,630 commitment cards turned in.

To mark Billy's eighty-third birthday on November 7, 2001, President and Mrs. Bush gave a private dinner for thirty at the White House for Billy and Ruth, inviting the Graham children and their spouses, together with a few friends including the Bev Sheas and the Cliff Barrows.

In December, to great pleasure throughout the world, Her Majesty the Queen conferred on Billy Graham an Honorary Knighthood as a Knight Commander of the Most Excellent Order of the British Empire. Honorary knighthoods, apart from the exchange of honors with heads of State, are sparingly given and do not confer a title. Billy would not be *Sir* William Franklin Graham but Dr. Billy Graham KBE (Hon.).

The British Ambassador in Washington, Sir Christopher Meyer, and Lady Meyer generously gave a dinner for seventy in honor of Billy and Ruth at the Ambassadorial Residence, the fine building designed by Lutyens in 1913, which had once been the whole embassy. The Meyers invited all the Graham children and grandchildren and spouses, with close associates and friends, including eight from England.

At the dinner on the evening of December 6, 2001, after a cloudless day of pleasant sunshine, in the embassy's state dining room with its porphyry pillars, portrait of the Queen, and at that season a big Christmas tree, the ambassador welcomed Billy "once again onto British soil." After humorously mentioning how "in 1946, he endured the darkest days of post-war British cooking" and how he survived the mystifying hostile headlines that greeted him in 1954, the ambassador gave a most gracious and perceptive overview of Billy's ministry, which touched him greatly:

"Dr. Graham has made an incalculable contribution to civic and religious life over sixty years. . . . He has pursued his calling with a straightforward passion and faithfulness. Along the way he has left us an extraordinary legacy.

"Billy Graham has preached the Gospel to more people in live audiences than anyone else in history. His ministry has been truly international. Millions of people throughout the world have found his message inspirational. Lives have been deeply touched and changed. In the furthest corners of the world, Billy Graham has blazed a remarkable trail of Christian commitment, marked by tolerance and respect for others. Dr. Graham's vision has kindled the continuing work of many thousands of others. . . .

"Here in the United States, where Dr. Graham has known every President since Harry Truman, Billy Graham is dearly loved. He especially is known and loved by all of you here tonight, as a husband of almost sixty years, a brother, father and grandfather, a friend, a lifelong partner in ministry.

"My country has also benefited from Dr. Graham's ministry. His commitment to the United Kingdom has been hugely significant. From his first meetings at Harringay Arena in 1954, and through ten later campaigns, he has been a popular visitor with a great love of Britain. He has repeatedly confounded our sturdy British skeptics. His meetings have filled arenas and football stadiums across the land.

Thousands have responded to his appeal to repentance and faith in Jesus Christ. In the Church of England alone, there are hundreds of clergy whose call to the Christian life of discipleship was first sparked by this humble man of God.

"Dr. Graham's gracious, informal, and straightforward character has, typically, allowed him to connect with people from across the full spectrum of life in Britain: social, political, and denominational. He has always established close partnerships with our local churches; but he has reached far beyond the boundaries of the institutional church.... Whether in Africa or Asia, with anti-establishment youngsters at the 1969 Miami Rock Festival, in the White House or in Buckingham Palace, Dr. Graham has remained true to himself and his calling. And this has allowed him to build bridges across so many of the most bitter divides in the world....

"Such is Dr. Graham's high reputation that he is often called a senior ambassador of Christ. As an ambassador of a mere temporal power, it is for me a special privilege to preside over this ceremony this evening.

"It is in recognition of the valuable services rendered to civic and religious life, that I am commanded by Her Majesty the Queen, in accordance with the powers vested in me as her ambassador, to confer on Dr. Billy Graham, the insignia of Honorary Knight Commander of the Most Excellent Order of the British Empire."

A British serviceman, in evening mess dress of scarlet jacket and blue trousers, stepped forward holding a large red cushion, from which Sir Christopher lifted the riband and insignia of the Order and placed it round Billy's neck. Billy stepped down from the dais, and television viewers saw him kiss Ruth in her wheelchair. Then he thanked the Ambassador and Lady Meyer very warmly for their hospitality and kindness and said, "I especially want to ask you, sir, to convey to Her Majesty the Queen, my deepest gratitude for the high honor she has graciously bestowed upon me this evening. I accept it with humility and unworthiness, and I take it as a symbol of the common historical ties that have bound our two nations together in war and in peace."

In the course of his response, Billy spoke of earlier days in Britain with humor and affection. He recalled his visits to Windsor and Sandringham. And he told of reading how Queen Victoria had said that she would like to lay her crown at the feet of Christ. "In the same way, I want to give God all the glory and all the praise for what has been accomplished in my life and those of my family and associates that are here tonight. I too look forward to the day when I can see Jesus face-to-face and lay at his feet any honor I've ever received because he deserves it all."

Before his final word of thanks, ending "May God bless Her Majesty the Queen," Billy spoke once again of Jesus: "We stand tonight beside this Christmas tree and earlier in the evening President Bush and two little children and his wife turned on the Christmas lights. And I thought about Jesus at Bethlehem as a little baby, growing up to go all the way through the life that he lived, the things he taught, the death he died, the fact that he rose from the dead. It reminds me of the great love that he has for all people. He not only loves the rest of the world, but he loves all people no matter what their ethnic or religious background is. He is a God of love."

35

"TOWARD THE FUTURE"

BAD HEALTH, WITH SEVERAL SPELLS IN THE HOSPITAL, RESTRICTED Billy Graham in the first half of 2002. When he mounted the podium at Paul Brown Stadium in Cincinnati, Ohio, on the stormy night of Thursday, June 27, receiving a great ovation, he said to the huge crowd, "This is the first sermon that I have attempted to preach in nine months, so I would appreciate your prayers that my throat will hold up." Their prayers were answered for all four nights of the Greater Cincinnati Northern Kentucky Mission. On the Friday, after the rain had gone and the temperature under the platform lights rose to 100 degrees, he had a moment of faintness before the time to preach, but it passed. Franklin, now one of America's leading evangelists in his own right, was at hand throughout and would have taken over.

Billy had last held a crusade in Cincinnati twenty-five years before, in 1977, using an indoor arena in the downtown of the beautiful city on the Ohio River. Many churches had worked together but over the years the unity had slipped and the evangelistic vision had dimmed. Racial tensions were strong. In April 2001, a white policeman shot an unarmed black man, sparking a week of rioting and violence. Press accounts touched Billy's heart, and he wondered whether he might return to Cincinnati for a stadium mission to reach the whole region on both sides of the river, which had become less of a dividing line. After the team had made inquiries, he gladly accepted a broad-based invitation for the summer of 2002.

An executive committee of pastors and business leaders began work under a prominent retired football league star. With the Cincinnati Bengals' Anthony Munoz as chairman and the pastor of a large African American congregation, Damon Lynch Jr., as vice chair, the committee did not make the mistake of 1977 when the black church leaders felt too excluded in the planning. This time all subcommittees had cochairs, one white and one from an ethnic minority.

The city authorities and community group were working to address racial issues, but a coalition of activists tried to accelerate reform by organizing a boycott of events in the city. Entertainers and conventions cancelled, but the Mission committee refused, affirming that the Billy Graham Mission "could address the very root of the problem—the need for reconciliation with God and with others through Jesus Christ."

This was already demonstrated by the gathering momentum of the preparation throughout the region. More than 900 churches from 67 denominations or groupings participated, crossing racial and ethnical divides, and more than 10,000 people attended the Christian Life and Witness classes. The Love-In-Action concept collected 750,000 pounds of food for distributing to needy families, encouraged volunteers to give time in community-youth projects for the months and years to come, and had one unusual initiative: "The Largest Soft Drink Giveaway Ever." On the Saturday before the mission, a hot and humid day, Christians gave out 300,000 soft drinks or bottles of water in the streets, each with the words, "This is to show you Christ's love in a practical way" and an invitation to the mission.

The boycott had no effect on preparations. Its leader, a young black pastor, was the son of the vice-chair of the mission's executive committee. When Billy Graham arrived in Cincinnati, he brought father and son together for a time of dialogue and prayer. Billy impressed all those he met personally by his willingness to listen. As he said in one of his sermons, "I'm praying that God is going to use this mission to help at least a little bit in the climate of love and understanding between all of us." He spoke too against anti-Semitism: "Bigotry of any kind is a sin in God's eyes."

The Graham organization was surprised by the huge attendance, including 50,000 on the Saturday at the youth concert, and the final evening on Sunday, June 30, which broke the Paul Brown Stadium's record. Billy was delighted by the response to his simple, clear presentation of the Gospel, preceded each night after singers or testimonies by one or more amusing stories that the people loved. Then pointing all in the vast stadium crowd to Christ, Billy said, "Jesus received those stripes across his back, nails in his hand, crown of thorns on his brow for you. If you were the only person in the world that needed him, he would have died for you. Because there's only one way that you can be justified before God and that's by the Cross. Jesus died in your place. But he didn't stay on the cross. On the third day he rose again, and tonight he's a living Christ. God is a God that loves you. He has a gift for you, waiting for you tonight to welcome you. I'm going to ask you to come and accept the invitation of the Father and the Son and the Holy Spirit." Over the four days, an average of more than 2,400 came forward, a total response of more than 11,000. As the mission director, Jeff Anderson, wrote: "The total impact of the mission will be known only to God."

Billy returned to Montreat. Ruth was still very sick and developed pneumonia. "For all these months that she's been so very ill," recalled Billy at the Charlotte ground-breaking that October, "I've had the privilege of talking to her every single day. And when she was in the hospital for so many weeks, I visited her every day for two or three or four or five hours. And I want to say to Ruth, my deepest love for a companion that's been with me ever since 1943 as my wife: I love her with all my heart." She returned home, cured of pneumonia. Although housebound, her health became better and her spirit was as strong as ever.

In mid-October Billy went to Texas for his second mission of 2002, the Metroplex Mission, centered in Dallas and Fort Worth in the Texas Stadium, built in 1971. The opening event had been the Greater Southwest crusade, with the late Tom Landry, legendary coach of the Dallas Cowboys, as executive chairman. In 1971 Billy had been two months short of his fifty-third birthday. He was now nearly eighty-four, yet he preached with authority and vigor. The BGEA's chief sound technician, who had kept a record of Billy's sound levels for the past fifteen years, reported that his voice was stronger at Dallas-Fort Worth than at any crusade or mission in the past five years.

Once again the statistics were overwhelming, with the stadium's attendance record broken on the Saturday, only to be broken again on the Sunday with 83,500. "And I thought to myself," commented Billy a few days later, "what God is doing. Cliff and Bev and I are getting a little older, and yet God used us in an unusual way with the help of our staff and the clergy and the people that prayed in Texas. I believe it touched all of Texas. The local clergy were quoted in the press as stating that they were pleased by the great number of people who made spiritual commitments who were under the age of twenty-five."

Rick Marshall of the team emphasized that as always "a mission with Billy Graham focuses on what we have in common, not our differences. This was vitally important in Texas where churches are large and highly visible. In fact, thirty-six of the largest one hundred churches in America are in the DFW Metroplex. Yet despite such visibility, it is a statistical fact that 60 percent of Texans are outside the grasp of the church. One leading pastor said, 'We don't know how to fish very well out of a pagan pond.'" After the Metroplex Mission, the pastors could follow up with 11,097 individuals.

Yet of all the highlights of the four nights in the stadium, perhaps the most memorable was the tribute by former President George Bush at the opening service. Responding to the great welcome from the crowd, he said that many wonderful things happen to a former president. "And for me today is one of the nicest, indeed, one of the best honors to have this opportunity to speak with each of you about a genuine American hero and a man the entire Bush family is proud to call a very dear friend. Of course, in this sense, my family is not unique. To Republican Presidents and Democratic Presidents, to Texans and Californians, to Southerners and Northerners, Billy Graham has been a personal pastor to America's first family since as long as I can remember. And all of us who have been privileged to call the White House home have gained strength and a greater sense of purpose from his healing ministry.

"I will never forget one evening eleven years ago, the night before an unprecedented international coalition for us began striking a desperate blow, decisive blow, against Iraq's aggression on Kuwait, to reverse an unprovoked attack, to liberate a country taken over brutally by its neighbor. And we called—Barbara and I had called—Rev. Billy Graham and asked him to come to the White House, and he prayed with us as the excruciating minutes to the moment the Kuwait liberation began ticked away. As we prayed that our coalition soldiers would be spared and that innocent Iraqi lives would be spared, I remember thinking at the time how Abraham Lincoln used to talk about the fact that you could not be President without spending some time on your knees appealing to a higher power.

"Whatever is to come, though, one thing is true: today we live in uncertain times in an unpredictable world. And yet as Americans we have faith—faith in our country; faith in the men and women of our armed services; faith in our leaders; and, just as important, faith in ourselves. And most important of all, thanks to the preaching of Rev. Billy Graham, we take faith in a loving God. The God we all pray to, as Billy would tell us, is a God of love and peace. And, of course, he's fond of saying, 'My one purpose in life is to help people find a personal relationship with God, which I believe comes through knowing Christ.' And here again—and here again—Dr. Graham has made a profound difference in the light of our nations and I expect in your family and certainly in my family."

Bush told how Billy went out of his way to show love and concern for the President's aged mother and to strengthen her already deep faith. "And Billy's ministry means an awful lot to this nation's forty-third President, believe me. He left his sickbed to come over with Franklin—Franklin flew him over, as a matter of fact—to Austin for a swearing-in as governor of Texas. And as he's done for many Presidents—he was on hand for the inauguration of both President forty-one and President forty-three, our son George. [But prevented on the day by ill health, Franklin substituted.] And my family will never forget.

"And so I'm afraid I can't remain impartial when it comes to Billy Graham. In this case, we Bushes plead a willing bias. We respect him, we cherish him, and we love him. And, like many of you, I'm sure I note with some sadness now that we have entered the third millennium of salvation history, and yet we see man committing many of the same barbaric acts that mark the more primitive eras in our existence. The atrocities that hit our nation last September 11 were a reminder that history is often a process of two steps forward and then one step back.

"Tonight in this place, thanks in large part to the selfless teachings of Billy Graham, we know we already dwell in the house of the Lord. We know we still live in his grace with his countless blessings. And like my beloved parents, like a precious little girl that Barbara and I lost almost fifty years to the day, we still rely on prayer in our family. Thankful prayers for our family, grateful prayers for the strength of faith in our country, and for esteemed friends like the Rev. Billy Graham."

Nine days after the end of the Metroplex Mission, Billy and Franklin Graham went to Charlotte, North Carolina, for the symbolic groundbreaking at the sixty-three-acre site for the planned new headquarters of the Billy Graham Evangelistic Association, which from mid–2004 would be moved permanently from Minneapolis to Charlotte. The ceremony on October 29, 2002, was attended by Governor Michael Easley of North Carolina, Mayor

Patrick McCrory of Charlotte, and many clergy and civic dignitaries, team and board members, friends and family, while Ruth was
present in spirit.

The past, the present, and the future touched each other that
day. Billy had in a sense come home to the place of his birth and
boyhood and of his conversion. He could look back on a ministry
of nearly sixty years, which reached across the world. The Billy
Graham Library, to be built in the same compound, would house
his personal memorabilia, chronicle by displays and exhibitions the
history of evangelism and the Graham story, and promote the message of the Gospel to the visiting public.

The chief building would take over from Minneapolis as the
main powerhouse and nerve center of the association's many and
varied ministries, domestic and overseas. Some of the staff had
already transferred to temporary offices close by. When the new
building is ready and the transition complete, the centers of the
three-fold, worldwide Graham vision of evangelism, discipleship,
and relief would all be in North Carolina: Billy's personal office at
Montreat, the Cove training center at Asheville, Blue Ridge Broadcasting at Black Mountain, Franklin's Samaritan's Purse offices at
Boone, and the main headquarters at Charlotte.

This, as Franklin emphasized in his speech of welcome to the
550 guests, "will be much more than an office facility. It's a center
for world evangelism that will allow us to train more than we've
ever been able to. It will allow us to grow and expand. . . . We want
to tell the world from one end to the other that God is a God of
love. And he will forgive us of sin if we are willing to put our faith
and trust in his Son Jesus Christ and to invite him to come into
our hearts and to our lives. This is the message we want to take
from here—Charlotte, North Carolina—to the ends of the earth."

The Governor of North Carolina and the Mayor of Charlotte
both praised Billy Graham warmly in their speeches, and he
received a standing ovation. With an echo of John the Baptist, he
turned the compliments, saying, "Jesus must increase, and I must

decrease. I sort of cringe when I hear my name called in something that I know has been the work of God through these years."

In a long address, he spoke of the past and of his love for Charlotte and the reasons for choosing the Billy Graham Evangelistic Association's new headquarters. He expressed sadness at leaving Minneapolis and thanked those who were transferring and those who could not. He went on: "A few minutes ago my friend Bishop Battle read these words from the New Testament: 'We are therefore Christ's ambassadors, as though God were making an appeal through us. We implore you on Christ's behalf: Be reconciled to God.' That is our message and that is our mission as Franklin has so well stated: to be Christ's ambassadors to the whole world, asking people to be reconciled to God. The primary message that I've tried to carry all over the world has been that God loves you. He gave his son to die for you. . . .

"We are living in an age of great spiritual hunger. And, I believe that this place is going to be a center for proclaiming that Gospel throughout the world. I wish we had time to tell you what has happened in Latin America where so many thousands of people have made their commitments to Christ just in the past few weeks." He was referring to the first, experimental *My Hope* strategy. Tens of thousands of Christians in countries of Central America invited friends to their homes on three nights to view television programs featuring one address by Billy, one by Franklin, and the third an appropriate World Wide Pictures film, all dubbed into Spanish. "More than 118,000 men, women, and children made decisions for Jesus Christ. It was one of our most successful television series ever, and we want to duplicate this in other parts of the world, continent by continent, in the coming years."

He went on: "We're also involved in many other areas of evangelism and disciple training throughout the world—through television, radio, film, the Internet, conferences, and other methods. And under Franklin's leadership, we are developing a much larger and deeper vision for the future.

"The building for which we are breaking ground today is an important step in making that future vision a reality."

In 2003, Billy Graham was listed again among the top ten men most admired by Americans, for the forty-fifth year—more than any other man since Gallup first polled the question in 1948. Pope John Paul II appeared twenty-five times.

At eighty-four, Billy was being greatly slowed by the natural aging process: He liked to quote Allan Emery's (the association's former president) remark that the "Golden Years" prove surprisingly to be the "Rusty Years." In addition, the physical limitations connected with the hydrocephalus (fluid on the brain) and the drainage shunt installed by surgery at the time of Amsterdam to remove the fluid, bring a daily handicap. The days pass with much less activity than in earlier years. "The vision is still there," commented one of his devoted personal staff in April 2003, "but day-to-day life takes most of his strength. Sermon preparation and correspondence are tackled on a good day, and set aside on days when physical challenges make it impossible to accomplish all that he would like.

"Ruth continues to be in rather frail health and largely confined to a wheelchair. She enjoys sitting by her window in her comfortable armchair, receiving visitors and continuing to deal with correspondence. A large screen television was recently installed because of vision difficulties, and she thoroughly enjoys watching good movies, since curling up with a book is no longer possible. As always, phone calls and visits from their large family mean a great deal to her—children, grandchildren, and great-grandchildren flow in and out of the house from time to time as their schedules and her strength allow."

The three daughters visited for a night or two when schedules allowed: All three had busy ministries as well as their own family responsibilities, Anne in particular with traveling in many parts of the world for her Bible conferences and her Just Give Me Jesus revivals. Ned and his wife, Christina, stayed with his parents for an extended period, helping at the time of transition as around the clock care became needed for Ruth. Franklin came over from Boone for Sunday lunch whenever he was home from his evangelistic festivals abroad and in the United States, and his leadership of Samaritan's Purse International, including the fight against AIDS and numerous other humanitarian and medical endeavors.

During the crisis and war, Billy and Ruth always prayed for the president in their daily devotions, remembering too those serving in the Coalition forces and their families. The historically close ties between the Grahams and the entire Bush family remained strong. They keep in touch from time to time with notes and phone calls.

As for ministry, Billy had hesitated to accept invitations for 2003 until after the Dallas-Fort Worth mission. The welcome and the response had been so overwhelming that he agreed to hold a four-day mission in San Diego, California, with its great naval and military presence, in May and a second in June at Oklahoma City, where he had preached at the memorable service after the tragic bombing. "My burden to proclaim the Gospel is as strong as ever," he said in a statement read at the Qualcomm Stadium in San Diego on January 9. "Therefore, health permitting, my associates and I will be glad to accept the invitation to come to California to join hands in proclaiming the Gospel." He added that he was pleasantly surprised that opportunities continued: "To be honest, I never expected to continue receiving invitations into my eighties." Fifty years earlier, in London at the start of Harringay, he had told the present writer that he did not expect to be able to continue in mass evangelism beyond the age of forty.

At San Diego, preparations that usually take a year were crammed into five months. The momentum gathered pace from the start as mission staff and civic and religious leaders worked together. On March 13, the *San Diego Union–Tribune* reported that "the response to the Christian Life and Witness Course being offered by Mission San Diego with Billy Graham has been staggering. Last week 20,000 people attended the opening session of the three-week course being taught in 16 churches from Oceanside to Chula Vista." That's twice as many people as originally anticipated and one of the largest turnouts ever, according to the Graham organizers. "We were just overwhelmed," said one pastor. "We lost count at 2,000." More than 3,000 attended another church. "Many say there is a sense of urgency about this event," commented the paper, urgent because it could be their last opportunity to see and hear Billy Graham, and urgent because of the faltering economy, and the war, which would directly affect so many San Diego families.

And so San Diego was ready when the three courageous veterans, who had served together for over fifty-four years, set out on their new adventure: Billy Graham at eighty-four, Cliff Barrows at eighty, and Bev Shea at ninety-four.

San Diego was their 413th crusade or mission together and broke several records. The 40,000 children and parents who attended the Kids Mix on the Saturday morning formed the largest audience of any Billy Graham service for children. The 74,000 youth who filled and spilled over at Saturday's concert broke the stadium's attendance record, held previously by the 1988 Superbowl. And the mission budget was met during the offering the second night so none was taken at the Saturday services and Sunday's collection was put toward televising the mission nationally, a gift for Billy Graham's next mission in Oklahoma City, and to funding future local evangelistic initiatives.

A festive air pervaded the mission because the war Operation Iraqi Freedom was over. Sailors and marines based in San Diego had formed 20 percent of the American forces deployed and as the mayor said in his welcome at a private leadership reception, "The timing of this mission couldn't be better with the return of local military forces from Iraq," although several households were in mourning.

Qualcomm Stadium had been turned into a high-tech cathedral with a multitude of jumbo screens facing the outdoor congregation and loudspeakers hanging from metal towers. Behind the platform, stretching across more than three sections and shading into left field, ranged the choir of 6,000, which Cliff Barrows conducted. The opening night, May 8, 2003, was unusually chilly. Billy wore an overcoat and the 54,000 people in the stands huddled close during the two-hour service of hymns, solos, and testimonies. Bev Shea led the congregation in "How Great Thou Art" and then sang to prepare all hearts for Billy's sermon. Billy was especially pleased to be back for his fourth crusade in San Diego, remembering also family vacations nearby in a house in Pauma Valley with its golf course and orange groves. He preached for thirty minutes, proclaiming once again the love of God and the need for every person to make the choice now, to accept or refuse "God's offer of forgiveness and mercy."

Billy then asked all who wanted to choose Christ to get out of their seats and come down to make their commitment to him. Men, women, and children came from all parts of the stadium to the field below the platform while the choir sang quietly the hymn "Just As I Am Without One Plea" and, surprisingly, many who remained in the stands cheered and applauded. Then Billy spoke to them, the benediction was given, and the counselors began their work. Long after Billy had left the podium on the arm of Franklin, the field was packed with inquirers and counselors huddled together. By the final count, 3,183 inquirers were counseled that night, offering nearly 700 churches with an immense field of new disciples to nurture.

The second night, "military night," was carried live over the Armed Forces Radio and Television Network to Iraq and every base and ship throughout the world. The next morning, in warm sunshine, came the Kids Mix and that evening the earsplitting Velocity: A Concert for Our Generation with 72,000 in the stadium and another 2,000 under a Jumbotron screen in the parking lot. The *San Diego Union–Tribune* reported: "It was not your grandmother's church service. The bands were loud, the beat fast, and the congregation rocked the house.... In addition to the packed stadium seats, about 5,000 people were allowed onto the field by the stage, where they clapped, shouted, hugged, and jumped up and down," led (and strictly but unobtrusively controlled) by Christian pop singers giving their services free, including Kirk Franklin, who then took them "into a deafening cheering fest for Jesus. And just when it couldn't get much louder, Franklin slowed it down with a ballad and then introduced a man that he called 'the bomb.' That's when the white-haired Graham made his way across the stage, with the help of his son, Franklin, to an ovation that lasted a full minute."

Billy called out, "Who is the man?" And they roared back "Jesus!" Then, for twenty-five minutes, 74,000 young people listened rapt, in total silence, to Billy speak of judgment and salvation and of the cost and joy of following Jesus. He said he was old enough to be their great-grandfather but had been at their age "when I received Christ into my heart and it changed my life." When Billy gave the invitation, more than 4,000 young people got out of their seats and even if, on the principle of the Parable of the Sower, no more than a quarter grow to maturity and bring forth fruit, America had gained a thousand future Christian leaders from that night.

On Sunday the stadium reverted to being an open-air cathedral with an immense congregation, including many hundreds who had handed their lives to Christ during one of the previous three days. Among the special guests, the widow of Colonel Rick Husband, who was killed in the recent Columbia space shuttle tragedy, spoke of her faith in Christ. "I do not understand," said Evelyn Husband, "why this happened, and I probably never will in my lifetime. And I don't have to, because I trust him. Because of Jesus, there can be joy—even in the midst of sorrow."

Later, Billy asked all for their prayers for his next mission in June at Oklahoma City, which had suffered grievously from the very recent tornadoes. "We've been praying," Billy told them, "and I've been so burdened for Oklahoma City these past few days I could hardly sleep. I don't have the answers, except to say that everything is in God's hands. Because he loves us, there must be a reason, but we may not know until we get to heaven."

When he reached Oklahoma City after a few short weeks at home, Billy was driven around the devastated area where 1,500 homes and businesses and nine churches had been damaged and 300 homes destroyed. "I could hardly believe my eyes . . . all on top of everything else here! And my heart goes out to you," as he said on the first night of the mission, June 12, 2003.

Billy's four-day mission at the new Ford Center was the latest in a historical sequence going back nearly fifty years. In 1956 Billy Graham, then aged thirty-seven, held a month-long crusade at the state fairgrounds speedway, which, in the opinion of a senior business man in 2003, "had a greater positive impact on Oklahoma City than any other event in the history of our city."

Kirk Humphreys, the city's mayor in 2003, who was chairman of the Billy Graham Mission Committee, had particular cause to remember the 1956 crusade. He was five years old at the time and his father, Jack Humphreys, a career-dominated businessman who allowed God only one day a week, had volunteered to be an usher, hoping, said his son, "to spend only one evening at the event. Instead he went every night as Billy's message of Christ's love took hold of his heart. . . . Dad's life started to change."

Jack Humphreys became a special friend of Billy's director of counseling, Charlie Riggs, who taught him a lot about the Christian life and how to witness. Many years later after retiring from his wholesale business, Humphreys spent four months every year for twenty-five years training counselors for Billy Graham crusades in the United States, Canada, and Australia. His son Kirk, the future mayor, came into a deep faith while at college and was one of the counselors when Billy held his second Oklahoma City crusade in 1983.

Ten years later, the city suffered the horror of the bomb that blew up the Alfred P. Murrah federal building with the loss of 178 lives. Oklahomans came together as never before to help the injured, the bereaved, and the survivors. They also arranged a memorial service four days later. President Clinton "and many other important people spoke," recalls survivor Brad Nesom. "Nothing seemed to help. Then Billy Graham got up to the speak God's Word in a simple, reassuring way that spoke right to me. A deep peace washed over me—the same peace I had experienced as a child when I dedicated my life to the Lord Jesus at a Billy Graham crusade. I knew that everything would be okay. God was still God."

"It is far better, " Billy had said, "to face something like this with God's strength than to face it alone without him." That service of hope connected the people of the region to Billy Graham in a very special way. And when disaster struck again with the tornadoes of May 2003, one month before the mission, many who might not otherwise have attended were ready to listen.

People lined up in the hot sun. The Ford Center, an indoor arena, filled rapidly with 18,000 people to its capacity. The latecomers, 11,000 people, were directed to the Cox Center. Billy spoke of the turmoil and the strife in the world and the suffering of so many Oklahomans. Then he spoke of the solution, the love of God through the Cross and resurrection of Christ and invited men, women, and children to put their trust in Christ. More than a thousand people responded.

On the next night, as is usual in a crusade or mission, numbers were less and the overflow building was not needed. One of the preliminary speakers was a former head of the Bureau of Indian Affairs, for Oklahoma is home to more Native Americans, and many were present, than any other state. Billy commented that Native Americans are a very spiritual people, many of whom know Christ, saving Oklahoma City some of the turmoil of other communities.

Groups were able to hear the mission in their own tongues, with translation and counseling in nine languages, including Spanish, Korean, Chinese, Farsi, and Russian. Before his father's address, Franklin spoke of the Samaritan's Purse's work to combat

AIDS and to help sufferers. He was scheduled to follow up the mission with a festival in September in Tulsa.

After the service for the children on Saturday morning, the high-decibel youth concert at night filled the Ford Center and spilled over into the Cox Center. It was dedicated to the memory of a Christian girl, Alicia Layne, who was only nineteen when she was killed in a car accident earlier in the month when she was driving home from the student's prayer rally around the arena. Her parents both gave their testimonies from the platform and promised to continue her witness for Christ. "I know God's got a tremendous work for our family. We're going to pick up the torch and go on," said her mother.

Billy began his address with the story of Solomon who was very wise. "But you cannot come to Christ with just your mind. You can't think your way to Jesus," he challenged his young audience. Solomon had wealth, women, and religion but no peace. Soon Billy had moved the focus from Solomon to Christ, and once again set Christ before them to lead them to the point of decision.

The final Sunday evening, after a hot day when the crowds patiently lined up for the unreserved seats and the buses came from all over the state, made a fitting climax to "four miraculous days." The two arenas echoed with song and prayer. Billy's younger brother Melvin, who liked to say he was "a nobody who wanted everybody to know that Somebody loves anybody," was one of the preliminary speakers: "You're going to hear a simple Gospel message. Billy preaches straightforward. He's going to tell you the only way you're going to get to heaven. Get all you can, 'cause this old boy might not get over here to preach again."

Billy preached on the Prodigal Son—how at his lowest point, he decided to repent and go home. *The Oklahoman* newspaper caught the drama of the moment:

"Looking out into the silent crowd, Graham said, 'You can come home. You can come home to God. . . . You've lived a life that somehow has failed but you can come home tonight. . . .'

" 'God will not reject a heart that's broken and sorry for sin,' he said. 'We give every person an opportunity here to take a step of repentance toward God. He's not waiting to condemn you, to judge you. He's waiting to kiss you, to say "I love you." '

"Several times throughout his message, Graham was forced to stop as the audience broke out in applause."

He spoke of Ruth, and his gratitude toward her. Their sixtieth wedding anniversary was just two months away. He also spoke of death: "The more I get older, the more I get closer to it, the happier I am. I am filled with anticipation—I'm looking forward to it. One reason is I'll get some rest! We're going to go ... before the next hundred years rolls around," he said to the laughter of the crowd. Finally, as always in a crusade or mission, he came to the invitation: "You must make a choice tonight. If you walk out of this arena tonight or the Cox Center without knowing Jesus in your heart, you will have made a choice. If you come forward, you have made a choice."

In the four days, 4,359 people made that choice. The Billy Graham Team members stayed through the summer to help the church. For, as Mayor Humphreys said on the last night, "This meeting is not the end of Mission Oklahoma City.... It's a transition point.... Our job is to see that the seed that has been scattered here takes root and grows and matures and multiplies, and that the fragrance of Jesus Christ is spread everywhere."

San Diego. Oklahoma City. Invitations to other cities in the future. There is no retirement in the Bible, Billy likes to point out. "I think God has called me to proclaim the Gospel as long as I have strength."

NOTES

1. See *A Foreign Devil in China: The Story of L. Nelson Bell* by John Pollock (Grand Rapids: Zondervan, 1971), (London: Hodder and Stoughton, 1972), revised edition (Minneapolis: World Wide Publications, 1988).

2. Historically it is a nice touch that the first conference organized by Billy Graham in Britain, of 250 persons, should have been held in the city where 37 years later 11,800 clergy and lay leaders converged from all over England to hear him, on 26 January 1984.

3. Quoted by gracious permission of Her Majesty the Queen.

4. For more detail about their origin, see *Billy Graham: Evangelist to the World* (San Francisco: HarperSanFrancisco, 1980), 130–32.

5. A full account of Billy Graham's South African visit is in *Evangelist to the World,* chapter 3.

6. A fuller account of the Korean crusade is in *Evangelist to the World,* chapters 4 and 5.

7. For Billy Graham's relations with Presidents Eisenhower, Kennedy, and Johnson, see *Evangelist to the World,* chapter 14.

8. For a full account of the preparation, course, and immediate aftermath of Lausanne, see *Evangelist to the World,* chapters 15, 16, and 19.

9. Franklin Graham, *Rebel with a Cause* (Nashville: Nelson, 1995), 123.

10. A fuller account is in *Evangelist to the World,* chapter 24.

11. The Church of England is not a state church but an established church, but few outside the United Kingdom comprehend the essential difference.

12. For an extended account of the origin of Mission England, see the final chapter of the 1984 edition of this book.

13. Self-supporting, Self-governing, Self-propagating.

INDEX

Abraham, Mark, 239
Adams, Lane, 91
Africa, 116–17, 124, 150, 221, 269–70, 279
Africa Enterprise, 116
African Children's Choir, 280
Akers, John, 175, 185, 188, 226
Alaska, 214
Albany, New York, 252, 256
Albuquerque, New Mexico, 131
Alexei, Patriarch, II, 263
All-Scotland Crusade, 78–83
Allan, Tom, 79
Altoona, Pennsylvania, 42
American Broadcasting Company (ABC), 33, 55, 59, 60, 70, 92
American Jewish Committee, 129
Amsterdam, 199–203, 237–43, 280, 281
Anderson, Jeff, 296
Andhra Pradesh Christian Relief and Rehabilitation, 157
anti-Semitism, 129–30, 296
apartheid, 116–17
Arulappa, Archbishop, 158
Asheville, North Carolina, 278, 280, 300
Asia, 184, 270, 279
atheism, 173, 182, 187, 230, 267
atheists, 151, 152, 176, 178–80, 184, 186, 187, 188, 190, 197, 223, 244, 248, 260
Auschwitz, 154–55
Australia, 96–103, 160–66

Baker, Stanley, 38–39
Baltic States, 184, 261, 268
Barnes, Ernest, 38–39
Barrows, Billie, 37–38
Barrows, Cliff, 37–38, 42, 47, 48, 52, 54, 60, 71, 77, 91, 98, 118, 163, 186, 202, 215, 217–18, 220, 235, 265, 272, 273, 275, 283, 290, 297, 304, 305
Barry, Marion, 232
Bartha, Bishop, 151
Battle, Bishop, 301
Beavan, Jerry, 65, 78, 96
Beijing, China, 244, 245, 248
Bell, Nelson, 63, 108, 249, 278
Bell, Ralph, 256
Bell, Ruth, 28. See also Graham, Ruth
Ben Lippen Bible Conference, 37
Bennett, Walter F., 55–57, 59, 92
Benny, Jack, 118
Berlin, 77, 133, 185, 186, 261
Berlin Wall, 77, 187, 261
Berry, Lowell, 110
Billy Graham, 8
Billy Graham Association, 185, 193, 199, 223
Billy Graham Center, 167
Billy Graham Center for World Evangelism, 299–300
Billy Graham: Evangelist to the World, 8
Billy Graham Evangelistic Association (BGEA), 9, 59, 61, 133, 152, 193, 199, 223, 271, 279, 282, 284, 289, 297
Billy Graham Library, 300
Billy Graham Mission Committee, 295, 307
Billy Graham Parkway, 282
Billy Graham Prayer Center, 289
Billy Graham Team, 8, 92–93, 100, 101, 173, 174, 176, 212, 310
Birmingham, Alabama, 112
Birmingham, England, 38–40, 70, 212, 219
Black Mountain, North Carolina, 300
Blackpool, England, 173, 211
Blewett, Bob, 109

Blinco, Joe, 39–40
Bolten, John, 54, 77
Boone, North Carolina, 300, 303
Borovoy, Vitaly, 174
Bostick, Florida, 22
Boston, Massachusetts, 52–54, 193, 195–97
Bradbury, Dr., 109
Brazil, 110–11, 114
Brinkley, David, 182
Bristol, England, 215–17, 220
Britain. *See* England
British Broadcasting Company (BBC), 69, 70, 71
Brock, Brunette, 23
Brooklyn Tabernacle Choir, 257
Brooks, Dallas, 99
Brown, Reese, 14
Bucharest, Romania, 224, 228, 230
Budapest, Hungary, 149, 150, 260
Buenos Aires, Argentina, 270
Buffalo, New York, 92–93, 252–54
Burklin, Werner, 200, 241
Burrell, William G., 255
Busby, Russ, 109
Bush, Anthony, 216
Bush, Barbara, 235, 290, 298, 299
Bush, George H. W., 167, 177, 234, 235, 259, 297–99, 303
Bush, George W., 7, 9, 282–83, 285, 290, 299, 303
Bychkov, Pastor, 177

California, 38, 42–51, 95, 108, 110, 118, 136, 289–90, 303–6
Cambridge, England, 70
Canterbury, Archbishop of, 71, 76, 83, 209, 280
Carey, Eileen, 83
Carey, George, 280
Carlson, Blair, 184, 261–62, 263, 264
Cash, Johnny, 257
Cash, June, 257
Cassidy, Michael, 116
Cavanaugh, Emily Regina, 24–25
Ceausescu, Nicholas, 223, 230

Central America, 301
Chapman, John, 161
Charlotte, North Carolina, 13, 15, 16, 17, 124, 126, 143, 282, 296, 299–301
Chattanooga, Tennessee, 113
Chesterton, G. K., 140
Chicago, Illinois, 28, 34, 92, 110
China, 244–51
China Christian Council, 244, 245
Christian Century, 88
Christian Embassy, 233
Christian Life and Witness Course, 215, 264, 295, 303
Christian Scientists, 52
Christianity Today, 108, 127
Church of England, 37, 182, 292
Church of Scotland, 81
Church of South India, 84
Churchill, Winston, 73
Cincinnati, Ohio, 157, 294–95
"citywide campaigns," 41–42, 44, 49, 50
Civil War, 13, 14
Clearwater, Florida, 21
Cleveland, Ohio, 272, 273, 275
Cleveland, Tennessee, 20
Clinton, Bill, 277, 308
Club Time, 33
Coe, Doug, 234
Coffey, Ben, 13
Coffey, Morrow, 13, 14
Columbia, South Carolina, 53–54
Colville, John, 73
Commonwealth of Independent States (CIS), 261, 262, 265, 267–68
Communism, 8, 148–49, 184, 230, 231, 260, 263
Congressional Gold Medal, 276, 277
Cornell, George, 90, 131, 141
Corts, John, 202
Crusade, 217
crusades and sermons, 7, 53–54;
    Alabama, 112; Alaska, 214;
    Amsterdam, 199–203, 237–43, 280, 281; Australia, 96–103, 160–66;

California, 42–51, 95, 108, 110, 118, 136, 289–90, 303–6; China, 244–51; Czechoslovakia, 184, 188–91; East Germany, 184–87; England, 64–83, 107, 136, 173, 211–13; Florida, 282; Hong Kong, 248, 256, 270; Illinois, 34, 110; India, 83–85, 156–59; Indiana, 196; Japan, 168–70; Kentucky, 283; Korea, 94, 120–23; Mexico, 171–72; Minnesota, 197; Nevada, 197; New England, 54, 192–98; New Mexico, 131; New York City, 87–95, 107, 114, 116, 256–58; New York State, 252–58; New Zealand, 96, 100; North Carolina, 124; Ohio, 157, 272–75, 294–95; Oklahoma, 197–98, 303, 304, 306–9; Oregon, 55–58; Pennsylvania, 42; Philippines, 156; Poland, 152–55; Romania, 221–31; Russia, 173–91, 259–68; Scotland, 78–83, 256, 261, 271; South America, 110–11, 114; South Carolina, 53–54; Switzerland, 132–36; Tennessee, 113, 126, 280; Texas, 62, 196, 275–76, 296–99, 303; Washington, D.C., 62, 232–36; Washington State, 113, 185
Cultural Revolution, 244, 247
Czechoslovakia, 184, 188–91

Daily Herald, 65
Daily Telegraph, 68
Dain, Jack, 132, 134, 160, 164
Dallas-Fort Worth Mission, 303
Dallas, Texas, 97, 275–76, 296–99, 303
Dao, Wang Ming, 247
dc Talk, 272, 275
Decision, 108–10
Decision Today, 280, 284
Delhi, India, 84–85
Derbyshire, England, 76
Dienert, Fred, 54, 55–57, 59, 92
disaster relief, 157–59, 202
Dortmund, West Germany, 108
Dudley-Smith, Timothy, 217

Duke, Charles, 263
Durban, South Africa, 116
Düsseldorf, Germany, 76

Easley, Michael, 299
East Anglia, England, 217–18
East Germany, 184–87
Eastern Europe, 7, 148–55, 175–76, 202, 252, 259, 261, 279
Edinburgh, Duke of, 82, 207–8
Edinburgh, Queen of, 82, 207–8
Edinburgh, Scotland, 81
Edman, V. Raymond, 28
Eisenhower, Dwight D., 62, 99, 113, 125, 232
Eisenhower, Julie Nixon, 124, 131
Elizabeth, Queen, 8–9, 74–75, 82, 208
Elsner, Theodore, 54–55
Emery, Allan, 193, 302
England, 8, 25, 37–40, 64–83, 107, 173, 207–22, 269, 291–93
ethnic issues, 130, 161, 225, 235, 257, 274, 286, 293, 295. _See also_ racial issues
Evans, Colleen Townsend, 233, 234
Evans, Louis, Jr., 233
Examiner, 47

Facing Death and the Life After, 289
Fairbanks, Douglas, 66
Fasig, Bill, 163
Faubus, Governor, 115
Federation of Evangelical Churches, 185
Fei, Pastor, 251
Ferm, Robert O., 90
Festival Hall, 97
Finney, Charles Grandison, 252, 254
Fisher, Geoffrey, 71, 76, 82
Florida, 20–24, 26, 27, 35, 125, 282
Florida Bible Institute, 20, 21
Ford, Leighton, 88, 168
Fort Worth, Texas, 62, 296–99, 303
Franklin, Kirk, 272, 306
Fresno, California, 289–90
Frost, David, 162

George, Lloyd, 70
Georgia, Soviet Union, 184
Germany, 76–77, 108, 184–87
Gerstung, Professor, 29
Gheorghita, Nic, 227
Gibson, Ernest R., 232, 233
Gill, Alan, 162
Gingrich, Newt, 277
Glasgow, Scotland, 70, 76, 78–83
Global Mission, 270
God: call of, 23–30; help from, 7, 15, 18–19, 25. See also crusades and sermons
Goetz, Marty, 257
Gomes, Peter, 194–95
Good News Festivals, 85, 156–57
Gorbachev, Mikhail, 260, 261
Gore, Al, 7, 277
Gough, Hugh, 66, 68
Graham, Anne, 63, 142, 147, 231, 280, 302
Graham, Billy: birth of, 13; children of, 36, 63, 107, 141, 142–43, 302–3; early years, 13–31; as father, 63, 86–87, 141–43; home of, 36, 63, 77, 86, 139–45; illnesses of, 35, 76–77, 97, 145, 254, 255, 280, 281, 294; marriage of, 32, 310. See also crusades and sermons
Graham, Bunny, 63, 142
Graham, Catherine, 14
Graham, Christina, 302
Graham, Clyde, 13
Graham, Frank, 14, 15
Graham, Franklin, 107, 143, 158, 202, 224, 244–45, 251, 280, 282–83, 299, 301, 303, 305–6, 308–9
Graham, Gigi (Virginia), 36, 107, 142, 144, 283
Graham, Jean, 14
Graham, Jimmy, 251
Graham, Melvin, 14, 309
Graham, Morrow Coffey, 13, 14
Graham, Ned, 107, 141, 185, 302
Graham, Ruth: birthplace of, 244, 249–50; children of, 36, 63, 107,

141, 142–43, 302–3; home of, 36, 63, 77, 86, 139–45; illnesses of, 283, 296; marriage of, 32, 310; as mother, 63–64, 107, 142–43
Graham, Sophie, 251
Graham, William Crook, 13
Graham, William Franklin, 13, 63
Graham, William Franklin, Jr., 13. See also Graham, Billy
Great Britain. See England
Greater Cincinnati Northern Kentucky Mission, 294–95
Greater London crusade. See London, England
Greater Southwest Crusade, 297
Greene, Buddy, 257
Grigolia, Alexander, 30
Guangzhou, China, 247, 248
Gustafson, Roy, 43, 101–2
Gustavson, Luverne, 93, 99

Hacking, Philip, 221
Haldeman, H. R., 128–29
Hall, Myrtle, 186
Halverson, Richard, 235
Ham, Mordecai Fowler, 17, 18, 19, 31
Hamblen, Stuart, 45–46, 47, 50
Hamblen, Suzy, 45–46
Hamburg, Germany, 119
Hamm, Viktor, 265–67, 281
Han, Dr., 122–23
Haqq, Akbar Abdul, 84–85, 157
Haraszti, Alexander S., 148, 150, 151, 174, 175, 181, 184–85, 188, 223, 225, 226, 229
Harringay, England, 67–69, 71, 73, 74, 78–82
Hartford, Connecticut, 252
Harvard, 194–95
Haymaker, Willis, 53, 60, 67
Hearst, William Randolph, 47
Heart Is a Rebel, The, 92
Heinrich, Chief, 187
Herald Express, 47
Herald Tribune, The, 90
Herring, Edmund, 100

Hinsdale, Illinois, 32
Hitler, Adolf, 77
Holland, 76, 200
Holley, Henry, 169
Hong Kong, 248, 256, 270
honorary awards, 155, 276, 290, 292
Houlton, Maine, 54
Hour of Decision, 59, 60, 61, 70, 265, 275, 280, 284
Houston, Texas, 196
Huaiyin, China, 249–50
Humphreys, Kirk, 307, 310
Hungary, 148–52, 155, 173, 225, 259–60
Husband, Evelyn, 306
Husband, Rick, 306
Huston, Sterling, 193–98, 252, 255, 256, 271
Hyde Park, 70

India, 83–85, 156–59
Indianapolis, Indiana, 196
International Conference of Itinerant Evangelists, 199–203
International Ministries, 237, 279
Ipswich, England, 218–20
Iraq, 298, 303, 304, 305
Ireland, 37
Israel, 128–30, 159
itinerant evangelists, 199–203

Jack, Victor, 217–18
Jacksonville, Florida, 282
Jacob, Bishop, 84
Japan, 168–70
Jesus, 26, 46, 51, 60. *See also* crusades and sermons
Jewish people, 115, 128–30
Johannesburg, South Africa, 116–17
Johnson, Jimmy, 20
Johnson, Lady Bird, 125
Johnson, Lyndon B., 114, 125, 126
Johnson, Torrey, 33, 34, 35, 37
Joslin, Norman E., 253–54

Kaldy, Bishop, 151
Karam, Jimmy, 114–15

Kent, Duchess of, 82
Kentucky, 283, 294
Kerstan, Reinhold, 186
Kharchev, Konstantin, 260
Khruschchev, Nikita, 174, 267
Kids Mix, 304, 305
Kiev, Ukraine, 260, 261, 264
Kim, Billy, 121, 281
King James Version, 140
King, Martin Luther, 114, 116
Kissinger, Henry, 176
Kivengere, Festo, 135
Knighthood, 290, 292
Knoxville, Tennessee, 126
Komendant, Grigori, 261, 264
Korea, 94, 120–23, 270, 271
Korean Choir, 257
Korean War, 60, 62, 120
Kriska, Jan, 188
Kuwait, 298

Landry, Tom, 297
Lane, Mortimer, 31
Lausanne Congress on World Evangelization, 132–36, 269
Layne, Alicia, 309
Lenin, Vladimir, 173
Leningrad, Russia, 260
Leninists, 176, 177
Lewis, C. S., 140
Lianyungang, 249
Life, 90
Lincoln, Abraham, 15, 298
Little Rock, Arkansas, 114–16
Livermore, Tom, 39
Liverpool, England, 219–20
Living Bible, The, 140
Loane, Marcus, 101, 160–61, 165, 166
London, England, 25, 39, 66–71, 83, 107, 136, 209, 221, 269
Long Island, New York, 252, 256
Los Angeles, California, 42–51, 118, 136
Lotz, Anne Graham, 231, 280, 302. *See also* Graham, Anne
Louisville, Kentucky, 283

Love-In-Action, 235, 255, 295
Luther, Martin, 27, 184
Lynch, Damon, Jr., 295

MacDonald, George, 140
MacInnes, David, 219
Mackay, President, 91
Madison Square Garden, 87, 89–92, 95, 107
Madras, India, 83, 84, 157
Maier, Walter A., 55
Maine, 54, 193
Malone, Neville, 164
Manchester, England, 37, 211
Mandela, Nelson, 117
Manila, Philippines, 156
Mao, Chairman, 251
Marcos, President, 156
Margaret, Princess, 82
Marina, Princess, 82
Marshall, Becki, 271
Marshall, Rick, 261, 271, 272, 273–74, 297
Marxists, 133, 168, 173, 176, 177, 185, 187, 190–91, 230, 244, 271
Massey, Charles, 25
Mayo Clinic, 256, 280, 281, 283
McCarrick, Cardinal, 289
McCrory, Patrick, 300
McKeehan, Toby, 275
McMakin, Albert, 17, 18
McMakin, Mr., 15
Mead, Bill, 56
Melbourne, Australia, 96–101, 103
Melrose, Florida, 22
Methodist Conference, 97
Metroplex Mission, 296–99
Mexico, 171–72, 239
Meyer, Christopher, 290–92
Meyer, Lady, 290–92
Middle East, 116
Miklos, Imre, 151
Minder, John, 21–22, 25, 27
Minneapolis, Minnesota, 9, 34, 38, 41–42, 44, 51, 58, 59, 65, 109, 110, 197, 276, 279–80, 282, 289, 300, 301

Mission England, 8, 207, 209, 211–22. See also England
Mission Metro New York, 256–58
Mission New York State, 252–58
Mission San Diego, 303–6
Mission Scotland, 78–83, 256, 261, 271
Mission World, 269
Mission World Asia, 270
missions. See crusades and sermons
Moffett, Samuel, 120
Moldavia, Romania, 224
Monogoram, Victor, 84
Monroe, North Carolina, 20
Montreat, North Carolina, 32, 36, 63, 77, 86, 296, 300
Moody, D. L., 24, 27, 30, 41
Moscow, Russia, 8, 173–91, 259–68
Moscow Times, 264
Moynihan, Daniel, 116
Mr. Texas, 62
Muggeridge, Malcolm, 69
Munoz, Anthony, 295
Murdoch, Rupert, 214
Murphy, Gerry, 207
My Answer, 62
My Hope, 301

Nagaland, India, 108, 150
Nanjing, China, 246
Nashville, Tennessee, 280
National Day of Prayer and Remembrance, 7, 276, 285
National Prayer Breakfasts, 234
National Religious Broadcasters, 54
Navigators, 62
Negrut, Paul, 227, 230, 281
Nesom, Brad, 308
New England, 52–54, 192–98
New Jersey, 252, 256
New York City, 77, 87–95, 107, 114, 116, 256–58
New York State, 252–58
New York Times, 90, 129, 257
New Zealand, 96, 100
News of the World, 72
Newsweek, 49

NeXt Generation, 272–76, 284
Niagara Falls, New York, 53, 253, 255
Niebuhr, Reinhold, 90–91
Nifon, Bishop, 224
Nixon, Richard, 124–31, 176
North Korea, 246
Northwestern Schools, 41–42, 58
Norwich, England, 217
nuclear disarmament, 154–55, 174–75, 180, 190, 259

Ocean City, New Jersey, 54
Oklahoma City, Oklahoma, 197–98, 303, 304, 306–9
Oklahoman, The, 309
Operation Andrew, 80, 96
Operation Iraqi Freedom, 303, 304
Oradea, Romania, 226–28, 230, 231
Osaka, Japan, 168, 170

Palatka, Florida, 22
Palau, Luis, 210
Palermo, Phil, 55
Palms, Roger, 110
Palotay, Sandor, 148
Paris, France, 77, 269
Pascal, Blaise, 140
Patti, Sandy, 257
Paul, Pope John, II, 152, 155, 156, 302
Paul, Pope, VI, 156
Pawlik, Zdzislaw, 155
peace between nations, 148, 154, 155, 156, 174, 178, 180, 187, 235, 259
Peace with God, 62, 135, 234
Pearl Harbor, 31
Pearson,Drew, 59
Peng, Li, 245–46, 248
Peniel, Florida, 27
Pentagon, 7, 285, 288
People, The, 66
Petersburgh, Mark, 233
Philip, Prince, 183
Philippines, 156
Phillips, Frank, 58
Pickford, Mary, 66
Pierce, Bob, 57
Pimen, Patriarch, 174, 175, 179, 261

Poland, 152–55
Ponomarev, Boris, 177
Popescu, Ion, 226
Portland, Oregon, 55–58
Potter, Dan, 94
Pravda, 178
prejudice, 114, 130, 219
Presidential Medal of Freedom, 277
Princeton Theological Seminary, 91
Protestant Council of New York, 87, 88, 94–95
Providence, Rhode Island, 194
Puerto Rico, 270

racial issues, 90, 112–16, 130, 277, 282, 290, 294–95. *See also* ethnic issues
radio shows, 7, 33, 45, 55–61, 70, 80, 96, 102, 117, 145, 190, 246, 253, 255, 262, 273, 275, 280, 284, 285, 301, 305
rallies. *See* crusades and sermons
Ramsay, Walter, 17
Rao, Devananda, 157
Reagan, Ronald, 177, 277
Rebel with a Cause, 143
Red Army Choir, 265
Reid, Gavin, 210, 214, 216
religious freedom, 173, 182–84, 245, 248, 259–61
Rennie, David, 221, 225, 226
Reno, Nevada, 197
Resue, Vera, 27
Rhode Island, 54, 193–94
Richard, Cliff, 281
Riggs, Charlie, 78, 80, 88, 197, 307
Riley, W. B., 41
Rio de Janeiro, Brazil, 110, 114
Roberts, Jim, 195
Rochester, Minnesota, 280
Rochester, New York, 252, 254–55
Romania, 221–31
Rome, 134, 152, 155
Rongji, Zhu, 246
Roosevelt, Franklin D., 52
Rowlandson, Maurice, 214
Runcie, Robert, 209

Russia, 8, 173–91, 259–68, 274. *See also* Soviet Union
Russian Orthodox Church, 173, 174, 261, 262, 268

Sachse, Hans-Günther, 187
St. John's Association, 27
St. Petersburg, Russia, 264
Salvation Army Band, 257
Samaritan's Purse, 158, 202, 282, 289, 300, 303, 308–9
San Diego, California, 303–6
San Diego Union–Tribune, 303, 305
San Francisco, California, 95, 108, 110
San Juan, Puerto Rico, 270
Sandringham, England, 8, 207–8
Scandinavia, 76
Scargill, Arthur, 220
Schultz, George, 234
Scotland, 37, 70, 73–74, 76, 78–83, 256, 261, 271
Selassie, Haile, 133
Seoul, Korea, 120–23, 270
September 11, 2001, 7, 285–90
sermons: delivering, 22, 25, 26, 31, 34, 48, 50–51, 67–68, 89, 93–94; preparing, 22, 26, 50–51, 87, 140–41, 302. *See also* crusades and sermons
Shanghai, China, 246–47
Shankley, Bill, 220
Shea, Bev, 33, 42, 47, 60, 72, 77, 79, 98, 102, 112, 118, 202, 257, 277, 283, 290, 297, 304, 305
Sheffield, England, 220–21, 269
Sheppard, David, 219
Siberia, Russia, 175, 177, 178, 180–82, 184
Smith, Michael W., 272, 274
Smyth, Walter H., 97, 144, 148, 158, 170, 175, 184, 185, 188, 200, 212, 223, 226, 237
Solzhenitsyn, Alexander, 140
Songs in the Night, 33
South Africa, 116–17, 124, 150, 221, 269–70, 279

South America, 110–11, 114, 150, 270, 271, 279
South India, 84
Southampton, England, 39, 64, 65
Southworth, Mike, 279
Soviet Union, 129, 148, 174, 176, 178, 182–84, 202, 220, 252–53, 259–63, 270. *See also* Russia
Spokane, Washington, 185
Springfield, Massachusetts, 53
Stafford, Crook, 19
Stalin, Joseph, 173, 266
Stewart, James, 80
Streater, Johnny, 28
Strom, Kersten Beck, 110
Suceava, Romania, 224
Sulphur Springs, Florida, 22
Sunday, Billy, 24, 63
Sunderland, England, 216–17, 220
Supreme Court, 113, 135, 253
Swaffer, Hannen, 65
Swearingen, Lawson L., 196
Sydney, Australia, 96, 100–103, 160–66
Sydney Morning Herald, 162
Syracuse, New York, 252, 255

Tacoma, Washington, 113
Tada, Joni Eareckson, 263
Take 6, 257
Tampa City Mission, 26
Tampa, Florida, 20
Tampa Gospel Tabernacle, 22, 27
Tanenbaum, Marc, 129
Tasmania, 100
telephone counseling, 196–97, 270
television coverage, 7, 80–81, 92–93, 97, 102, 108, 111, 155, 166, 182, 188, 190, 193, 196, 197, 209, 219, 221, 253, 255, 258, 259, 260, 270, 273, 277, 285, 301
Temple Terrace, Florida, 20, 21, 23, 24
Templeton, Charles, 42
terrorism, 190, 285, 290
Thailand, 199
Thatcher, Margaret, 209

Thielicke, Helmut, 119
Thomson, D. P., 81
Three Self Patriotic Movement, 244, 246, 247, 248
Tibet, China, 30
Time, 49
Time for Decision, A, 165
Times Square, 94
Times, The, 178, 214
Timisoara, Romania, 223, 228–29
Ting, Bishop, 245
Tokyo, Japan, 168–70
Toronto, Canada, 52
Transylvania, Romania, 225
Trinity College, 21
Trotman, Dawson, 62, 88
Truman, Harry, 291
Trusting Jesus, 163
Tsingkiangpu, China, 244, 249–50
Tulsa, Oklahoma, 309
TV Mirror, 81

Underwood, Cecil, 22, 27
United Gospel Tabernacle of Wheaton and Glen Ellyn, 31
United States Army, 35

Van Kampen, Bob, 32
Vaught, W. O., 115–16
Vaus, Alice, 47–49
Vaus, Jim, 47–49
Velocity: A Concert for Our Generation, 305–6
Venice, Florida, 26
Verona, 225
Victoria, Australia, 99, 100
"Vozrozhdeniye 92," 262–63, 267

"Wall of Death," 154
Ward, Charles, 172
Warlock, Derek, 219
Washington, D.C., 62, 232–36
Washington, George, 276
Washington, Walter, 232
Watchman–Examiner, 109
Watergate, 124, 126–28, 131
Waters, Ethel, 91–92

Watson, W. T., 20
Wayne, John, 50
Wembley, 71–82
Wesley, Charles, 27
Wesley, John, 215
West Germany, 76–77, 108
West Melbourne, 97
Western Springs, Illinois, 31, 33
Wheaton College, 28, 30–31, 112, 113, 167
White City, England, 71
White, John Wesley, 195
Whitefield, George, 194, 215
Williams, Bob, 237, 241
Wilson, Billy, 38
Wilson, George, 34, 38, 42, 58, 59
Wilson, Grady, 18, 20, 46, 56–58, 60, 98, 141, 267
Wilson, T. W., 214, 216, 283
Winchell, Walter, 59
Wirt, Sherwood Eliot, 108, 110
Wittenberg, East Germany, 182, 184
Wojtyla, Cardinal, 152
Wood, Maurice, 83, 217
Worcester, Massachusetts, 53
World Council of Churches, 174
World Emergency Fund, 159, 223
world evangelism, 133, 299–300
World Medical Missions, 158
World Relief Fund, 157
World Trade Center, 7, 285, 288
World Vision, 57
World War I, 14
World War II, 149, 169, 173
World Wide Pictures, 108

Xiangao, Lin, 247, 248

Yeltson, Boris, 261, 263
Yoido Island, Korea, 120–21
Youth for Christ, 34–38, 42, 47, 97, 200, 273

Zamperini, Louis, 49, 50
Zhang, Ambassador, 244–45
Zurich, Switzerland, 261